CATTLE MANAGEMENT

Cheryl May

CATTLE MANAGEMENT

Reston Publishing Company, Inc.
A Prentice-Hall Company
Reston, Virginia

Library of Congress Cataloging in Publication Data

May, Cheryl.
    Cattle management.

    Includes index.
    1. Cattle.   I. Title.
SF197.M393   636.2   80–27161
ISBN 0–8359–0721–X

© 1981 by Reston Publishing Company, Inc.
A *Prentice-Hall Company*
Reston, Virginia 22090

1   3   5   7   9   10   8   6   4   2

PRINTED IN THE UNITED STATES OF AMERICA

This book is for Gary and Jared.

Table of Contents

Preface

Working with beef or dairy cattle offers the young person one of the most exciting and interesting careers available. Often, though, a student who might develop a basic interest in this field into a firm career goal becomes stymied by reading complicated technical materials too soon. It is the author's view that a student who obtains a background in cattle information by studying a basic, easily understood text will be better able to cope with more technical material later on. This book has been written for the student with the hope that by reading this text, he or she will keep alive an all-important excitement for and interest in the cattle industry.

This book is intended as a starting point for a lifetime of learning about beef and dairy cattle. Basic information is included on a variety of cattle-related topics to expose the student to as many facets of cattle raising as possible. Spurred by this background information, it is hoped that the student will go on to explore specific interests in greater detail.

The book also is intended to make the task of the instructor a more creative one by freeing him or her from spending time simplifying complicated material and, instead, allowing the opportunity to explore the more interesting and exciting aspects of beef and dairy cattle management.

Special thanks to Charles Norton, professor of animal science at Kansas State University for his assistance with this manuscript. Other educators and cattle experts helped also to make this text accurate and up-to-date. These professionals know the joys of working with cattle. We all hope that through this introductory volume we can communicate some of that excitement to the beginning student.

CHERYL MAY

CATTLE MANAGEMENT

Introduction to
Cattle Breeding

The development of cattle breeds for specific purposes such as milking, providing meat, and working as draft animals stands as a tribute to the ingenuity of mankind. For hundreds of years outstanding bulls have been bred to outstanding cows to develop the special characteristics needed in different areas of the world. Although today cattle producers take for granted the obvious advantages of careful selection for breeding, early pioneers in selective breeding took a few chances. Certainly it must have taken a strong spirit to have been the first in one's town to decide that, in one's own herd at least, certain characteristics were desirable and others were not. Unknown pioneers developed outstanding breeds like the Ayrshire, the Brown Swiss, the Angus, the Pinzgauer, and others. Today, American cattle producers reap the harvest of the efforts of those who have gone before them. Today's American cattle producers are not lacking in the courage and foresight required for breeding top quality cattle; they have developed polled versions of Hereford and Shorthorn cattle, and crossbred established breeds to develop the Barzona, the Braford, the Brangus, the Beefmaster, the Charbray, and the Santa Gertrudis. By taking advantage of the recessive red gene in Angus and in Brangus, the Red Angus and the Red Brangus breed were developed.

Additionally, many cattle producers whose herds are comprised of specimens of the British breeds such as Angus, Hereford, and Shorthorn, crossbreed their animals with various breeds, both new and old, in an effort to improve their herds.

Some of the "new" breeds, or *exotics*, as they are sometimes called, are not really new at all. They are merely new to us in the United States. Cattle breeds like Charolais, Marchigiana, and Simmental are relatively new to American cattle producers but have been bred selectively for generations in their native countries. For this reason, many of their breeders frown on the use of the term "exotic" to describe these cattle. Like the more tradi-

1

tional British breeds of Angus, Hereford, Shorthorn, and Devon, the new breeds all are members of the species *Bos taurus.*

The other species of cattle, *Bos indicus,* is represented in America by the Brahman, a breed established here in 1854 from several strains of Zebu, or Indian humped cattle.

In this book, the cattle breeds are divided into two categories: dairy cattle and beef cattle. All of the dairy breeds with the exception of the Normande have been established in the United States since at least 1912. Half-blood Normandes arrived in America in 1974 and certainly can be classified as members of a "new" breed.

Since the term exotic is used so frequently to describe various breeds of beef cattle, a listing of these new breeds might be helpful. A partial list includes: Blonde d'Aquitaine, Charolais, Chianina, Gelbvieh, Limousin, Maine-Anjou, Marchigiana, Murray Grey, Pinzgauer, Romagnola, Simmental, and Tarentaise. More breeds are arriving all the time, so any listing becomes incomplete as quickly as it is written.

Beef breeds developed in the United States include Barzona, Beefmaster, Braford, Brahman, Brangus, Polled Hereford, Red Brangus, Santa Gertrudis, and Polled Shorthorn.

British beef breeds consist of Angus, Red Angus, Devon, Galloway, Hereford, Shorthorn, and Scotch Highland.

An old breed that has been rediscovered and sometimes is termed an exotic is the Texas Longhorn. A descendant of Spanish Andalusian cattle, the Longhorn has been a part of U.S. cattle history since the 1600's but had been almost forgotten in recent years. An ambitious preservation effort has revitalized the breed.

In dairy cattle, the Normande is the lone newcomer. The little Dexter, originally from Ireland, is the second most recent addition to the American dairy cattle scene. That breed arrived in 1912. The other dairy breeds, the Ayrshire of Scotland, the Brown Swiss of Switzerland, the Dutch Belted of Holland, the Guernsey and the Jersey from the English Channel Islands bearing their names, the Holstein from the Rhine delta region of Europe, and the Milking Shorthorn, all arrived in the United States in the late 1700's or the 1800's.

With so many breeds from which to choose, the average American cattle producer often faces a dilemma in trying to find the "perfect" breed for his or her own ranch situation. Since there is no "perfect" breed, the decision is all the more difficult for now the advantages and disadvantages of each breed must be weighed and then matched with such factors as climate, type of cattle operation, finances, and the like. Making a close comparison of cattle qualities may help, as is done in the two following comparison charts.

CHART 1.   U.S. DAIRY CATTLE BREEDS COMPARED:
Date Introduced & Country of Origin

	Color	Horns	Weight (lbs.)
AYRSHIRE: 1822 (Ayr, Scotland, before 1800)	Red and white, mahogany, brown, or combination of these colors	Incline upward, refined, medium length. Taper toward tips	Cows: 1,200 Bulls: 1,850
BROWN SWISS: 1869 (Switzerland, as early as the Bronze Age)	Solid brown, varying from light to dark	Incline upward, slightly, medium length tapering toward tips	Cows: 1,500 Bulls: 2,000 +
DEXTER: 1912 (Ireland)	Solid black, occasionally red	Incline upward, medium length, taper toward tips	Cows: 650 Bulls: 800
DUTCH BELTED: 1838 (Holland prior to 17th century)	Black with band of white encircling the body	Yes	Cows: 900 to 1,500 Bulls: 2,000 +
GUERNSEY: 1831 (Guernsey Isle, English Channel, about A.D. 960)	Fawn with clearly defined white markings. Golden yellow pigmentation	Yes	Cows: 1,100 Bulls: 1,700
HOLSTEIN: mid-1850's (Rhine delta region of Europe about the time of Christ)	Black and white or red and white clearly defined markings	Yes	Cows: 1,500 Bulls: 2,200
JERSEY: 1815 (Jersey Isle, English Channel, about A.D. 960)	Fawn, with or without white markings	Curve inward, medium length, taper toward tips	Cows: 1,000 Bulls: 1,500
MILKING SHORTHORN: also known as Illawarra and Durham, 1783 (England about 1600)	Roan, red, red and white	Horned or polled. Horns flat and well set	Cows: 1,400 to 1,600 Bulls: up to 2,300
NORMANDE: 1974, half-bloods (France)	Dark red and white with colored patches around the eyes	Short. On cows, incurving and tapering toward tips	Cows: 1,500 to 1,600 Bulls: 2,500

CHART 2.   U.S. BEEF CATTLE BREEDS COMPARED:
Date Introduced & Country of Origin

	Color	Horns	Weight (lbs.)
ABONDANCE: 1976 (Semen from France)	Red and white	Medium length upright horns	Cows: 1,210 to 1,365 Bulls: 1,980 to 2,200
AFRICANDER: 1931 Breed has now disappeared from the U.S. (South Africa)	Red, lt. red, lt. tan, yellow and gray	Long horns with upturned ends. Also a polled strain.	Cows: 1,400 Bulls: 2,000
ANGUS: 1883 (Aberdeen and Angus shires in Scotland)	Black	Polled	Cows: 1,000 to 1,300 Bulls: 2,000 +
BARZONA: 1942 (Developed by F. N. Bard at Yavapai County, Arizona)	Solid red, varying from light to deep some white on underline	Short, curved horns	Cows: 1,100 to 1,250 Bulls: 1,800
BEEFALO: 1970 (in California)	Varying colors	Polled	Bulls: up to 3,800
BEEFMASTER: 1931 (by Tom Lasater in Texas from Hereford/Short-horn/Brahman)	Red, dun, others	Most horned	Cows: 1,400 Bulls: 2,200
BLONDE d'AQUITAINE: Semen to U.S. in 1971 (18th century from the Garonnais cattle of France)	Solid wheat color —light to dark	Horned	Cows: 1,650 Bulls: 2,530
BRAFORD: 1948 (by Alto Adams, Jr., at Ft. Pierce, Fla. from 5/8 Hereford, 3/8 Brahman	Shades of red to yellow; pigment around the eyes	Horned	Cows: 1,200 to 1,300 Bulls: 1,800

CHART 2. U.S. BEEF CATTLE BREEDS COMPARED:
Date Introduced & Country of Origin (*continued*)

	Color	Horns	Weight (lbs.)
BRAHMAN: 1854 (from several strains of Indian "Zebu" cattle)	Vary from light to gray or red to almost black	Short, straight horns	Cows: 1,000 to 1,400 Bulls: 1,600 to 2,200
BRANGUS: 1912 (Developed from 3/8 Brahman and 5/8 Angus at USDA Experiment Station at Jeanerette, La.)	Black (Red Brangus is red resulting from recessive red gene)	Polled	Cows: 1,200 to 1,400 Bulls: 1,900 to 2,050
CHARBRAY: 1930's (Developed in Rio Grande Valley from 13/16 Charolais and 3/16 Brahman)	White to light straw	Small horns	Cows: 2,000 to 2,200 Bulls: 2,800 to 3,200
CHAROLAIS: 1936 (Developed as early as A.D. 878 in Charolles, France)	White to light straw color	Small horns in horned specimens; also a polled strain	Cows: 1,600 to 1,800 Bulls: 2,500
CHIANINA: Semen in 1971 (Developed in the Chiana Valley of Italy before the Roman Empire)	Porcelain white hair, black tongue and palate, black nose and eye area, and a black switch	Horns curve downward	Cows: to 2,400 Bulls: to 4,000
DEVON: 1623 with colonists: First polled mutant developed in 1915 (Devonshire, England)	Ruby red hair, yellow skin	Horned strain has creamy white horns with black tips; also a polled strain	Cows: 1,200 Bulls: 1,800 to 2,000

CHART 2.   U.S. BEEF CATTLE BREEDS COMPARED:
Date Introduced & Country of Origin (*continued*)

	Color	Horns	Weight (lbs.)
GALLOWAY: 1870 First belted specimen arrived in 1948 (Vikings brought them to Scotland in 9th century)	Black, dun, white, red, belted (black with white belt)	Polled	Cows: 1,000 Bulls: 1,450
GELBVIEH: Semen in 1971 (N. Bavaria, West Germany)	Cream to reddish yellow	Horned	Cows: 1,400 to 1,800 Bulls: 2,225 to 2,900
HAYS CONVERTER No major imports yet (Developed by Sen. Harry Hays in Canada, 1952)	Black with white face or red with white face	Horned	Cows: 1,800 Bulls: 2,700
HEREFORD: 1817 Imported by Henry Clay (Hereford County, England)	Red with white face	Medium size, curved horns	Cows: 1,100 to 1,400 Bulls: 1,800 to 2,500
KOBE: 1978 Four Bulls (Japan)	Black	Short, upturned horns	Cows: 1,300 to 1,400 Bulls: 2,200 to 2,500
LIMOUSIN: Semen from Canada in 1968 (Developed in Limousin, France: Cave drawings record their history)	Light yellow with lighter areas around eyes and muzzle	Horns are horizontal, then spread upward	Cows: 1,300 to 1,400 Bulls: 2,200 to 2,500
LINCOLN RED: (Lincolnshire, England)	Red with occasional white markings	Horned and polled	Cows: 1,400 Bulls: 1,800 to 2,000

CHART 2.   U.S. BEEF CATTLE BREEDS COMPARED:
Date Introduced & Country of Origin (*continued*)

	Color	Horns	Weight (lbs.)
MAINE-ANJOU: Semen from Canada in 1969 (Durham and Mancelle Cattle crossed in France in 1830)	Dark red and white	Medium size, forward curving horns; some polled specimens	Cows: 1,650 to 1,960 Bulls: 2,600 to 3,000
MARCHIGIANA: Semen in 1972 (In the 5th century with the fall of the Roman Empire barbarians brought their cattle into Italy)	Gray	Horned	Cows: 1,300 to 1,500 Bulls: 2,500 to 3,000
MURRAY GREY: Semen in 1969 (First specimen born in 1905 in Australia to Angus sire and light roan Shorthorn dam)	Silver to dark gray, or dun	Polled	Cows: 1,500 Bulls: 1,800 to 2,000
NORWEGIAN RED: 1973 (Norway)	Solid red or red and white	Horned	Cows: 1,210 to 1,430 Bulls: 2,200 to 2,640
PARTHENAISE: 1970 (France)	Fawn with black background		Cows: 1,350 Bulls: 2,400
PIEDMONT— Piedmontese (Po Valley of Italy)	Light gray to cream color with black points	Small horns	Cows: 1,400 Bulls: 1,950
PINZGAUER: Semen in 1972 (Developed in late 1700's in Pinzgau Valley of Austria)	Reddish chestnut with white on back, tail, and barrel	Short, thick horns	Cows: 1,320 to 1,650 Bulls: 2,200 to 2,800

CHART 2.   U.S. BEEF CATTLE BREEDS COMPARED:
Date Introduced & Country of Origin (*continued*)

	Color	Horns	Weight (lbs.)
POLLED HEREFORD: 1900 (Developed when Warren Gammon collected herd of polled mutants for breeding)	Red with white face	Polled	Cows: 1,100 to 1,400 Bulls: 1,800 to 2,500
RANGER: 1950's (Developed in Wyoming and California by Ranger Cattle Co.)	Any color, solid or mottled	Small horns	Cows: 1,200 to 1,400 Bulls: 1,800 to 2,000
RED ANGUS: 1890 22 reds registered in Angus herd book (Red a recessive gene in black Angus herds)	Red	Polled	Cows: 1,500 Bulls: 1,900
RED BRANGUS: First recognized as separate breed in Texas in 1946 (Red a recessive gene in black Brangus herds)	Red	Polled	Cows: 1,200 to 1,400 Bulls: 1,900 to 2,050
RED POLL: 1873 by G. F. Taber (Norfolk and Suffolk, England, developed in 1846)	Light to dark red, white in tail switch	Polled	Cows: 1,400 Bulls: 2,100
ROMAGNOLA: 1974 (Po Valley of Italy)	Solid light gray with black patch around eyes, bulls have darker shade around neck, black tail brush	Horned	Cows: 1,450 to 1,750 Bulls: 2,500

CHART 2.   U.S. BEEF CATTLE BREEDS COMPARED:
Date Introduced & Country of Origin (*continued*)

	Color	Horns	Weight (lbs.)
SAHIWAL: No imports yet: included here as example of Zebu cattle. (West Pakistan)	Red with varying amounts of white on the neck, black tail brush	Horned and polled	Cows: 1,300 Bulls: 2,000
SALERS: North America 1973, U.S. 1978 (Mountainous regions of Salers, France)	Dark cherry red	Lyre-shaped horns	Cows: 1,430 to 1,760 Bulls: 2,000 to 2,650
SANTA GERTRUDIS: 1910 (by Robert J. Kleberg, Jr., on King Ranch from 3/8 Brahman and 5/8 Shorthorn)	Cherry red	Horned primarily, some polled specimens	Cows: 1,350 to 1,850 Bulls: 2,000 to 2,400
SCOTCH HIGHLAND: mid 1800's (Highlands of Scotland)	Black, brindle, red, light red, yellow, dun, and silver	Long, horizontal then upward curving horns	Cows: 900 to 1,400 Bulls: 1,300 to 2,000
SHORTHORN, POLLED SHORTHORN: 1783; Polled developed about 1870 (Developed about 1600 in the Tees River valley on the Northeastern coast of England)	Red, white, or roan	Short, refined horns that curve inward; polled Shorthorns are polled, of course	Cows: 1,600 to 2,000 Bulls: 2,200 +

CHART 2.   U.S. BEEF CATTLE BREEDS COMPARED:
Date Introduced & Country of Origin (*continued*)

	Color	Horns	Weight (lbs.)
SIMMENTAL: Semen from Canada in 1969 (Developed in western Switzerland)	White to light straw faces with red to dark red spotted bodies	Medium-size horns	Cows: 1,300 to 1,800 Bulls: 2,400 to 2,800
SOUTH DEVON: 1969 (Established in western England since 16th century)	Light red	Small, incurving horns	Cows: 1,500 to 1,700 Bulls: up to 3,000
SUSSEX: 1884 (Counties of Sussex and Kent in England)	Solid, medium red	Horned and polled	Cows: 1,450 Bulls: 2,000 +
TARENTAISE: 1972; Alpin, first bull to North America (Derived from ancient Alpine strain in Southeast France in 1859)	Reddish chestnut with darker pigment around eyes; bulls have darker pigment around neck and a dark tail brush	Horned, some polled specimens	Cows: 1,500 Bulls: 2,000
TEXAS LONGHORN: Crossed the Rio Grande with the Spanish in the 1600's (Originated from the Spanish Andalusian cattle that Columbus brought to Santo Domingo in 1493)	Brindle, roan, dark red, dark brown, dun, sand-hill crane, or grulla	Very, very long curved horns; steers grow the longest horns	Cows: 1,300 Bulls: 1,700 to 2,045
WELSH BLACK: 1960's (Developed in Wales as early as the 1300's)	Black	Horned	Cows: 1,000 to 1,300 Bulls: 1,800 to 2,000

Section One

THE DAIRY BREEDS

- Ayrshire • Brown Swiss • Dexter
- Dutch Belted • Guernsey • Holstein
- Jersey • Milking Shorthorn • Normande

Figure I-1 Indian Lake M. Lady Diane represents the typical Ayrshire. *(Courtesy of The Ayrshire Digest)*

Figure I-2 The Brown Swiss. *(Courtesy of the Brown Swiss Association)*

AYRSHIRE

The Ayrshire breed originated in the county of Ayr in Scotland sometime prior to 1800. It was through a long-term practice of selection for hardiness, superior quality udders, and efficiency of milk production from native stock that the breed was developed. To date, more than 800,000 Ayrshires have been issued certificates of ancestral heritage of pure-breed bloodlines by the American breed association since its organization in 1875.

The Ayrshire Breeders' Association has approved sire and dam programs to aid in selection of superior breeding stock. A selective registry program emphasizes top siring bulls for milk production based on official records in their pedigree.

Ayrshires are red and white. Mature cows weigh more than 1,200 pounds. They are especially strong in the heart girth with large, capacious middles. A hardy, rugged breed, they have well-attached udders and sound feet and legs. This breed has excellent lifetime production and longevity records. Under average conditions, a mature cow may produce more than 12,000 pounds of 4 percent milk. Through progressive feeding and management practices, hundreds of Ayrshires have produced at levels above 10,000 quarts, or 20,000 pounds of milk in their normal 10-month lactation periods. Some single lactation records in excess of 30,000 pounds have been officially recorded by the Ayrshire Breeders' Association.

The first American importation of Ayrshires was made by H. W. Hills of Windsor, Connecticut, around 1822. After becoming established in New England, dairy farmers from other parts of the country purchased breeding stock and established herds throughout the United States. Today, New York, Pennsylvania, Minnesota, Ohio, Kansas, Wisconsin, and Vermont have the highest concentrations of Ayrshires.

Economy of production, hardiness, reproduction persistency, and longevity are the basic Ayrshire qualities that make them popular.

BROWN SWISS

The Brown Swiss breed is one of the oldest of the dairy breeds and is descended from cattle used in the valleys and mountain slopes of Switzerland since before historic records began. The origins still further back are somewhat doubtful. Some think that the breed goes back eventually to Oriental origins, having been introduced into Europe from the steppes and valleys of western Asia. On the other hand, cattle bones found in the ruins of the Swiss Lake Dwellers are very similar to the bones of present Brown Swiss cattle and are evidence that a type of cattle closely related to the Brown Swiss existed in Switzerland during the Bronze Age. It is believed that there has been little or no infusion of foreign blood, no apparent crossing of the breed with other cattle, throughout its development.

The first Brown Swiss cattle to be introduced into America were brought in by Henry M. Clark, of Belmont, Massachusetts, in the winter of 1869–70. The first importation consisted of one bull and seven females from the canton of Schwyz, Switzerland. An additional bull and female from a different area were imported at the same time. From total importations numbering only 155 head, the breed has grown and prospered in the United States.

Early breed growth in the United States was limited to New England, but the breed gradually found itself growing in popularity. Today the breed is represented in every state, Canada, Mexico, South America, and South Africa.

Advantages of Brown Swiss include long productive lives, quiet temperament, good milk production, and quality legs. A research study at Iowa State University comparing major dairy breeds for "cow life" found Brown Swiss to be the longest lived.

Brown Swiss color is a solid brown varying from very light to dark. Mature cows weigh 1300 to 1500 pounds. Mature bulls weigh about 2000 pounds. Breeders have been striving to improve the quality of Brown Swiss udders.

DEXTER

One of the rarest breeds found in the United States is the Irish Dexter. First imported in 1912, the Dexter is the smallest American breed. Cows average 650 pounds, bulls about 800 pounds. Their shortness is accentuated by the shortness of their legs between the knee and the dewclaw. Originally a mountain breed, Dexters adapt well to climatic variations.

Figure I-3   The diminutive Dexter. *(Courtesy of the American Dexter Cattle Association)*

In spite of their small size, milk yields of 400 to 600 gallons a year are considered normal. Dexters sometimes are utilized as a dual-purpose breed for beef as well as milk. Since the breed matures early, steers can be grown out at minimum cost.

Dexters have been exported to many parts of the world. In South Africa the breed has been used for many years and probably arrived on ships where they had been kept for supplying passengers with milk en route.

Today Dexters for sale are scarce. Only about 150 breeders in the United States maintain herds.

Dexter breeders are outcrossing to other breeds to overcome a genetic problem. There is a high incidence of births of "bulldog" calves, a lethal condition to the calf that causes it to be dropped anytime between the fifth and ninth month of pregnancy. The flow of milk from the cow is roughly proportional to the time the calf has been carried. The cow recovers its normal lactation at its next normal calving. Some breeders slaughter breeding stock that bear "bulldogs."

DUTCH BELTED

Dutch Belted cattle originated in Holland prior to the seventeenth century. From the records available it seems they were bred by the nobility who conceived the idea of breeding animals of all kinds to a particular color, mainly with a band of white in the center and both ends black. For more than 100 years they and their descendants worked on this color pattern until they produced belted cattle, rabbits, goats, poultry, and swine. The resulting animals are today known as Dutch Belted cattle, Dutch belted rabbits, Dutch belted goats, Lakenvelder poultry of England and America, Lanche swine of Holland and Germany, and Hampshire swine of America. (Hampshire swine are said to have originated in Hampshire, England but are descendants of the Holland herds.)

Dutch Belted cattle are jet black except for the white belt that should begin a little back of the shoulder and extend not quite to the hips and entirely circle the body.

Mature bulls often weigh more than 2,000 pounds. Cows weigh from 900 to 1,500 pounds.

Cows have large udders and prominent milk veins and are good milkers. Their milk tests 3.5 to 5.5 percent butterfat.

The first importation of Dutch Belted cattle into the United States was made by the U.S. Consul of Holland, D. H. Haight, in 1838. In 1840, P. T. Barnum, of circus fame, imported several head from a nobleman to be used for exhibition as a feature of his circus. Barnum's herd was exhibited for several years, but he found them to be so valuable as milkers that he placed them on his farm in Orange County, New York.

Figure I-4   A wide white band around the midsection characterizes the Dutch Belted. *(Courtesy of the Dutch Belted Cattle Association of America, Inc.)*

In 1848, H. W. Coleman of Cornwall, Pennsylvania, imported several animals. A later importation was made in 1906 by W. H. Lance of Peapack, New Jersey. From these beginnings, Dutch Belted cattle spread throughout the United States. Several herds from this country have been exported to Canada, Cuba, Mexico, Argentina, Brazil, England. The breed is horned.

GUERNSEY

Guernsey cattle trace their ancestry back a thousand years to the Isle of Guernsey in the English Channel. The island covers only 24 square miles but is the birthplace of today's worldwide population of Guernsey cattle.

Monks sent to colonize the island, civilize the natives, and drive marauding pirates from the shores, sent for two breeds of French dairy cattle and began crossing the two. The two breeds, the Fromont du Leon from Brittany, and the Norman Brindles from Normandy, are believed to be the same foundation stock used for the development of the Jersey breed on neighboring Jersey, another of the Channel Islands.

The native Guernsey cattle were bred selectively by the monks for years before being exported to other lands. In 1831 Captain Prince, an American sailing captain from Boston, Massachusetts, visited Guernsey on his way back to America from France. He was impressed with the quality of Guernsey milk and bought a cow and bull to take back to America. These first Guernseys to reach America were known as the Pillsbury cow and bull. They were taken to New Hampshire, to an island in the middle of Lake Winnepesaukee later named Guernsey Island.

The American Guernsey Cattle Club was formed on February 7, 1877, at the Astor House in New York City. The club provides a Guernsey registry, promotes the breed throughout the United States and abroad, and offers a complete group of breed improvement and service programs. One of the most basic of club programs is production testing. In addition, a program of sire evaluation is maintained, and an annual performance register is published by the club.

A Gold Star Recognition Program was organized to recognize outstanding sires, dams, breeders, and herds.

Figure I-5 Golden Acres Dari Lillian is a representative Guernsey. *(Courtesy of the American Guernsey Cattle Club)*

The Gold Star Dam Award designates approximately the top one percent of registered Guernsey cows that have met high requirements. To be a Gold Star Dam, a cow must have a minimum of two production records, have a USDA Cow Index of more than 750 pounds of milk at 32 percent repeatability, and be officially classified very good or excellent for conformation. Other Gold Star Recognition Programs demand similar high achievements.

With its youth program, the American Guernsey Cattle Club sponsors a junior production contest and presents several recognition awards annually to outstanding junior Guernsey breeders.

Guernsey cows should weigh 1,100 pounds or more at maturity. Mature bulls weigh up to 1,800 pounds. The breed is a shade of fawn in color with white markings clearly defined. The breed is horned.

HOLSTEIN

The Holstein cow originated in Europe, the daughter of the black cows and the white cows of the Bavarians and the Friesians, two migrant European tribes that moved together into the fertile Rhine delta region about 2,000 years ago. That Rhineland region became the Netherlands, and for 2,000 years the Holstein cow was bred to obtain animals that could make the best use of the area's most abundant resource—grass.

The Holstein has made quite an impact on the American cattle scene as well. The frequently seen black and white Holstein is the most numerous dairy breed in the United States, representing 80 percent of the milk cows in America today.

The first Holstein in America arrived on a Dutch sailing ship in the 1850's. Winthrop Chenery, a Massachusetts cattle breeder, purchased a Holland cow from the master of the sailing vessel who had landed his ship at the port of Boston. The cow had furnished the crew with fresh milk during the voyage. She proved to be such a satisfactory producer that Chenery made later importations in 1857, 1859, and 1861.

After about 8,800 animals had been imported, foot-and-mouth disease broke out in Europe. United States government regulations prohibited imports from affected countries. To maintain Holstein standards, American breeders gathered together, formed their associations, and in 1885 merged them into the Holstein-Friesian Association of America. With their own herd book, their own association, and their own foundation stock, they set about the task of building their own Holstein breed.

Holstein calves weigh about 90 pounds at birth. Bulls grow to about 2,200 pounds at maturity, cows to about 1,500 pounds.

Figure I-6 Rinehart Apollo Dawfin, a representative Holstein. *(Courtesy of the Holstein-Friesian Association of America)*

A USDA test of American Holstein cows of all ages for a 5-year period showed an actual average per cow of 12,900 pounds of milk in 305 days with 3.68 percent fat content. Two year olds calving at 24 months averaged 11,055 pounds milk, while cows calving at 7 years produced an average 14,300 pounds of milk. Cows that calved at 13 years averaged 12,676 pounds of milk. A cow population of 3,386,876 animals was used in the test.

With nutrition and management practices improving all the time, milk production records can be expected to be surpassed in the future.

JERSEY

In 1815, the first Jersey cows came to America from the Island of Jersey, the largest of the English Channel islands. More Jerseys were imported in 1850, and it was these that became the first animals to be registered in the *American Jersey Cattle Club Herd Book* when the club was established in 1868.

Figure I-7   The Jersey breed is fawn-colored like Generators Topsy. *(Courtesy of the American Jersey Cattle Club)*

Jerseys vary greatly in color, but the characteristic color is some shade of fawn with optional white markings. The muzzle is black encircled by a light-colored ring. The tongue and switch may be either white or black. If horns are present on the Jersey they characteristically incline forward and are incurving. They should be refined, of medium length, and taper toward the tips. No discrimination is made by Jersey judges for absence of horns.

Advantages of Jerseys include well-shaped udders and strong udder attachments. They have an angular conformation and tend to be free of excessive tissue.

The ideal mature weight for Jersey cows in milk is about 1,000 pounds. Bulls weigh about 1,500 pounds.

Selective breeding has been used for generations to develop a typical Jersey cow. The first unified attempts at improving the conformation of Jersey animals began in 1834 on Jersey Island. A scale of points was drawn up during that year and the first district show was held.

Careful selection techniques continue today with Dairy Herd Improvement Registry records used as a basis for sire selection.

In 1973, all registered Jerseys on official test averaged 10,304 pounds of milk and 514 pounds fat. That year Generators Topsy was Grand Champion female with 25,010 pounds of milk. In each succeeding year, individual cows topped that record. By 1976, Basil Lucy Minnie Pansy achieved a record of 32,660 pounds of milk and 1,589 pounds fat. By now that record most likely will have been surpassed.

Dairy bulls have a reputation for dangerous tempers and Jerseys are among the most notorious of all. For safety's sake, however, no bull should be trusted.

MILKING SHORTHORNS

Milking Shorthorns originated from the same stock as their beef Shorthorn cousins on the northeastern coast of England in the counties of Northumberland, Durham, York, and Lincoln, with the first real development of the breed being in the valley of the Tees River about 1600. The Shorthorns that spread to Scotland were developed as beef animals. Those remaining in England were selected more for dual-purpose qualities—milk and meat.

Milk breed Shorthorns first came to America in 1783, landing in Virginia. Called Durhams, they were used not only for milk and meat, but also for power. Even today, in some sections of the country, fair goers can see Durham oxen in pulling contests.

Figure I-8 The Milking Shorthorn developed from the Shorthorn breed. *(Courtesy of the American Milking Shorthorn Society)*

In 1882 the American Shorthorn Breeders Association was formed to register and promote both Milking and Scotch (beef) Shorthorns. In 1912 a group of Milking Shorthorn breeders formed the Milking Shorthorn Club to work within the framework of the American Shorthorn Breeders Association. This relationship continued until 1948 when the American Milking Shorthorn Society was incorporated and took over the registration and promotion of Milking Shorthorns.

Like beef Shorthorns, Milking Shorthorns can be either polled or horned. Cows are stretchy, maintaining depth of body to present a balanced profile. Mature cows weigh 1,400 to 1,600 pounds. Bulls weigh up to 2,300 pounds. Bulls are taller than their beef counterparts and tend to have longer, more angular bodies.

Milking Shorthorns sometimes are referred to as Durhams or as Illawarras, though their official name is Milking Shorthorns.

Top records in milk production for the breed are in excess of 20,000 pounds.

Figure I-9   The newest dairy breed in America is the Normande. *(Courtesy of the American Normande Association)*

NORMANDE

The Normande breed originated in France where today there is a high density of the breed in the areas of Normandy, Brittany, and Maine. The breed has been exported for many years, especially to Latin America. Normandes were present in Colombia as early as 1877.

The first half-blood Normandes in the United States arrived in 1974. The Normandes are primarily dark red and white in color, the proportion of their respective color in the coat varies with the animal so that some have very dark coats while others show a lighter coloring.

Advantages of Normande include good milking ability, good beef quality, tolerance of cold weather, hardiness, adaptability, and calving ease. Birth weights average 83 pounds for females and 92 pounds for males. Mature bulls average 2,500 pounds.

Colored patches around the eyes give them resistance to pinkeye and cancer eye. A pigmented udder helps prevent sunburn.

The average Normande cow produces 9,240 pounds of milk per year. Mature cows generally reach weights of 1,500 to 1,600 pounds. Despite their size, Normande cows are known for their docile dispositions. Appendix A gives a listing of dairy cattle breed associations.

STUDY QUESTIONS

1. Breeds like Angus and Hereford are members of the _____ species. (*Bos taurus*)
2. *Bos indicus* cattle are recognized by _____. (a hump)
3. Cattle identified by a wide white band around their middle are known as _____. (Dutch Belted)
4. The _____ breed is the most numerous dairy breed in the United States today. (Holstein)
5. Illawarra, or Durham, refer to the breed known officially as _____. (Milking Shorthorns)
6. The newest breed of dairy cattle, the _____, came to the United States from France. (Normande)

Section Two

THE BEEF BREEDS

- Abondance • Africander • Angus • Barzona
- Beefalo • Beefmaster • Belted Galloway
- Blonde d'Aquitaine • Braford • Brahman
- Brangus • Charbray • Charolais • Chiangus
- Chianina • Devon • Galloway • Gelbvieh
- Hays Converter • Hereford • Kobe • Limousin
- Lincoln Red • Maine-Anjou • Marchigiana
- Murray Grey • Norwegian Red • Parthenaise
- Piedmont • Pinzgauer • Polled Hereford
- Ranger • Red Angus • Red Brangus • Red Poll
- Romagnola • Sahiwal • Salers • Santa Gertrudis
- Scotch Highland • Shorthorn • Simmental
- South Devon • Sussex • Tarentaise
- Texas Longhorn • Welsh Black

ABONDANCE

The Abondance is a red and white dual purpose breed from the mountainous regions of France. The cattle are highly adapted to rugged terrain. They originated from three isolated groups of cattle: the Valdotaine cattle of Italy, the Boheme cattle of Czechoslovakia, and the red cattle from the Black Forest of Germany. The French Abondance herd book was established in 1894.

Advantages of the Abondance include their excellent milk production and their adaptability to the mountain climate of France. The breed has been criticized for lack of stature and late maturity. Average mature cows weigh from 1,210 to 1,365 pounds, while bulls may vary from 1,980 to 2,200 pounds.

Some promoters in the United States have called the Abondance a strain of Simmental cattle. However, other sources who have conducted research studying the three groups of cattle from which the Abondance sprang say that none of the breeds appears closely related to Simmental. The controversy continues.

Many Abondance cattle have a typical red patch around their eyes.

Figure II-1 A red eye patch is characteristic of the **Abondance.** *(Courtesy of Hy-Cross Beef Breeders Ltd.)*

AFRICANDER

Hundreds of years ago when the Portuguese landed in South Africa they brought with them their cattle, the Alentejana. These cattle mated with native South African cattle. The result was the animal known today as the Africander. These Zebu-type, humped cattle have been known in South Africa as a distinct breed since before 1900. When Dutch settlers arrived in South Africa they used selective breeding to develop the Africander first for draft use and later for beef production.

A polled strain of the breed has been developed, but most animals are horned—long horns with upturned ends. Colors within the breed include red, light red, light tan, yellow and gray.

Mature cows weigh about 1,400 pounds, with bulls averaging about 2,000 pounds.

The Africander first reached the United States in 1931, when the King Ranch of Texas imported 16 bulls and 11 cows. The breed was used in a number of experimental breeding programs and was successfully used in the development of the Barzona breed.

The King Ranch of Kingsville, Texas, was the last remaining bastion of the Africander in the United States. The last of the purebred Africanders died in 1974. Only a few half-bloods remain on the King Ranch today and they are very old.

ANGUS

Black, polled cattle are said to have existed in Scotland long before the 1700's. The breed known today as Angus however, was developed in the shires of Aberdeen and Angus. The breed still is known as the Aberdeen-Angus in many countries, though the name in most places has been shortened for simplicity.

As early as 1707 beef from Scotland was prized in England for its flavor. Scotch farmers took advantage of the demand and selected their animals for beef-stock traits.

Hugh Watson of Keillor, Scotland, took some black, hornless cattle from his father's herd, added 11 of his own, and set about breeding the best animals to each other. His inbreeding program resulted in animals that still are famous today. His most well-known cow, Old Grannie, lived to age 36 after producing 29 calves. In 1859 she died, not as a result of illness or old age, but in a thunderstorm.

William McCombie, another pioneer of the Angus breed, is credited with being a dynamic factor in building the breed. Like Watson, he too utilized inbreeding to fix type, outcrossing for improvement later. From 1847 to 1878 McCombie brought fame to the breed through show ring wins.

Figure II-2   The Angus is known for its excellent quality carcass. *(Courtesy of the American Angus Association)*

Called the perfector of Angus type, Sir George MacPherson-Grant of Ballindalloch, Scotland, became involved with Angus breeding in 1861 when he purchased a well-bred cow, Erica. Prior to his death in 1907, MacPherson-Grant made numerous contributions to the development of the breed.

Angus came to the United States through the efforts of George Grant, a native Briton who envisioned establishing a colony of Britishers in the middle of Kansas. He purchased land, developed a town that he named after his queen, Victoria, and imported four Angus bulls. The bulls arrived in 1873 and were first used on Texas Longhorn cows. Later, in 1876, George Brown, a professor at Kansas State University, imported additional Angus. The first registered Angus were imported by James Anderson and George Findlay, of Lake Forest, Illinois. Both men were Scots, knowledgeable in the breed.

Today Angus herds have been established throughout the world, including Argentina, South Africa, New Zealand, Japan, North and South America, and Europe.

Mature bulls sometimes top 2,000 pounds, cows average 1,300 to 1,500 pounds.

Angus are best known for their high-quality carcasses. Additional desirable traits include easy calving, good mothering ability, early maturity, and lengthy, productive lives. Critics of Angus cite lack of size as a breed fault. Also, bulls are not as aggressive breeders as bulls of some breeds.

Figure II-3 This Barzona, Mr. Mafes 6234, weighed 1500 pounds at two years of age. *(Courtesy of Barzona Breeders Association of America and Mississippi State University)*

BARZONA

Development of the Barzona breed of beef cattle was begun in 1942 by F. N. Bard in the Castle Hot Springs area of Yavapai County, Arizona. Bard Ranch, a sprawling 400 sections, ranged from actual deserts at 1,000-foot elevations to rough, rocky foothills, up to very rugged mountains at about 6,000 feet. Temperatures were extreme, rainfall was sparse and irregular, and waters were widely scattered. Available feed consisted of shrubs and browse plants, some perennial grasses at the higher elevations, plus annual weeds following occasional wet spells. Annual carrying capacity was rated at two to eight head to the section. Fundamental economics dictated a need to develop an animal that would live, grow, and reproduce regularly under these stressful conditions. In 1946, E. S. (Jack) Humphrey, a geneticist, was chosen by the Bard Ranch to head the breeding program.

Breeding selection was based on a need for natural fertility, aggressive breeding habits, easy calving, strong mothering instinct, feet and legs to handle rough country, and ability to utilize a large quantity of browse in the diet.

The first breeding step was to cross Africander bulls on mountain-raised Hereford cows. Shorthorn and Brahman blood were added by breeding Santa Gertrudis with the first cross. With the infusion of some Angus blood to add carcass quality, small birth weights, milk, and muscle, the gene pool was complete. The herd was closed in the mid-1950's.

The Barzona Breeders Association of America was established in 1968. From those Arizona beginnings, Barzona have moved to herds throughout the United States.

The Barzona is a medium-sized beef animal with actual adult size varying somewhat with the environment. Cows average 1,100 to 1,200 pounds, with mature bulls weighing up to 1,800 pounds. Barzonas have smooth, long bodies with longish heads. Normal color is solid, medium red, but may vary from a deep to a light red. Occasionally white may appear on the animal's underline or switch. The dark-pigmented loose hide and straight, short hair help make the Barzona heat tolerant and insect resistant. Pinkeye and related conditions are seldom heard of in these cattle. Barzonas may be either horned or polled. The breed has developed relatively long legs, strong medium-sized bone, and tight, very hard feet. The animals graze large areas efficiently and are naturally able to utilize a high percentage of browse in their diet.

Although the breed has excellent heat tolerance, it has been criticized for not withstanding cold weather as well as some other breeds.

Figure II-4   The Beefalo is a hybrid cross of cattle and buffalo. *(Courtesy of American Beefalo Association)*

BEEFALO

A Beefalo is an animal comprised of three-eighths buffalo, three-eighths Charolais, and one-fourth Hereford. Because the chromosome structures of cattle and buffalo are not the same, researchers spent years attempting a cross that would result in a fertile hybrid. Initial attempts resulted in sterile animals, like mules, which are the hybrid of horses and donkeys. The F, female is fertile but the f, bull is not. Some Beefalo bulls have exceeded 3,800 pounds in weight.

Advantages of the Beefalo include good cold tolerance because they have fur instead of regular cow hides with 15,000 to 18,000 hairs per square inch compared with regular cattle which have 3,000 to 5,000 hairs per square inch. Additionally, Beefalo calves are born weighing 40 to 65 pounds. The breed has excellent winter foraging ability according to research by H. F. Peters and S. B. Slen of the Canada Department of Agriculture.

The Beefalo, however, does not perform as well in the feedlot as conventional cattle, its meat is leaner and lacks the marbling that consumers have come to expect in tender meat. Because of the lack of marbling, Beefalo carcasses tend to grade lower also.

BEEFMASTER

The Beefmaster breed was developed by the Lasater Ranch, formerly of Falfurrias, Texas. The breeding program leading to their development was started by Ed C. Lasater in 1908 when he purchased Brahman bulls to use on his commercial herd of Hereford and Shorthorn cattle. Three strains of Brahman blood were used in the program, Gir, Nellore, and Guzerat. Throughout the program, milk production was stressed. Later there was a combination of breeding among the Brahman and Hereford cattle with a limited introduction of registered Shorthorn.

The exact pedigree of the foundation cattle is unknown. Estimates are that at present the cattle carry slightly less than one-half Brahman blood and slightly more than one-fourth each of Hereford and Shorthorn blood.

Breeding operations were carried on in multiple-sire herds. Culling was based on "Beefmasters' Six Essentials": disposition, fertility, weight, conformation, hardiness, and milk production. Emphasis was on the production of pounds of beef. No attention has been given to characteristics that do not affect the carcass, such as horns, hide, and color, although red is a predominant color for the breed.

Weight for mature cows averages 1,400 pounds; bulls average 2,200 pounds.

Beefmaster has been criticized for a lack of uniformity when compared to longer established breeds.

Figure II-5   The Beefmaster developed from Hereford, Shorthorn, and Brahman crosses. *(Courtesy of Beefmaster Breeders Universal)*

The breed association, Beefmaster Breeders Universal, was established in 1961 with headquarters in San Antonio, Texas. Cattle are not registered in the conventional sense, although a breeder can secure a Certificate of Breeding if desired. Beefmaster Breeders Universal no longer requires that cattle come directly from the foundation Lasater herd to be designated as Beefmasters. Cattle must be either "purebred" descendants of the foundation herd or they must be produced by three consecutive crosses of recognized Beefmaster breeding, a process known as *grading up*.

Beefmaster Breeders Universal offers both a voluntary classification program and a voluntary approved sales program. In the voluntary classification program, the animal is rated, or classified, according to breed guidelines. There are three categories: U, for superior purebreds; commercial, for commercial herds; and X, indicating the animal is disqualified due to inherited deformities or a combination of discriminations that would be a detriment to the breed. The voluntary approved sales program specifies that all cattle to be sold be inspected by the BBU executive vice-president, official classifier, or field inspector to insure that all cattle are properly identified according to their Certificates of Breeding. Any cattle exhibiting genetic defects, signs of infertility, or any other faults detrimental to the breed are removed from the sale offering.

BELTED GALLOWAYS

Belted Galloways are an old Scottish breed characterized by the unique combination of certain special qualities including hardiness, adaptability to cold climates due to their thick, double coat, and a wide white belt around their midsection.

Foundation stock of the present Belted Galloway herds in the United States and Canada apparently date back to an importation from Scotland in 1948. Since that time, whenever there have been no import restrictions, additional stock has been imported and established throughout the United States.

"Belties" are members of the Galloway family of hill cattle, one of the oldest breeds. The Galloway district of Scotland includes some of the most mountainous, cold, and austere land in Britain. Having been developed under these conditions, they adapt well to cold climates. Their double coat consists of a fine, short, thick undercoat and a rough, long overcoat. Their long coat makes them less tolerant of heat, though.

"Beltie" cows are aggressive protectors of their calves but with proper management are quiet and docile.

Advantages of the Belted Galloway include good browsing ability, cows with large udders for good milk production, and hardiness in inclement weather. The cattle are similar to Angus, are polled, but have a long curly coat. Smaller than their Scotch cousins, "Belties" average 1,100 to 1,500 pounds for mature bulls. Cows generally average less than 1,000 pounds. (*See also* "Galloway.")

Figure II-6   Belted Galloway are distinguished by a wide, white belt around their midsections. *(Courtesy of Belted Galloway Society, Inc.)*

Figure II-7   The Blonde d'Aquitaine is a large French breed. *(Courtesy of the American Blonde d'Aquitaine Association)*

BLONDE D'AQUITAINE

The Blonde d'Aquitaine breed originated in the southwestern part of France in the eighteenth century. The Blonde breed of today descended from a group of light-colored cattle with pale mucous membranes, the Garonnais of the plain and the Garonnais of the hills, later known as "Le Quercy."

The Garonnais herd book was established in 1898. However it was not until the end of World War II that those responsible for the herd book began selective breeding for meat production. Until that time, Blondes had primarily been used as working animals.

The breed was introduced to the North American continent in September 1971. Semen became available in December 1971, for use in crossbreeding programs. Breeding cattle or semen have been exported to the United States, Canada, Australia, New Zealand, Argentina, and 15 other countries throughout the world.

Blonde coloring is a solid wheat ranging from light to dark with lighter rings often occurring around the eyes and muzzle, on the inner side of the legs, under the belly and the shins. The horns are light-colored, darkening at the tips. The hooves also are light-colored.

Structurally, the breed standard calls for a long-bodied, heavy, long-muscled animal with a parallel top and underline. Blondes have moderate bone for a large breed.

Mature bulls weigh 2,500 pounds and more. Average mature cows weigh about 1,650 pounds.

Advantages of the breed include good mothering ability. Cows produce large quantities of high butterfat milk. Additionally, Blondes display good heat tolerance, good quality carcass, and high fertility.

BRAFORD

The Braford was one of the first successful crosses to be used in Florida and the Gulf Coast. The Adams Ranch Braford program was begun in 1948 when a group of Kansas Hereford bulls were bred to Brahman cows by Alto Adams, Jr., at his Fort Pierce, Florida, ranch. By the middle 1950's, five-eighths Hereford, three-eighths Brahman bulls were mated with similar cows in a program geared to produce a heavy (550 to 750 pounds) calf that could go to slaughter, grass, or directly to the feedlot.

By producing a heavy weaned calf, stockmen are able to put the steer calves directly on feed. Calves have a high feed efficiency, reducing production costs.

Figure II-8 The Braford was developed to combine qualities of Brahmans and Herefords. *(Courtesy of International Braford Association)*

Characteristically Brafords have the short hair, eye pigment, and good milking qualities of the Brahman. From the Hereford they get bone, body, good disposition, and fertility. The Brahman hump has been eliminated. The color is various shades of red to yellow as distinguished from the brindle found in the early crosses. There is some white in the face with pigmented eyes.

The Adams ranch program has involved from 5,000 to 9,000 cows annually. Many lines of Hereford bulls were used to develop five largely unrelated families of Braford cattle. This has made possible selection from a wide base. From the beginning, selection has been based on productivity. Bulls have been weighed for nearly 30 years and have been replaced as soon as a superior son has been produced. This has resulted in rapid improvement and many generations of selection on the bull side. Cows are turned over more slowly and old cows are kept to insure that the longevity of the original crosses is maintained.

Today selection emphasizes early maturity, both in breeding animals and finishing steers. The International Braford Association emphasizes that the goal of breeders is toward more efficient cattle with good feed conversion. Adaptation to warm climates and practical commercial conditions also is a must. Cattle kept for breeding are raised in the same manner as commercial cattle, with no special treatment.

Braford herds have been established in southern and central Florida and exported to Puerto Rico and South America. They are used as far north as Tennessee, and in Texas, New Mexico, and the Southwest.

The International Braford Association was incorporated by Alto Adams, Jr., in 1969. Founder memberships still are open. The five-part Braford program involves the following points:

1. Cattle must be bred in the environment in which they are to be raised.
2. Selection is based on traits having the greatest dollar value.
3. Natural selection is used.
4. Selection of herd sire bulls is made from the widest possible base.
5. Group the best cows—breed the best herd sire bulls to the best cows.

Where hot weather, insects, and other feedlot and range conditions prevail, Braford have adapted effectively. They do not perform well in cold climates, however.

BRAHMAN

The humped cattle of India—sometimes called Zebu—have served humanity for thousands of years. Throughout their history they have endured famine, insect pests, diseases, and the extremely hot climates of India and other countries. Some 30 well-defined breeds or strains of humped cattle are found in India. They vary in type and characteristics according to the needs and fancy of the people in the regions where they are found. Only a few of the breeds of India contributed to the development of the American Brahman.

The American Brahman breed was developed in the southern part of the United States. The breed was developed from approximately 266 bulls and 22 cows of several strains of Indian humped cattle imported to the United States between 1854 and 1926.

The first Indian cattle were imported in 1849 by Dr. James Bolton Davis of Fairfield County, South Carolina. However, their identity was lost during the Civil War. In 1854, two Indian bulls were presented to Richard Barrow, sugar and cotton planter of Louisiana, as a gift from the government of Great Britain. Barrow bred the cattle and their fame spread.

In 1878 a speculator bought four Indian bulls and a cow to sell at the port of Indianola, Texas. Additional imports were made in 1885, 1895, and 1906. At this same time, many animals were being exported from India to Brazil, providing an additional purchase point for American cattle producers. In 1924 the American Brahman Breeders Association was organized, a herd book established, and a standard of excellence adopted. The name "Brahman" was suggested by J. W. Sartwelle, first secretary of the association.

Figure II-9 The Brahman was developed from Indian cattle. *(Courtesy of American Brahman Breeders Association)*

Mature bulls weigh from 1,600 to 2,200 pounds, mature cows from 1,000 to 1,400 pounds. Calves are small at birth, weighing 60 to 65 pounds.

Brahmans vary in color from a very light gray or red to almost black. The preferred color is a light to medium shade of gray. Mature bulls are normally darker than cows and usually have dark areas on the neck, shoulders, lower thighs, and flanks. Red color has become increasingly popular. White or dark spots on a gray or red background are acceptable but not popular. So-called albinos, characterized by unpigmented skin, white nose, light colored hooves, and white switch are disqualified for registration as are brindle colors.

The Brahman has a genetic resistance to some diseases including pinkeye, tick fever, anaplasmosis, and lumpy jaw. The complete absence of eye cancer is due in part to the dark pigmented skin. Scientists believe that a genetic resistance also is involved. The Brahman also has natural protection against blood-sucking insects due to unique physiological characteristics, including an ability to twitch the skin, a dense hide, a sebum secretion, and a short haircoat.

Advantages of Brahman include mothering ability, with cows giving milk with a butterfat content of more than 5 percent, good rustling ability, calving ease due to low birth weights, and longevity.

Brahman are somewhat slow to mature sexually, with bulls used in limited service at age 2 on 10 to 12 females. By age 3, Brahmans are given a breeding herd of 25 to 30 females. Some say Brahmans have a trait of breeding each cow only once, and that being at her most conceptual period of heat.

Brahmans have excellent heat tolerance, but do not tolerate cold climates very well.

Disposition of Brahman cattle sometimes is questioned. They are high-spirited and energetic and need to be handled with care and kindness. The "Brahma" bull used in rodeo competition should not be considered representative of the Brahman beef breed any more than rodeo broncs are representative of various horse breeds.

BRANGUS

The first crosses of Brahman and Angus cattle were made as far back as 1912 at the USDA Experiment Station at Jeanerette, Louisiana. During the same period, Clear Creek Ranch of Welch, Oklahoma, the Essar Ranch of San Antonio, Texas, and a few individual breeders were carrying on private experimental breeding programs. These Brangus pioneers were looking for a desirable beef-type animal with the Brahman's climatic adaptability and

Figure II-10 The Brangus was developed from the Brahman and the Angus breeds. *(Courtesy of International Brangus Breeders Association)*

the Angus's high-quality carcass. In 1949 breeders from 16 states and Canada gathered in Vinita, Oklahoma and formed the American Brangus Breeders Association, later renamed the International Brangus Breeders Association.

Proven individuals of the two parent breeds serve as the foundation for establishing new bloodlines. Registered Brangus must be three-eighths Brahman and five-eighths Angus, solid black, polled, and have passed inspection by an association inspector as to conformation and breed character.

Brangus have adapted to many and varied climates. Breeders cite the fact that the parent breeds were developed for such varying climates as the reason for their tolerance for all kinds of weather. They seem to be better adapted than either parent breed to desert or semidesert country. Their attributes include mothering ability, good feedlot performance, and good carcasses. Brangus bulls average 1,900 to 2,100 pounds. Cows average 1,200 to 1,400 pounds.

Critics say the Brangus has a poor temperament.

Figure II-11   The Charbray is a cross of the Brahman and Charolais breeds. *(Courtesy of the American-International Charolais Association)*

CHARBRAY

In an effort to combine the growth rates of the Charolais with the heat and insect resistance of the Brahman, a crossing of the two was made and the resultant animal is recorded as a Charbray. Although no specific requirements are made in terms of percentage blood, the preferred combination is thirteen-sixteenths Charolais and three-sixteenths Brahman. First crossbreeding efforts to develop the Charbray were conducted in the Rio Grande Valley of Texas in the late 1930's.

Charbrays are horned and creamy white in color. Mature cows average 2,000 to 2,200 pounds, with bulls ranging from 2,800 to 3,200 pounds.

The American-International Charolais Association registers Charbray having at least one-fourth Brahman blood.

CHAROLAIS

One of the oldest of the several breeds of French cattle, the Charolais was developed in the district around Charolles in central France.

The breed became established there and had achieved considerable regard as a meat producer by the sixteenth or seventeenth century. There is

Figure II-12 The Charolais was one of the first new breeds imported to the United States. *(Courtesy of the American-International Charolais Association)*

also historical evidence that the white cattle were being noticed as early as A.D. 878.

The cattle were confined to that general area until after the French Revolution. However, in 1773 Claude Mathieu, a farmer and cattle breeder from the Charolle region, moved to Anlezy in the province of Nievre, bringing with him his herd of white cattle.

The breed flourished there and the region prospered. In fact, the cattle did so well in their new home that for a time they were more widely known as Nivernais cattle than by their original name of Charolais.

In 1882, Charolais breeders in the vicinity of Charolles set up a herd book for recording pedigrees of the breed in their region; this followed a move by Count Charles de Bouille in 1864 to keep a herd book of his own Charolais at his stable at Villars, France. The two societies merged in 1919 to overcome confusion of pedigrees, with the older organization taking the records of the newer group into their headquarters at Nevers, the capital of the Nievre province.

From these early beginnings the breed spread outward to nearly every part of France and to nearly every continent. By 1964 when the French herd book was 100 years old, there were some 2,200,000 head of Charolais cattle in France, making it one of the most important French breeds.

Central France continues to be the heart of the foundation herds of the breed. The grandson of the founder of the French herd book, the present

Count Roger de Bouille, still operates the estates and continues the Charolais herd.

The first cattle of the Charolais breed to enter the North American continent were imported to Mexico by Jean Pugibet soon after World War I. He had seen the Charolais cattle while serving as a French army volunteer and was impressed with their appearance and productivity. He arranged for a shipment of 2 bulls and 10 heifers to Mexico in 1930. Later shipments in 1931 and 1937 increased his herd. Until recently, all of the Charolais in Mexico, the United States, and Canada were descendants of this initial Pugibet herd. Not long after the last shipment, Pugibet died and no further imports were attempted.

The mid-1940's outbreak of foot-and-mouth disease barred further North American imports until 1965 when Canada opened imports via rigid quarantine restrictions both in Canada and in the country of origin.

Advantages of Charolais include a high rate of growth, feed efficiency, a minimum of excess fat at a young age, and good climatic adaptability.

Mature cows weigh 1,250 to 1,600 pounds with mature bulls ranging from 2,000 to 2,500 pounds.

Animals registered by the national association, the American-International Charolais Association, can be polled or horned. The color of the breed is a characteristic white or very light straw color.

CHIANGUS

The crossing of a Chianina and an Angus has been recognized as a Chiangus by the American Chianina Association. The Chiangus is black, with white allowed only on the underline, polled, and contains a minimum of 25 percent and a maximum of 75 percent blood of either breed.

The infusion of Chianina blood into the Angus breed resulting in this new crossbreed results in an animal considerably larger than the Angus, but smaller than the Chianina, one of the largest breeds of cattle.

The Chiangus can be expected to weigh roughly 1,900 pounds for a mature cow and approximately 2,800 pounds for a mature bull. The Chiangus is a relatively new breed and so is not as uniform in performance as some of the more established breeds. The breed does, however, have the advantage of hybrid vigor resulting from crossing the two different breeds.

The American Chianina Association plans additional "Chi" programs with other breeds in the future, but none are formulated yet.

CHIANINA

Chianina cattle are the oldest breed of cattle in Italy and probably one of the oldest in the world, dating back before the Roman Empire. They obtain their name from the Chiana valley in the province of Tuscany in central

Figure II-13   The Chianina is one of the largest breeds. *(Courtesy of the American Chianina Association)*

Italy, famous for Chianti grapes and wine. Chianina (pronounced Key-a-nee-na) is the principal breed for work and beef production in Italy. The Chianina breed accounts for approximately 6 percent of the total meat-milk-draft cattle in Italy, but a much higher percentage of these cattle are used for beef only. The Val di Chiana cattle are acknowledged to be the largest breed of cattle in the world.

Mature full-blood Italian Chianina bulls stand up to 72 inches at the withers and weigh up to 4,000 pounds, while females can weigh a maximum of 2,400 pounds and stand 60 to 68 inches at the withers. Even the smallest infusion of Chianina blood adds size to offspring when crossed with conventional breeds.

Structurally the Chianina is a taller, longer, leaner type of cattle than most breeds. Chianina exhibit trimness of the middle and absence of excessive dewlap and brisket.

Hair color for full-bloods ranges from white to steel gray with black pigmentation of the tongue, palate, nose, switch, and anus, and around the eyes.

Chianina are long-boned and long-muscled. They are generally free of double muscling.

The first Chianina semen to enter the United States arrived in 1971 and on January 31, 1972, the first half-blood Chianina was born on U.S. soil.

Although the American Chianina Association allows for registration of percentage Chianina cattle from any base breed, some members felt a need for a unified registration program originating from the cross of Chianina and another particular breed with specific guidelines in regard to color and percentage structures.

The first "Chi" program is the Chiangus registration. Any cross or its reciprocal cross between the two breeds (only) of Chianina and Angus that results in a black (white allowed only on underline), polled (or scurred) animal containing a minimum of 25 percent and a maximum of 75 percent blood of either breed is eligible for registration in the American Chianina Association as a Chiangus. The association plans additional "Chi" programs with other foundation breeds.

DEVON

Historically the Devon is the oldest purebred breed in the United States. Devon cattle came to America with the Pilgrims in 1623. At that time, their hardy foraging ability fit the uncertain grass conditions; their moderate but rich milking ability favored the substance of both calf and family. Their docility and strength adapted them for use as oxen. As the pioneers pushed westward, Devon cattle went with them, drawing them along the grass line. In 1884 the American Devon Cattle Club was established. Records for the

Figure II-14.   The Devon is a deep, ruby red. *(Courtesy of the Devon Cattle Association, Inc.)*

Devon as a pure breed began when Colonel John T. Davy of Rose Ash in North Devon, England, published the first volume of *Davy's Devon Herd Book* in 1850. The breed, however, traces its existence back to records of the Red Cattle of North Devon, England, in 23 B.C.

Polled Devons came into existence in 1915 when a mutant bull was born without horns. This bull, Missouri 9097, offered the Devon breed an opportunity to develop a polled strain without outcrossing and breeding up from polled animals of another breed.

Devons are noted for their traveling ability, covering ground in any terrain, and good mothering ability.

Devon bulls average 1,800 to 2,000 pounds, cows weigh about 1,200 pounds. Calves crossbred to Devon have averaged 65 pounds at birth. They have creamy white horns with dark or black tips. They exhibit slow growth and poor feedlot performance in many cases.

GALLOWAY

The Galloway breed came to the United States from its native Scotland in 1870. Because of the moist, cold climate of Scotland, the Galloway developed an ability to withstand harsh climatic conditions.

Galloways resemble Angus, but their black coat is comprised of soft, wavy long hair and a thick, mossy undercoat. The breed is polled and similar in size to Angus.

Advantages of the breed include good carcass quality, ability to withstand harsh climates, and good foraging ability.

The breed's characteristics result largely from environment. Lowland Scotia's year-long chill from cold winds laden with sea salt promoted long, wavy outercoats over thick fur. Sparse forage and feed low in nutrition adjusted digestive tracts to a higher level of feed efficiency.

Breed characteristics are said to have been stabilized since the eleventh century. Although black is the most common and most popular color, Galloways can be red, dun, white, and belted. (*See also* "Belted Galloway.")

Their heavy coats, so helpful in cold climates, limit their productivity in warmer areas.

GELBVIEH

The Gelbvieh breed began making its mark on the American cattle scene when the first semen imports were made into North America in 1971. Leness Hall, former general manager of Carnation Farms Breeding Service, now Carnation Genetics, was responsible for the initial imports. He visited the bull stud at Nuestadt Aisch in Germany and spotted the Gelbvieh. His initial impression was of a well-muscled, solid red bull that was an excellent meat-type animal.

Figure II-15   The Gelbvieh is a new breed from Austria and Germany. *(Courtesy of Dr. Gary L. Minish, Virginia Polytechnic Institute and State University)*

The Gelbvieh was developed from four triple-purpose yellow breeds of cattle: the Glan-Donnersburg, the Yellow Franconian, the Limburg, and the Lahn, which all developed about 1850. By 1920 the four were developed into a single breed—the Gelbvieh. Initial development occurred in Austria and Germany.

Physically, the Gelbvieh is of medium size and stature. Coat color varies from cream to reddish-yellow.

Gelbvieh enthusiasts cite low birth weights and high weaning weights as the primary assets of the breed. The high weaning weights can be attributed to the fact that Gelbvieh cows often produce 8,800 pounds of milk with a 4.12 percent butterfat content to feed their calves. Other advantages of the breed include high fertility and good feedlot efficiency.

The breed has been primarily developed through the use of artificial insemination in their home of northern Bavaria, West Germany. Practically all of the breeding has been done by artificial insemination for several generations. Performance requirements are necessary for registration.

HAYS CONVERTER

Careful crossbreeding of Holstein-Hereford and Brown Swiss-Hereford cattle enabled former senator Harrys Hays of Canada to develop his own breed, the Hays Converter. Senator Hays, a former minister of agriculture, practiced a selection process emphasizing weaning and yearling weights along

Figure II-16 The Hays Converter from Canada. *(Courtesy of Western Breeders Ltd.)*

with selection for good udders on replacement heifers. Although no selections were made based on color, the Hays Converter normally is black with a white face. Occasionally red animals with white faces are seen also.

Mature weight of cows is about 1,800 pounds, with bulls weighing about 2,700 pounds.

The Hays Converter is a hardy breed with good milk production and efficient growth rates.

HEREFORD

About two and a half centuries ago farmers living in the county of Hereford, near Herefordshire in England, determined to produce beef for their share of the expanding food market created by Britain's eighteenth-century industrial revolution.

To succeed, these early cattle producers realized they needed cattle that could convert their native grass to beef at a profit. Some felt there was no breed in existence that could fill that need, so the farmers of Herefordshire molded their cattle for a high yield of beef and economy of production.

These pioneers started with cattle of unknown origin common in their area, most of which were draft animals. These cattle had been mixed with white cattle from Flanders. History indicates a red bull with a white face was introduced from Yorkshire about 1750.

Figure II-17 The Hereford may be the best known breed in America. *(Courtesy of the American Hereford Association)*

Benjamin Tomkins started the effort of breeding for beef in Herefordshire in 1742. This was 18 years before Robert Bakewell advanced the first theories of animal breeding and 104 years before the *English Hereford Herd Book* was started. Tomkins' father had bequeathed him a cow called Silver and her calf. His breeding program began later with two cows and a bull descendant of the old Silver cow. Tomkins's cattle were dark, many with mottled faces, and from the beginning were selected for early maturity and ease of fleshing. Tomkins and his son continued the herd until 1819.

Following the Tomkins's lead, a herd was founded by William Galliers, presumably using the same bloodlines. The first public sale of Herefords of which there is a detailed account was that of Galliers held October 15, 1795.

Herefords of the early days in England were much larger than today's Herefords. Mature animals weighing 3,000 pounds were not uncommon. Gradually the type and conformation changed to less extreme weight with more smoothness and quality. Herefords became popular and by the 1840's the Hereford was exported to the United States and to more than 20 countries. The first Herefords to arrive here from England were imported to Kentucky by Henry Clay, the statesman. The first Hereford blood was not kept pure and was diffused into the native cattle of the area.

The first Hereford breeding herd in the United States was established by William H. Sotham and Erastus Corning of Albany, New York, in 1840.

By 1850 Herefords were established at Maryland's Hayfields Farms, owned by John Merryman. His descendants still breed Herefords at the farm.

The westward advance of Herefords took them to Ohio and beyond. Only about 200 head of Herefords were imported up to 1880, but more than 3,500 came to America in the 1880 to 1889 period.

Herefords have adapted to a wide range of climates, calve easily, and do well in the feedlot. Their docile dispositions contribute to their continued popularity.

Mature cows range in weight from 1,100 to 1,400 pounds, while bulls weigh from 1,800 to 2,400 pounds.

Like other breeds with white around their eyes, Herefords are particularly susceptible to pinkeye and cancer eye. Another criticism of the breed has been a difficulty in withstanding a hot, humid environment.

KOBE

The name synonymous with prime top-quality beef to visitors of Japan is Kobe beef. Wagyu (Kobe) cattle are the native cattle of Japan. They have been genetically selected for years to develop top-quality beef. In Japan, Kobe beef means prime quality steaks with extreme marbling and a unique flavor.

Japanese caretakers massage their Kobe animals and feed them rations of grain and beer.

At present there are only four Kobe bulls in the United States, although their half-blood offspring are on the ground.

The Japanese feed mature virgin cows (four years old) a fattening ration for one year and even longer. The end result is beef with more marbling than the USDA prime grade in this country. It is doubtful that American cattle producers could justify the effort in terms of economic returns.

LIMOUSIN

The history of the Limousin may very well be as old as that of any European breed. Cattle found in cave drawings estimated to be 20,000 years old in the Lascaux Cave near Montignac, France, have a resemblance to today's Limousin.

These golden-red cattle are native to the south-central part of France in the regions of Limousin and Marche. The terrain of their homeland is rugged and rolling with rocky soil and a harsh climate. A lack of natural resources enabled the region to remain relatively isolated and the farmers free to develop their cattle with little outside genetic interference.

Limousin cattle are thought to be related to Spanish cattle and to the French Blonde d'Aquitaine. In the early years of their development, Limousin

Figure II-18   The Limousin is one of several new breeds from France. *(Courtesy of the North American Limousin Foundation)*

cattle received little attention as they were used primarily as beasts of burden and for the production of manure. Only at the end of their working life were the Limousin fattened for slaughter. They were small animals, reflecting the fact that little feed was available for them besides the forage they could obtain themselves.

Little selection was used. The best animals were sold or slaughtered for each farmer's own use. Legend says the only bulls kept for breeding purposes were the ones the farmer could not sell.

Finally a foresighted cattleman, Charles de Leobary and his herdsman, Royer, began a campaign for herd improvement through natural selection. Through a tough selection process, the two developed an outstanding herd of "purebred" Limousin. From 1854 to 1896 the Leobary herd won a total of 265 ribbons at prestigious French cattle shows.

In November, 1896, the first Limousin herd book was established. By July, 1914, the total number of animals registered in the herd book was 5,416. Through the late 1800's and the early 1900's, Limousin breeders paid close attention to conformation as the breed developed. The medium size of these cattle sets them apart from most other European breeds. Other traits selected for include a dark golden-red hide with wheat-colored underpinnings, a deep chest, strong top-line, well-placed tail, and head and strongly muscled hindquarter.

The first Limousin arrived in Canada in 1968. He was followed in 1969 by a group of five additional sires. These bulls formed the base for the North American Limousin herds. The first Limousin bulls imported permanently into the United States arrived in the fall of 1971. Anticipating that arrival, 15 cattle producers formed the North American Limousin Foundation in 1968 at a Denver, Colorado, meeting.

Advantages of Limousin include feedlot efficiency, mothering ability, fertility, and aggressiveness of bulls. Limousins tend to be rather late maturing, a fault breeders are working to correct.

LINCOLN RED

Developed in Lincolnshire on the eastern coast of England, the Lincoln Red is similar to the Shorthorn from which it sprang. As its name implies, the breed is red, with occasional white markings. Both horned and polled animals exist within the breed.

Slightly larger than the Shorthorn, the Lincoln Red is a docile breed with good maternal instincts.

The Lincoln Red had been segregated in its place of origin in Lincoln County and surrounding areas for about 100 years. Until the 1960's the breed was used primarily as a dairy animal.

Mature cows weigh about 1,400 pounds, while mature bulls range from 1,800 to 2,000 pounds.

Figure II-19 The Lincoln Red. *(Courtesy of Shaver Holdings, Ltd.)*

Figure II-20   The Maine-Anjou is a large beef breed from France. *(Courtesy of the American Maine-Anjou Association)*

MAINE-ANJOU

Primarily known as a beef breed in the United States, the Maine-Anjou is utilized as a dual-purpose breed in its native France. The development of milk production in what was basically a beef breed originally was sought as a solution to the poor climatic adaptability of French milk breeds. French cattle breeders noted that through the years cows of a milk breed suffered dramatically in milk production and condition during hot summer months and could not recuperate sufficiently to produce at their best even when conditions improved. The Maine-Anjou, with her somewhat larger frame and substance, was less affected by weather extremes and managed to maintain a supply of milk not substantially reduced by hot, dry weather or sparse pastures.

The breed we know today resulted from the crossing of the English Durham and the Mancelle of west-central France. In the first part of the nineteenth century the idea of separating beef stock from draft stock for better beef production was gradually gaining popularity. Leclere-Thouin, a French agriculturalist, wrote in 1843 that on the community pastures of the Auge Valley, the Mancelle were the last to be put onto the grass but were the first to be sent to market. Two other Frenchmen, M. Jamet and Count de Falloux, saw even greater possibilities in crossing the Mancelle with the Durham cattle of England. They introduced the first Durham bull to the

Mancelle region in 1839. The Durham-Mancelle cross combined the Mancelle's hardiness, vigor and milking ability, even under adverse conditions, with the Durham's quality carcass and rapid growth. By 1850 Durham-Mancelle crossbreds were winning championships at Le Concourse de Poissy, the forerunner to the modern French General Agricultural Fair. The name Maine-Anjou was adopted in 1909.

The first purebred Maine-Anjou to enter the North American continent arrived in 1969 through quarantine stations into Canada. Nearly all of the imported sires were placed in artificial insemination centers for semen collection. In the summer of 1969, the first semen was collected and utilized in crossbreeding programs in the United States and Canada. By fall, Americans had formed their own Maine-Anjou Society, with the name later changed to the American Maine-Anjou Association.

The average mature Maine-Anjou bull weighs 2,750 pounds and the mature female 1,980. Yearling weight is about 1,025 pounds. Maine-Anjou carry their weight on squarely balanced frames with firm, long muscle structure, and a typically straight topline.

Color is mahogany and white. The head is predominantly red and the eyes always surrounded by red. Horns are short.

Advantages include a docile disposition, good feed efficiency, and good mothering ability.

MARCHIGIANA

With the fall of the Roman Empire in the fifth century, barbarians streamed into Rome and surrounding provinces. With them came cattle. From these cattle—believed to be *Bos indicus*—came the basic foundation stock for the most numerous breed now in Italy, the Marchigiana (pronounced Mar-key-jah-nah).

The Marchigiana population is concentrated in the rough Marche region around Rome. The breed now makes up about 45 percent of Italy's total cattle population.

Italy now records more than 1,072,000 purebred Marchigiana cattle in the official herd book. A program of recording breed progeny weights at 6, 12, and 18 months has documented greatly increased average weaning, yearling, and 18-month weights during recent years. The herd book also judges animals on 10 index areas for conformation. Animals are recommended to have a minimum of a 75/100 score for registry.

Promoted in the United States primarily as a terminal cross, the mature Marchigiana bull weighs up to 3,000 pounds, cows about 1,500 pounds.

Marchigiana semen first was imported into the United States in 1972, but it was not until 1976 that actual purebred animals reached America, due to quarantine restrictions. Currently no exportation of purebreds from

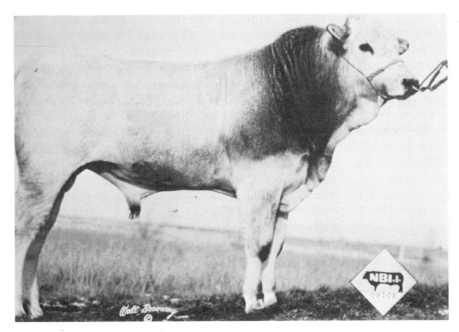

Figure II-21   The Marchigiana, or "Markey" comes from Italy. *(Courtesy of New Breeds Industries. Photo by Walt Browarny)*

Italy can be made due to an outbreak there of foot-and-mouth disease. American breeders organized the American International Marchigiana Society in 1973.

Advantages of Marchigiana cattle are high growth rates, skeletal strength and muscling, thrifty use of poor roughages, and good milking quality.

MURRAY GREY

Murray Grey, the silver cattle from Australia, are a natural genetic phenomenon that was by chance recognized and preserved. In 1905 on the Thologolong property of Peter Sutherland in southern New South Wales, a particular roan Shorthorn cow, when bred to various Aberdeen-Angus bulls, dropped only gray calves, 12 of them by 1917. Because Mrs. Eva Sutherland liked these gray calves, her husband did not slaughter them although he feared they would reflect poorly on his black Angus herd.

When her husband died in 1929, Mrs. Sutherland sold the herd of greys to her cousin, Helen Sutherland, who started a systematic breeding with eight cows and four bulls.

In the early 1940's, Mervyn Gadd started a second Murray Grey herd as a commercial venture, using a gray bull from the Sutherlands and breeding up from Angus cows. Gadd was convinced that the Greys were better and more efficient weight gainers, but it was not until 1957 that a demand for them developed. In 1962, 50 breeders banded together to form the Murray Grey Beef Cattle Club of Australia. They named the cattle for their color and the fact that they developed along the Murray River.

The Murray Greys began to win shows several years ago, mostly carcass competitions, but in 1974 they won a championship or reserve championship in each of the seven Royal Shows in Australia.

Semen first was imported into the United States in 1969. The first imports of live cattle were in May 1972, when two head of young cattle, a bull calf and a yearling heifer, arrived in Denver. Since that time there have been 28 purebred bulls and 9 purebred heifers imported from New Zealand or from Australia via New Zealand.

The American Murray Grey Association was formed and chartered in August 1970, in Texas.

Weight for mature bulls averages 1,800 to 2,000 pounds and mature cows about 1,500. Birth weight is about 60 to 70 pounds.

Advantages of the Murray Grey include calving ease due to the smallness of the calves at birth, lively calves, high fertility, adaptability, and docility. The breed is polled.

Figure II-22   The Murray Grey breed originated in Australia. *(Courtesy of the American Murray Grey Association)*

NORWEGIAN RED

As recently as the 1930's in Norway, every district in the country had its own breed of cattle, with each supposedly suited to its own area. The various districts were, at that time, rather isolated from each other with limited communications. In 1935, a small group of Norwegian cattle breeders started a cattle society aimed at improving Norwegian cattle as milk and beef producers. Since that time, most of the local breed societies have joined the association, called the Norwegian Red Cattle Association. The association in Norway maintains complete breed records from conception to carcass results. In 1972 the Norwegian Red Cattle Association recorded 25,000 herds and 249,217 cows constituting 60.1 percent of all Norwegian cows.

The breed entered the United States when Southern Cattle Corporation of Memphis, Tennessee, imported 6 young Norwegian Red bulls and 46 bred Norwegian Red heifers. The animals were brought directly to the USDA quarantine station at Clifton, New Jersey, from their native Norway.

The average mature Norwegian Red bull weighs 2,200 to 2,640 pounds, with cows ranging from 1,210 to 1,430 pounds.

These horned animals can be either solid red or red and white.

A dual-purpose breed, the advantages include good mothering ability and calving ease.

Figure II-23   The Norwegian Red is a product of Norway.

Figure II-24   The Parthenaise. *(Courtesy of Shaver Holdings, Ltd.)*

PARTHENAISE

The Parthenaise currently is being promoted in Canada. A native of France, the breed is known for its ability to thrive under adverse weather and nutritional conditions. Birth weights among purebreds are in the 60 to 80 pound range. The calves grow moderately, but do not have the high weight gains of the larger European breeds.

Conformation is very similar to that of the Limousin. Hide coloring in the purebred is fawn with a black background and black on the nose, eyelids, edge of the ears, and around the eyes. In the crossbred, the predominant color is that of the dam.

Parthenaise milk yield runs from a low of 5,500 pounds per lactation to a high of 11,400 pounds, with a fat content of 4.38 percent.

PIEDMONT

The Piedmont (or Piemontese) originated in the Po valley of Italy. Similar to the Romagnola, the Piedmont has light gray to cream-colored hair with black points. Double-muscling is very prevalent in the breed, but Italian cattle producers have utilized this trait to good advantage and consider it a plus rather than a minus. Certainly with this kind of double-muscled animal a great deal of care must be taken to avoid calving problems.

At one time these cattle were used for both draft and beef production. Today, however, they are grown primarily for meat.

Mature cows weigh about 1,400 pounds and mature bulls about 1,950 pounds.

PINZGAUER

Pinzgauer cattle descended from the European mountain breeds and originated in the Pinzgau valley in Austria and in adjacent areas of Bavaria, Germany, and Tyrol, Italy. Pinzgauer breeders made their first attempts at selective breeding for milk and meat as early as the late 1700's. The first cattle were exported in the 1820's to neighboring Rumania, Czechoslovakia, and Yugoslavia.

Known for their genetic purity, Pinzgauers maintain that standard through rigid rules of registration enforced by the International Pinzgauer Cattle Breeders Association in Salzburg, Austria.

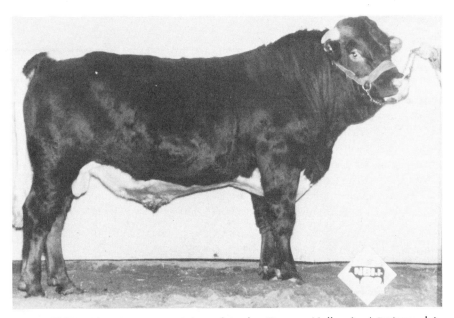

Figure II-25 The Pinzgauer originated in the Pinzgau Valley in Austria and in adjacent areas of Bavaria, Germany, and Tyrol, Italy. *(Courtesy of New Breeds Industries. Photo by Walt Browarny)*

Pinzgauers were introduced into North America in 1972. The American Pinzgauer Association is the registration and promotional organization, headquartered in Norman, Oklahoma. Throughout the world, Pinzgauer cattle total more than 3 million head in 22 countries throughout Europe, Africa, North and South America, Asia, and Australia.

The Pinzgauer has a reddish chestnut coat with a variety of white markings on the back, tail, and barrel. Dark pigmented skin, strong legs, and hard, dark hooves are other characteristics of the breed.

Average birth weight of calves is 80 pounds for females and 85 pounds for males. Mature bulls weigh 2,000 to 2,860 pounds. Mature cows average 1,320 to 1,650.

No accurate records for milk production have been kept in the United States; however, in Austria the milk yield of herd book cows is approximately 8,800 pounds with 4.02 percent fat.

Advantages of the Pinzgauer include feed efficiency, carcass quality, and adaptability.

POLLED HEREFORD

Polled Herefords originated in the United States, the second major beef cattle breed able to make that claim. The breed was founded in 1901 in Des Moines, Iowa, when Warren Gammon and his son Bert bought 11 head of registered Herefords that were naturally polled (mutants). The breed quickly gained acceptance.

Herefords, polled and horned, have a number of attributes in common. They are well adapted to wide ranges of climates, calve easily, and do well in the feedlot. They have a reputation for docility. Because of their constitution, hardiness, and adaptability, whiteface cattle predominate the commercial cattle industry.

Mature bulls weigh from 1,800 to 2,400 pounds. Cows average 1,100 to 1,400 pounds.

At one time the two breeds were represented by one breed organization, the American Hereford Association. The polled segment began keeping its own registry records in 1903. As recently as 1968 the AHA and the American Polled Hereford Association participated in a single joint certification program.

There have been talks between the two organizations about a consolidation, but since both groups operate from a profitable base, there has been no need for the move. Current attitudes call for a continued spirit of cooperation rather than a consolidation.

A unique feature of the two breeds is that they are the only two breeds known that can exchange germ plasm without calling the exchange crossbreeding.

Figure II-26   Hereford breeders who wanted a polled version of the breed developed the Polled Hereford. *(Courtesy of the American Polled Hereford Association)*

Since occasional horned calves are born to polled parents and vice versa, each association can and does register animals that might, by description, be better listed with the other association. The ancestors of all the animals involved can be traced to the same animals in the English herd book.

The major criticism of Herefords is their lack of pigmentation around the eyes, making them targets for cases of pinkeye and cancer eye.

Traditionally, Polled Herefords have been light in the hindquarters as well.

RANGER

In the early 1950's a number of cattle producers began breeding for an animal with high productivity, high quality carcass, low operating cost, and requiring minimum management adapted to all the western range areas. These cattle producers from Wyoming, Colorado, and California, formed Ranger Cattle Company and developed what is today the Ranger breed. The Ranger was developed from crosses of Milking Shorthorn and Hereford bulls, with later additions of Red Angus and Brahman blood. By 1959, the producers added the Scotch Highland, using both bulls and females. In 1965

Charolais blood was introduced. Cattle containing Charolais blood, however, are maintained as a separate line. Beefmaster blood also was added in 1965.

Cattle are of moderate size and may be of any color, solid or mottled.

Advantages of the Ranger are its adaptability to western range conditions and ease of calving. Unassisted calving has been an inflexible requirement for a cow to stay in the Ranger herds.

RED ANGUS

Breeders of Red Angus cattle believe that the red strain of their beef breed came about sometime in the eighteenth century in Scotland. At that time draft oxen were needed as work animals, and the black Scottish cattle, the Aberdeen-Angus, were too light in weight to pull large loads. It is thought that larger English longhorns, predominantly red in color, were imported and crossed with the native black, hornless breed. The offspring from this cross were all black and polled, since black is genetically predominant over red. The offspring did, however, carry a recessive red gene. Subsequent inbreeding produced an average of one red calf in four. Red calves occur when both parents are red, when one parent is red and the other black, carrying a recessive red gene, or when both parents are black, but both carry a red

Figure II-27 Red Angus developed from black Angus herds. *(Courtesy of the Red Angus Association of America)*

gene. The latter situation occurs in modern black Angus herds at a ratio of 500 to 1.

The first Aberdeen-Angus herd book, published in Scotland in 1862, recorded both black and reds without distinction. Even today in England and Scotland both colors are recorded together in the herd book.

When the first Angus were imported into the United States in the 1870's, recordkeeping began. The first American herd book was published in 1886 and made no mention of color. A second edition two years later followed the same practice. In 1890 color was mentioned and 22 reds of approximately 2,700 animals were recorded that year. Finally, in 1917, the *American Aberdeen-Angus Herd Book* limited registration to black animals only. From 1917 until the early 1950's red progeny from purebred Angus cattle were not considered recordable by the existing Angus registry.

In March, 1954, Red Angus breeders formed the Red Angus Association of America. Coming entirely from registered black Angus bloodlines, size and characteristics are the same as their black counterparts.

Advantages of the Red Angus include the same excellent carcass quality of the black Angus, good mothering ability, and ease of calving. Their red color, a homozygous recessive characteristic, causes them to breed true when bred to other red cattle. Red color is said to reflect sunlight better than black, making Red Angus less susceptible to heat in the tropics. Breeders in tropical climates use Africander and other Brahman-type red native cattle in crossbreeding programs with the Red Angus to maintain the red color.

Size of Red Angus compares closely to that of the black Angus. Mature bulls weigh approximately 2,000 pounds and mature cows average 1,300 to 1,500 pounds.

Figure II-28   The Red Brangus also is the result of recessive red genes in black Brangus herds. *(Courtesy of the American Red Brangus Association)*

RED BRANGUS

In much the same way that red genetic mutations caused the development of the Red Angus breed, so too did a recessive red gene result in the Red Brangus breed. Size and characteristics are similar to the black Brangus. The Red Brangus first was recognized as a separate breed in 1946 in Texas.

The Red Brangus, unlike the black, need not be precisely five-eighths Angus and three-eighths Brahman, but must show characteristics of both breeds.

RED POLL

Red Poll cattle originated in England prior to 1800 where they were bred for dual qualities of milk and beef production. Importations were made into the United States prior to 1880 and have continued at intermittent periods.

The cattle are naturally polled, red in color, docile, and adaptable to climatic variances. Because of their dual-purpose history, cows are good milkers.

The Red Poll bull is prepotent: when bred to horned cattle he is said to be a 95 to 100 percent dehorner. Subsequent crosses on his offspring with purebred Red Poll bulls produce a herd of polled, solid red cattle.

Figure II-29 Pinpur Broadcaster was the grand champion Red Poll bull at the 1972 national Red Poll show. *(Courtesy of American Red Poll Association)*

For many years the breed in the United States was concentrated on Cornbelt farms. The majority of breeders for the past several decades have been breeding for beef production. The breed has spread from the general farming areas of the Midwest to ranching areas of the West and Southwest and finally to the South and Southeast.

The trend toward beef production led to the incorporation of the Red Poll Beef International. Several leading breeders joined together for the promotion of the breed as a true beef breed, keeping in mind the necessity of maintaining the mothering ability in Red Poll cows.

Red Poll cattle have good mothering ability, good disposition, uniform color, and no horns.

Mature bulls weigh about 2,100 pounds. Cows weigh up to 1,500 pounds.

ROMAGNOLA

First bred as a dual-purpose breed for both meat and draft work, the Romagnola has evolved into primarily a beef breed. Although the breed has not yet become widely known in the United States, Romagnolas have been bred selectively for the past hundred years in the Romagna district of northern Italy. Their native area is known for its rugged terrain and its sparse

Figure II-30   Romagnola is a native of northern Italy. *(Courtesy of Western Breeders. Photo by Walt Browarny)*

vegetation. In many cases animals had to cover a great deal of area to obtain food. The Romagnola breed first received national attention in Italy in 1884 when a specimen of the breed was awarded first prize at the National Exhibition of Turin.

Physically the Romagnola is an extremely muscular animal with legs that appear short in relation to its body. The head is small. Eyes are dark in most specimens. The horns are of medium length and curved.

Advantages of the breed include feed efficiency and good milk production.

SAHIWAL

Used primarily as a dairy animal in its native West Pakistan, the Sahiwal was imported to Australia in 1952 for use in a crossbreeding program intended to develop a dual-purpose animal with an easier temperament than the Zebus that had been exported from America into Australia in 1932 but still retaining a similar hardiness and tick resistance. Better size and confor-

Figure II-31 The Sahiwal is a good example of a Zebu breed. *(Courtesy of New Breeds Industries)*

mation also were sought. After several experiments, it was decided to utilize the Jersey in a crossbreeding program to develop a tropical dairy breed. The result was the Australian Milking Zebu, which has not been imported to the United States.

Some cattle producers are expressing an interest in importing the Sahiwal for use as a dual-purpose (milk and beef) breed.

The Sahiwal is generally red in color with varying amounts of white on the neck, underline, and even the body. In males, the color darkens toward the extremities that may even be black. In the male the hump should be well developed, the dewlap voluminous, and the sheath not overly pendulous. Many specimens are horned.

The Sahiwal represents an excellent example of a typical Zebu animal.

SALERS

The Salers (pronounced say-lair) was developed in the southwest center of France in the rough, mountainous region of Salers. The breed is characterized by a solid, dark cherry-red coat, and black hooves.

The first Salers to reach North America were imported to Canada in 1973. In their native France they are utilized as a dual-purpose animal for meat and milk.

Figure II-32   The Salers was developed in the mountainous region of France near Salers. *(Courtesy of New Breeds Industries. Photo by Walt Browarny)*

The breed displays a medium size, triangular head with a short face. The breed has a straight topline and a wide rump. Average mature weight of cows ranges between 1,430 to 1,760 pounds, and between 2,000 and 2,650 for bulls. The breed is horned.

The largest importation to date of Salers into the United States was a group of 47 full-bloods, with 45 head going to the Rocking M Cattle Company of Weiser, Idaho. An American Salers Association has been established with headquarters in Weiser.

SANTA GERTRUDIS

Developed in the United States on the King Ranch in southern Texas, the Santa Gertrudis is the result of crosses between beef-type Shorthorn cows and Brahman bulls. Robert J. Kleberg, Jr., president of King Ranch is credited with development of the breed.

Actually, the crossbreeding of the two species of cattle, *Bos taurus* represented by the beef-type Shorthorn cows, and *Bos indicus,* the Brahman bulls, began in 1910. In the first stage of the breeding program, bulls with various percentages of Brahman blood were crossed with cows of British breeds. After years of evaluating the success of this program, actual steps toward formation of a new breed were begun in 1918. In 1920 a bull calf of three-eighths Brahman blood and five-eighths Shorthorn blood was born. This calf, named Monkey, displayed many of the qualities desired by King Ranch in their new breed. Monkey became the foundation sire of the breed and all Santa Gertrudis cattle descend from him. Luckily he was a prepotent sire and produced more than 150 useful sons prior to his death in 1932.

The breed has attained considerable popularity in the United States, particularly in the South, and has been exported to 59 countries throughout the world.

Santa Gertrudis Breeders International was organized in 1951 to promote, record, and improve the breed.

Santa Gertrudis bulls accepted by the breed association as "certified purebred" must meet the standard of excellence for the breed, upon inspection by the association's classifiers. Bulls that meet the requirements are branded with an "S" and those not meeting the minimum requirements are rejected and not branded. Females are classified similarly. In order to maintain quality in purebred Santa Gertrudis, the classifier inspects cattle, compares them with a minimum culling level called the Standard of Excellence, and places the official association "S" or "S Bar" brand on each that passes the test. Also, only those animals that are out of Certified or Accredited females—those already inspected by a classifier and branded—or are the offspring of a grading-up program in which Certified bulls are used for four successive generations, or are the product of a female top-cross grading-up program are eligible to be branded.

Figure II-33   The Santa Gertrudis was developed in Texas. *(Courtesy of Santa Gertrudis Breeders International)*

Santa Gertrudis are cherry-red animals with loose hides, neck folds, and sheath or navel flap. Most specimens are horned, but polled cattle can be registered. The hair is short in moderate climates and grows longer where the weather is cold. Among the advantages of Santa Gertrudis are a resistance to ticks and biting insects and a good heat tolerance.

Cows weigh 1,350 to 1,850 pounds at maturity, with bulls ranging from 2,000 to 2,400 pounds.

Critics of the breed cite low fertility in some bulls and a nervous disposition as faults.

SCOTCH HIGHLAND

The Scotch Highland breed originated in Scotland. Records of the shaggy cattle go back as far as the twelfth century. Originally there were two distinct strains of the breed: the West Highlander, known as the Kyloe, was smaller, shaggier, and mostly black in color, while the Mainland Highlander had a shorter coat in colors of brindle, red, yellow, dun, silver, and black. The Highland name derives from their origin in the Highlands and west coastal islands of Scotland.

The Highland Society of Scotland was formed in 1884 and the first herd book was published the following year. Reports differ, but it is generally agreed that Highland cattle were first imported to the United States sometime between 1850 and 1900. In the 1920's more were imported into the East Coast and Montana. In the 1930's many of the Highlands were dispersed and many were sent to market. With a growing interest in the breed in the 1940's, the XX Ranch of South Dakota gathered a few of the Scotch Highlands from across America for a small herd. In the fall of 1948 a group of ranchers met at Belvidere, South Dakota, to form the American Scotch Highland Breeders' Association.

Highland cattle are rather unusual looking when compared with other European beef breeds. They are straight above and below, deep in flanks and thighs, long in quarters, short in legs, and broad in hock. The shaggy coat is the Highland's most distinctive feature and actually consists of two coats —a downy undercoat and a long outercoat that may reach 13 inches.

Scotch Highland cattle tend to face into snow and wind during a storm, much like Buffalo. Their long foretops protect their faces and the wind blows the long coat flat instead of ruffling it up as would happen if they turned their backs to the wind.

Highland bulls weigh 1,600 to 1,800 pounds at maturity; cows weigh about 1,000 pounds.

Females are early maturing and have been known to calve at 14 months of age, although most calve for the first time at age 2. Highland dams have good mothering ability and are extremely protective of their calves.

Other advantages of the breed include their hardiness in very cold climates, lack of calving problems, and good marbling of their meat.

Due to their heavy coats, Scotch Highlands have less heat tolerance than some other breeds.

The breed is horned. In bulls the horns should be strong and come level out of the head, slightly inclining forward and also slightly rising toward the points, although some breeders have a preference for a downward curve. The horns of cows can follow two directions: some come out squarer from the head than in the male, rise sooner, and are slightly longer; others come more level from the head with a back set curve and a very wide sweep.

Because they have the smallest calves at birth of any breed, Scotch Highlands are popular in the Dakotas for use on first-calf heifers.

SHORTHORN

The Shorthorn breed originated on the northeastern coast of England in the counties of Northumberland, Durham, York, and Lincoln, with the first real development of the breed being in the valley of the Tees River about 1600.

The breed later spread to Scotland and then to America in 1783. When first brought to Virginia, the breed was called Durham. It was the first improved beef breed to be imported here and the qualities that the

Figure II-34　The Shorthorn is known as a top feedlot performer. *(Courtesy of American Shorthorn Association)*

animals possessed put them in great demand. Two years after their arrival in Virginia, they crossed the Blue Ridge Mountains into Kentucky and followed the wagon trains across the Great Plains into the West and Northwest.

Breeding of the Shorthorn with the Spanish Andalusian cattle brought to the North American continent by the Spanish conquistadors probably occurred in Kansas during the Civil War era when the great beef trails boomed from Texas to the Kansas railroad cattle towns. Legend has it that Longhorns actually sprang from Shorthorns crossed with the Spanish cattle. As early as 1854, producers in the United States were making direct importations of Shorthorns from Scotland.

Although Shorthorns came first, Midwesterners in 1870 discovered "natural hornless" cattle occurred from time to time in horned herds. Thus polled Shorthorns were discovered and are one of the first major beef breeds to be developed in the United States, originating on the Colonel McCormick Reeve farm in Minnesota. (Brahman were established in the United States about 1854.)

The first herd book record established for any breed of cattle was for Shorthorns. It was called the *Coates Herd Book*, founded in 1822. In 1874, it was acquired by the Shorthorn Society of Great Britain and Ireland, with headquarters in London. The *American Shorthorn Herd Book* was the first to be published in this country and was started in 1846 by Lewis Allen. The

American Shorthorn Association followed in 1872 when breeders from nine states formulated the organization as both an advisory, service outlet and to keep track of registration and recorded ancestry of the Shorthorn.

Both Shorthorns and Polled Shorthorns record in the same herd book, so breeders can infuse the blood of both branches of the breed into their programs.

Shorthorn cattle may be various shades of red, completely white, or roan in color. Mature cows average 1,200 pounds and are expected to raise a minimum of 10 calves in their lifetimes. Average mature weight for bulls is 2,000 pounds with an expected minimum useful range life of 6 years. Calves average 75 to 80 pounds at birth.

The American Shorthorn Association offers a Sire Evaluation Program to provide information, through a controlled situation, on a bull's ability to transmit economically important traits to his progeny.

Additionally, several performance programs and awards are offered, including some for youth. A women's auxiliary is called the National Shorthorn Lassies.

Shorthorns are known for their excellent feedlot performance, but may develop a coarse carcass if fed beyond optimum slaughter weight.

SIMMENTAL

The Simmental takes its name from its place of origin, the Simme Valley in the Bernese Oberland of Switzerland. Early property records discuss red and white cattle, the forerunners of today's Simmental. In the 1700's a demand was created for these cattle because of their rapid growth. In addition to their use as beef animals, early Simmentals were used for milking and as draft oxen. The breed spread throughout Europe when representatives of European royalty visited Switzerland to purchase the increasingly well-known cattle.

The government of Berne, Switzerland, set up a herd book in 1806 that included a requirement for performance information. The rules specified that all Simmentals of breeding age be evaluated by an official commission of judges before they could be registered in the herd book.

Those standards carried over to the United States when, on October 14, 1968, the American Simmental Association was formed as the registration and promotion organization of this country. The association registers Simmental and Brahmental, both horned and polled. The Brahman crossbreds take advantage of the Brahman resistance to heat and insects.

Additionally, Simmental in other countries known locally as Pie Rouge, Abondance, and Montbeliard in France; Fleckvieh in Germany and Austria; and Pezzata Rosa Fruilana in Italy are accepted for entry into the herd book.

Figure II-35 Although the Simmental is a new breed it has become popular in crossbreeding programs. *(Courtesy of the American Simmental Association. Photo by Walt Browarny)*

Simmental are found in numbers in other countries as well. In Czechoslovakia, 4 million head comprise 94 percent of the cattle population. In Hungary, nearly 2 million head make up 92 percent of the total cattle population. Simmental also are found in Africa, where they first arrived in 1895, and in South America, Australia, New Zealand, Iraq, and Japan.

Simmental cows mature to a weight of 1,300 to 1,800 pounds. Mature bull weights range from 2,400 to 2,800 pounds. Birth weight ranges from 85 to 100 pounds.

There are no color restrictions for registration in the American Simmental herd book. Simmentals vary from yellowish-brown or straw color to a dark red with white. Often they have red spots around their eyes. Legs and tail generally are white and there may be white patches on the body. The breed is horned.

Milk performance remains one of the most important criteria for selection in Europe. The average Simmental cow gives 9,000 pounds of milk annually with a 4 percent or better butterfat content.

Advantages of Simmental include a rapid growth rate, good milking ability, high fertility, a docile disposition, and carcass quality.

Figure II-36 This is the Grand Champion female at the 1978 national South Devon show. *(Courtesy of North American South Devon Association)*

SOUTH DEVON

Herds of South Devon cattle have been established in western England since the sixteenth century, although the origin of the breed remains a mystery. Not to be confused with the Devon breed, the South Devon is light red in color. The famous Devonshire cream of the United Kingdom is from these cattle.

The South Devon is the largest of the British breeds with cows weighing 1,500 to 1,700 pounds and bulls weighing up to 3,000 pounds. First major importations of the breed into the United States were made by Arthur N. Palmer in 1969.

Originally used as a draft animal and milk producer, the South Devon is the only breed in the United Kingdom that qualifies for a premium on milk as well as for the official beef calf subsidy on both its heifer and steer calves. The breed is horned, with small, incurving horns.

South Devon breeders stress mothering ability and milk production as advantages of the breed. Herd averages of 10,000 pounds of milk at 4.20 percent butterfat per lactation have been recorded. One cow recently recorded 23,000 pounds at 5.21 percent butterfat in 365 days.

Figure II-37   The Sussex. *(Courtesy of the Sussex Cattle Association)*

SUSSEX

The Sussex originated in the counties of Sussex and Kent in England. The breed is said to have descended from the red cattle of the area as early as the eleventh century. The breed was imported into the United States in 1884.

The breed is a solid, medium red. Some specimens have a white switch. There are both horned and polled Sussex, the polled strain developed by the infusion of the blood of a Red Angus bull.

Mature cows weigh about 1,450 pounds and bulls can weigh 2,000 pounds and more.

TARENTAISE

Derived from an ancient Alpine strain, the Tarentaise breed first was described by name in 1859. Coming from southeastern France where the land's beauty is second only to its contrasts, the breed adapted to life in the region where Mont Blanc towers more than 15,000 feet over lowlands of 500 feet elevation.

Official breed classification began in 1866 in conjunction with the first breed congress. The herd book was started in 1888, and since then the breed has grown and been exported to Italy, Spain, North Africa, Canada, and the United States.

The first Tarentaise bull to arrive in North America was Alpin, who was imported in 1972. Tarentaise originally were imported for the purpose

Figure II-38　Iroune is an example of a Tarentaise bull. *(Courtesy of the American Tarentaise Association)*

of complementing domestic breeds through crossbreeding. Specifically, Tarentaise is the same biological type as our domestic breeds with strong maternal traits.

Advantages of the Tarentaise include good milk production, early maturity, hardiness, and carcass quality. Calves are moderate size at birth.

Tarentaise bulls weigh up to 2,000 pounds at maturity, cows approximate 1,500 pounds.

TEXAS LONGHORN

Ancestors of the Texas Longhorn, Spanish Andalusian cattle, first arrived in the New World with Christopher Columbus on his second voyage to Santo Domingo in 1493. In 1521 descendants of these cattle were brought into Mexico by Gregorio de Villalobos. By the late 1600's and early 1700's, the Spanish were crossing the Rio Grande into what is now Texas, establishing missions and ranches. As was their custom, the Spanish took their cattle with them, and from this foundation stock evolved the wild and colorful Texas Longhorn of legend and Western lore.

After the Civil War Texans found that they had a marketable commodity in their Texas Longhorns. To the north there was a beef market and deep in the brush and across the vast reaches of the Texas ranges were millions of Longhorn cattle. During the 1870's and 1880's, the great cattle industry boomed. An estimated 10 million head of Texas Longhorns were

Figure II-39   The characteristic horns of the Texas Longhorn grow longest on steers. *(Courtesy of the Texas Longhorn Breeders Association)*

trailed north by many different routes. The Goodnight-Loving Trail and the 800-mile long Chisholm Trail from San Antonio, Texas, to Abilene, Kansas, were two of the most famous routes. In 1871, 600,000 head traveled up the Chisholm Trail.

The northern-bound herds usually numbered about 2,500 to 3,000; however, when crossing through hostile Indian territory, herds often would group together for protection. A combined herd might contain as many as 15,000 animals and 200 people. The Longhorn was well suited for the harsh drives. They had a natural instinct for survival and could travel long distances and swim wide rivers.

By 1895 the great northern trails were closing. Open ranges were being fenced, and, most importantly, a better strain of beef cattle had been introduced.

By 1920 the Longhorn was nearing extinction. Well-known western author J. Frank Dobie began an effort to save the Longhorn. He assembled a small herd in the early 1920's for the state of Texas. In 1927 Senator John B. Kendrick of Wyoming was instrumental in urging Congress to pass a special appropriation to establish a herd on the Wichita National Forest. Both herds remain established today.

In May, 1964, a Texas Longhorn Breeders Association of America was founded to recognize and promote the breed. Charles Schreiner III, Mountain Home, Texas, is considered the founding father of the association.

Advantages of the Texas Longhorn include longevity, mothering instinct, disease resistance, a high percentage browse utilization, calving ease, and an ability to survive and thrive under adverse conditions.

Today's Longhorn carries the genetics of only the 100 percent unassisted survivors, breeders point out. Steers grow much longer horns than cows or bulls. The traditional Longhorn is usually represented by the steer. Bulls are shorter of stature and more muscular, while cows are feminine. Cows often have longer horn measurements than bulls, but the bull horn is much thicker.

Mature bulls weigh from 1,700 to 2,045 pounds.

Horns are a source of pride and enjoyment for breeders and horns frequently are measured from tip to tip.

Texas Longhorns come in a variety of colors, including brindle, roan, grulla (or sandhill crane), dark red, and dark brown.

WELSH BLACK

The Welsh Black is one of the oldest of the British breeds, with its development in Wales dating as far back as the 1300's. The hill country of Wales is known for its poor grazing and bad weather conditions. Being on the west coast of Britain, it is continuously exposed to North Atlantic storms. It is in this environment that the breed was developed. Consequently, the Welsh Black developed a shaggy hair coat to protect itself from cold, inclement weather. The breed performs well in cold, harsh climates, but because of its long coat does not have good heat tolerance.

Legend has it that the Welsh Black breed descended from cattle raised and domesticated in ancient Britain before the Roman Conquest in 55 B.C. A researcher in North Wales concluded that the ancestors of the Welsh Blacks were of the species *Bos longifrons* as opposed to the species *Bos urus*, which the invading tribes of Northern Europe brought to Britain with them. These invaders drove the Celtic Britains, along with their oxen, (the *Bos longrifons*) into the mountains and the almost inaccessible parts of western Britain—Wales. Since the Celts of Wales were never entirely subdued by their invaders, for many centuries there was little mixing of the two species of cattle. The Welsh breed—the Welsh Black—maintained many of its ancient characteristics such as hardiness, longevity, and the ability to thrive on poor-quality feeds. From the ancient cattle two types emerged:

Figure II-40   The Welsh Black is one of the oldest of the British breeds. *(Courtesy of New Breeds Industries. Photo by Walt Browarny)*

the North Wales type, compact and sturdy, and the Castlemartin breed of South West Wales, a little larger. Both breeds were triple-purpose for draft, milk, and beef.

The Welsh Black of North America is horned. The solid black animals average a weight of 1,000 to 1,300 pounds for mature cows. Mature bulls range from 1,800 to 2,000 pounds.

STUDY QUESTIONS

1. Best known for its high quality carcass is the _____. (Angus)
2. The _____ combines ancestry from cattle and buffalo. (Beefalo)
3. The giant _____ breed is believed to have originated before the time of the Roman Empire. (Chianina)
4. _____ cattle came to America with the Pilgrims in 1623. (Devon)
5. The _____ was developed in Canada by Senator Harry Hays. (Hays Converter)
6. The _____ breed was developed to convert grass to beef at a profit. (Hereford)
7. _____ are known for their excellent performance in the feedlot. (Shorthorns)

Section Three

MANAGEMENT TECHNIQUES

TABLE 1-A.   CATTLE CYCLES IN THE U.S. SINCE 1930

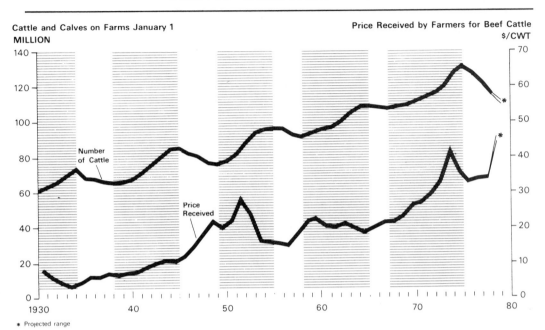

Cattle and Calves on Farms January 1
MILLION

Price Received by Farmers for Beef Cattle
$/CWT

* Projected range

Cattle numbers have been fluctuating cyclically since 1890. The five cycles since 1930 are shown above. The shaded sections are periods of herd building. Prices tended to be highest when cattle numbers were low and increasing. Other important price-making factors were consumer buying power and supplies of competing meats.

Source: *The Farmers' Newsletter,* "Livestock," Aug. 1978.

1

Taking Care of Business

The early 1980's offer the beginning cattle producer an excellent opportunity to get into the cattle business and establish at the outset a profitable operation. Contrary to what many believe, cattle production can be a profitable business. To ensure that a given cattle operation runs profitably, however, one must set up an intelligent management system and run the cattle business just as one would run any other business: with a careful eye on the financial aspects of the ranching operation.

Like many other businesses, the cattle business runs in cycles. Cycles run 10 to 12 years from one low point in cattle numbers to the next. During one part of the cycle, cattle numbers and the national cow herd increase as hundreds of thousands of individual farmers and ranchers react to favorable prices by expanding their herds or by entering the cattle business for the first time. When cattle numbers get too large, there is more beef than consumers can buy, or are willing to buy, at a price that is profitable for the producer. This situation causes producers to liquidate their herds. Liquidation temporarily compounds the problem of oversupply, and further decreases prices. That situation occurred within the last few years. The speedup of cattle slaughter during recent years overloaded retail meat counters. Consumers bought all the beef that was produced, but prices did not provide adequate profits for the cattle producer. After accounting for inflation, the farm price of cattle declined during 1975, 1976, and 1977.

As a result, many cattle producers sold their breeding stock, plowed up their pastures, and planted cash crops. Many of these people may be reluctant to reenter the cattle business even when prices rise and the prospects begin to look brighter.

The changes in the cattle cycle will alter the beef cattle situation substantially. Since 1975, when cattle numbers peaked, cattle producers have been selling more cattle than the national cattle herd produced. Now the national herd is smaller and has correspondingly less beef-producing capacity than before. When herd rebuilding begins, producers will sell fewer cattle than they produce.

Judging from previous cattle cycles, herd expansion can be expected to continue for six years, or even longer. The first substantial increase in marketing of cattle usually occurs during the third or fourth year of herd increase. To be among those individuals who can survive the ups and downs of the cattle industry and maintain a profitable cattle operation, the rancher must pay attention to the business side of cattle production.

BUSINESS ORGANIZATION

Deciding what form the farm business takes is an important part of setting up a successful cattle operation. Basically, there are three forms of farm business organizations: the sole proprietorship, the partnership, and the corporation.

The *sole proprietorship*, as one might surmise, is a one-person operation. There may be many workers, but the proprietor owns, operates, and manages the farm business.

With the sole proprietorship, the business terminates upon the death of the owner. In case of any liabilities, the owner is personally liable. To obtain financing, the sole proprietor must obtain money through loans or personal investments. Of course, there are advantages. When business decisions are to be made, no one else need be consulted. The proprietor makes his or her own decisions and places his or her own limits on the activities of the business. Any income from the business is taxed to the individual. The proprietor can take a 50 percent deduction for long-term capital gains.

The *partnership* consists of a group of owners. Two or more persons contribute assets and share management profits and losses. In a general partnership, each person is liable for the actions of all partners within the scope of partnership activities. In some states a limited partnership also is permitted. This special partnership may have one or more nonmanagerial partners. Their liability for partnership debts and obligations is limited to their investment in the farm business.

A partnership is defined in most states as an association of two or more persons who carry on a business together as co-owners to make a profit.

While a minor may generally be a partner with an adult in a partnership, the minor's contract of partnership is voidable and may be disaffirmed. This is an important point to keep in mind when utilizing the partnership to give a child or other person an opportunity to get started in farming. Another frequent reason for use of the partnership is to permit a senior partner an opportunity to reduce his or her labor without interrupting the business operation. A third reason for forming a partnership is the goal of combining resources for a larger and more efficient unit.

Before forming a partnership, several points should be considered. First, the partners must develop a written agreement allowing for fair and equitable treatment of everyone involved. The agreement should specify a buy-sell agreement to protect surviving partners in case of the death of one of the individuals involved. Additionally, the agreement should include a method of dissolving the partnership at a specified time. Partners must agree in advance on the method of keeping adequate records and plan for an annual financial reconciliation between partners for cash position and farm profit.

To establish a 50–50 partnership, all assets of the farm should be appraised. That value should be added to the value of working capital and tallied on the beginning date of the new business. Outstanding debts should be subtracted from the total. The new partner gives the other an interest-bearing note for one-half the net equity in all the working capital and resources. As a partner he or she assumes one-half the outstanding indebtedness on it.

A partnership operates as an independent third party. The partnership should have a bank account separate from the accounts of the individuals involved. All receipts should be deposited into the partnership bank account and all expenses paid from it. A provision should be made for withdrawals to be made to the personal accounts of the partners as funds accumulate in the partnership account.

At the end of the year a complete and detailed settlement of the accounts should be made, taking into account the net cash income of the business, the amounts withdrawn by each partner, the rent and interest due the senior partner, and the payments made on the note by the new partner.

This partnership agreement assumes that the senior partner is the parent, taking a child into the farm business. The child's only resource might be labor. If one partner assumes more than half of the labor, there should be a wage adjustment to that partner. In cases where one partner is not willing to assume the financial responsibility of one-half of the senior partner's equity in working capital and one-half of additional borrowed funds, a fixed contribution approach may be used.

For people interested in limiting their liability for partnership debts and obligations, some states allow the establishment of a limited partnership. In this form of partnership, the liability of one or more partners for debts and obligations incurred by the partnership is limited to their investment in the business. A limited partner can act only as an investor, not as a manager. Once a limited partner becomes active in management, he or she becomes liable for all partnership obligations as a general partner. A limited partnership must also have at least one general partner who handles the management of the business and is fully liable for all partnership debts and obligations. A farm business could not consist of only limited partners.

Where both partners are actively engaged in the farm business, a limited partnership will not fit the situation. This would be a general partnership. In some instances, however, people involved in a general partnership may want to switch to a limited partnership. For instance, if a father and son operated a ranch together in a general partnership, when the father wanted to retire, limiting his contribution to a monetary one only, they would establish a limited partnership, with the son assuming the liabilities of the partnership.

If a limited partnership is desired, necessary forms and information can be obtained from the office of the secretary of state. Normally, copies are filed with the local county registrar of deeds as well.

Forming a *corporation* may be the best form of business organization for large farms and for those involving high risks. There are several advantages to forming a corporation. First of all, there is usually no income tax on transferring assets to the corporation. A regular corporation pays annual income taxes on farm profits, and often, is able to obtain tax benefits not available to partnerships. Since tax laws vary from state to state and change annually at the federal level, no discussion of specific tax benefits will be made here. Basically, though, there are some advantages available to the corporation.

One of the most important characteristics of the corporation is the limited liability of the shareholders for acts or obligations of the corporation. Because the corporation is a separate legal entity that exists apart from its shareholders, the shareholders themselves are not personally liable for the obligations or responsibilities of the corporation. It is the corporation that is liable for damages arising from any negligence on the part of its officers and employees within the scope of employment. If, however, a shareholder is required to sign personally for corporate obligations, he or she extends personal credit and, in this case, would be personally liable if the corporation fails.

A corporation, unlike a sole proprietorship or a partnership, exists as long as the shareholders desire. The life of a corporation is not dependent upon the lives of people. Many states permit such perpetual corporations. There are several advantages to a corporation based on the corporation's continuity of existence. For one, ownership transfer is simplified. The increasing size of farm businesses poses some problems in transferring property to the next generation. Shares of stock provide a simple and convenient way to make lifetime and death transfers. A share of stock may be sold, given away, or transferred by will. Stock transfers can be made without disrupting the ranch business. The ease of orderly and gradual transfer of a growing farm business by transfer of shares of stock can provide a progressive shift in ownership and management. Control arrangements are flexible.

An additional benefit of a corporation consists of allowing the shareholders to obtain employee benefits. Since neither sole proprietors nor partners can be employees of themselves or of their partnerships, the corporation offers shareholders the unique opportunity to obtain certain retirement plans, medical benefits, and group term life insurance.

Despite the benefits, a few features exclusive to corporations are cited by farmers as disadvantages to incorporating. For instance, shareholder-employees of the corporation are subject to Social Security taxes as employees, not as self-employed farmers. The combined employer and employee tax is higher than an individual's self-employment tax. Additionally, any wages paid to a child under the age of 21 who is working for his or her parent are not subject to Social Security tax. Wages paid to children by their parent's corporation are subject to Social Security tax.

Additionally, under current tax laws, a farm corporation is limited to half the amount of extra first-year 20-percent depreciation that a married sole proprietor filing jointly can claim. Under current regulations, a farm corporation and a farm partnership are limited to $2,000 of extra first-year 20-percent depreciation, whereas a married sole proprietor filing jointly may claim up to $4,000 of such extra first-year depreciation.

Another difficulty with the corporation might arise if all assets such as land, machinery, livestock, and so on, are included in the corporation. Retired couples, surviving spouses, and minority stockholders—especially those off the farm—might not be able to extract income because assets are locked in the corporation.

A tax-option, or Sub-Chapter S Corporation is a creation of federal law. It is a corporation in all respects except that it does not pay income tax because each shareholder-owner reports a share of corporate income for tax purposes. The corporation itself files only an informational tax return.

Only by carefully weighing the advantages and disadvantages of each form of farm business can the rancher determine the best method of organization. Since the ultimate decision is such an important one, it is wise to consult with a trusted advisor, such as a banker, accountant, or other tax specialist.

TAXES

People involved in agriculture, whether as investors, farmers, or ranchers, receive a number of tax advantages as a result of their participation in the cattle business. A few of the tax advantages of owning cattle include: conversion of ordinary tax deductions into capital gain income, tax deferral through accelerated depreciation methods, and tax saving and/or tax deferral through investment credit. According to a prominent CPA, the net effect of tax deferral is that taxpayers grant themselves an interest-free loan from the federal government during the period of tax deferral. For instance, if a taxpayer has $100,000 of accelerated deductions and invests the tax savings in a 7 percent tax-exempt bond the money will double in less than 11 years. Of course, tax laws change constantly so that the advice of a competent accountant always will be a necessity.

The Revenue Act of 1978, signed into law on November 7, 1978, offers some relief to agricultural taxpayers. One of the most significant changes in the investment tax credit for agriculture is its extension for the first time to certain farm buildings. By specifically making newly built milking parlors, confinement buildings, and the like eligible, the new law settles a long-running debate between farmers and the IRS.

To qualify for the credit, a livestock structure must be specifically designed, constructed, used, and equipped for the housing, raising, and feeding of livestock. This includes facilities to produce milk from dairy cows or to produce feeder cattle. Also, the structure must be used only for the qualifying purpose. It does not qualify, for example, if part of it is used for storing equipment. If later the building is converted, or any part of the building is converted, from its qualifying use, the IRS may recapture the credit granted earlier.

Although the credit was made retroactive to August 15, 1971, IRS regulations allow farmers to file an amended return no more than three years after the original deadline, or two years after the tax was paid, whichever was later. The exception: If any year back to 1971 remains an "open year" because the farmer was involved in a dispute with the IRS and waived the statute of limitations, the farmer may still be able to claim a refund for that year based on this provision.

Cattle producers or dairymen who have been considering expansion may find an additional tax break and a fresh incentive in the new regulations. The tax credit will not only partially offset the cost of new facilities, but should also be considered in figuring the prospective return on the investment.

As a bonus to all businesses, but with wide application to agriculture, the new law extends tax credit eligibility to old buildings. For tax years ending October, 1978, capital expenditures made after that date in connection with rehabilitating buildings to be used for business or production are eligible for the credit, providing the structure has been in use for 20 years or more. Residential housing does not qualify, nor do the costs of buying, completing, or enlarging a building.

Costs for renovating old barns or general storage buildings, as well as livestock facilities, are eligible for the credit if the improvements have a useful life of 5 years or more and the other qualifications are met. However, no credit is allowed if more than 25 percent of the exterior walls are replaced.

As an example, if a farmer decides to replace interior partitions and electrical wiring as part of the rehabilitation of a barn that has been in use for at least 20 years, the farmer could get a $400 credit against taxes for a

$4,000 investment in the renovations. For specific answers regarding whether or not an improvement on a certain farm building would qualify for a tax credit, one should check with the local IRS office.

INVESTMENT CREDIT

To encourage investment in productive assets such as machinery and equipment, the new tax law retains the 10 percent investment credit rate. The credit is figured based on the investment cost, or the qualifying portion of it. The rate had been scheduled to drop to 7 percent by 1981. The limit on the cost of newly acquired, used productive assets that can qualify for the 10 percent investment credit will remain at $100,000 for any one year, instead of declining to $50,000. This means a maximum credit of $10,000 on a tax return (10 percent of $100,000) for all used property put in service during the year.

There is no limit on expenditures for new productive assets eligible for the credit. However, an individual's total investment credit was limited in 1978 to the lesser of tax liability, or $25,000 plus 50 percent of tax liability over $25,000. For tax years ending in 1979, the percentage of tax liability over $25,000 that can be offset by credit increases to 60 percent and then by 10 percentage points each year until 1982 when it will reach a permanent 90 percent.

Credits are subtracted from an individual's tax liability, not from income. Although they cannot exceed one's liability, excess credits can be carried back to the three preceding tax years and the balance still unused in those years can be carried forward to the seven succeeding tax years.

To qualify for a tax credit, property must be depreciable, be used in one's business, and have a useful life of at least 3 years.

COMPUTING INVESTMENT TAX CREDIT

The useful life of qualifying property is important in figuring the amount of the investment that is eligible for the tax credit. If the useful life is 3 or 4 years, only one-third of the investment cost is eligible for the credit. If the useful life is 5 or 6 years, two-thirds of the cost is eligible. If the useful life is 7 years or more, the full credit may be claimed.

As an example, Farmer Brown bought a used farm tractor, three milk cows, and a bull for breeding during 1978. The tractor cost $3,000 and has an expected life of 4 years. Each cow cost $600 and has an expected useful life of 5 years, and had not been used for dairying before this purchase. The bull cost $1,400, has an expected useful life of 8 years, and had not previously been used for breeding. Based on these investments, Mr. Brown would be entitled to deduct from his tax bill a 10 percent investment tax credit of $360 on a qualified investment of $3,600.

$1,000 (⅓ of tractor cost)
 1,200 (⅔ of cost of three cows)
 1,400 (Full cost of bull)
──────
$3,600 (Total)

Ten percent of $3,600 is $360, Farmer Brown's total investment tax credit.

If Brown had sold or disposed of any of these investments during the year, he could not use that investment to qualify for the tax credit. Also, if he had disposed of substantially identical livestock as defined by sex, age, and use, during the 1-year period beginning 6 months before his purchase of the cows and bull, he would have to subtract the amount he received for the animals he sold from his investment figure for the newly purchased livestock.

Also, Brown needs to remember the "recapture rule." If he disposes of an asset before the end of the estimated useful life he originally used in computing his credit, he must recompute the credit using the actual useful life—the time he owned it. He would then have to make up any difference between the credit he took and the recomputed credit.

Although land does not qualify for the investment tax credit, several other items do. Among those that have qualified for the credit in the past are farm machinery and vehicles, including automobiles used in the farm business; livestock, except horses; fences for livestock; and others.

CASH-FLOW PROJECTIONS

Successful investment decisions are critical to the financial health of the farm business. To determine the advisability of making any purchase before doing so can no doubt save money and possible mistakes. Many modern farmers use some of the same tools of analysis that accountants for big business use to decide if a given move will be good for the business or bad. In making any investment, two factors must be considered. First, will the change be profitable in the short run, that is, in the first 1 to 5 years of the investment? Secondly, will the move be profitable in the long run, 8 to 10 years, or even further, down the road?

Because the financial aspects of farm businesses are so important to the profitability of the operation, every management tool must be used to its best advantage. A helpful tool for determining short-term profitability of a proposed change in the farm business is called a *cash-flow projection*. For years, accountants at firms throughout the country have used the cash-flow projection to give them an idea of the short-term practicality of implementing various changes in their businesses. The dairy farmer and beef cattle producer can use this same accounting tool to help determine the same kind of information for their own businesses. The cash-flow projection tells the farmer if the management change he is contemplating will be profitable in the near future.

If the rancher wants to determine long-term profitability, which he most probably will, he will study budgets. In proposed budgets, capital expenditures are prorated over the life of the assets by various arbitrary depreciation methods.

Both short-term and long-term profitability should be studied before making a business decision. Some business changes are capable of being profitable in the long run, but cannot meet short-run demands for cash. This is particularly true when payment requirements for capital expenditures are concentrated in the early years of an investment.

A cash-flow projection is made on a period basis. The farmer decides if it will be monthly, bimonthly, quarterly, semiannual or annual. Basically, a cash-flow projection garners information from several sources such as past cash-flow records, tax returns, and price and yield estimates. The projection gathers the information in one spot and creates an organized picture of the proposed investment which helps the farmer decide the advisability of various changes in the farm situation.

The cash-flow projection compares incoming cash with outgoing cash to get an overall picture of the farm financial situation.

FINANCIAL RATIOS

Another accounting tool that is being used more frequently in farm businesses is the financial ratio. Put simply, a financial ratio is a comparison of two measurements of the business to each other. For example, a farm with a net income of $25,000 and a gross income of $100,000 has a net income to gross income ratio of 1 : 4. Expressed in percentage terms, the farm has a net income that is 25 percent of gross income. Data for some financial ratios come from the balance sheet. Data for other financial ratios come from the income statement. Some ratios use data from both the balance sheet and the income statement.

Financial ratios can be used in many ways. They are helpful in analyzing the financial situation of the farm, they can be used by a lending institution to determine the advisability of loaning money to the farmer, and they may be used by an investor in investment analysis.

Financial ratios often are used to determine the soundness of the farm business. Taking data from the balance sheet, one can figure the current ratio this way:

$$\text{Current Ratio} = \frac{\text{Current Loans}}{\text{Current Assets}}$$

Current assets are those assets that turn over in a normal year's operation. An example would be livestock held for sale.

Another ratio that relates adequacy of capital is the intermediate ratio:

$$\text{Intermediate Ratio} = \frac{\text{Intermediate Loans}}{\text{Intermediate Assets}}$$

Intermediate assets include machinery, equipment, and stock in cooperatives. Intermediate loans are usually for a period of 1 to 7 years.

A third ratio to determine adequacy of capital and soundness of the farm business is the long-term ratio:

$$\text{Long-Term Ratio} = \frac{\text{Long-Term Loans}}{\text{Long-Term Assets}}$$

Long-term assets are needed to produce income but may not be easily converted to cash in the ordinary business process. These include land and buildings. Long-term loans include land contracts and mortgages on land and farm improvements. The long-term ratio relates the long-term loans to the long-term assets.

Combining all the loans and all the assets makes possible the calculation of the total ratio:

$$\text{Total Ratio} = \frac{\text{Total Assets}}{\text{Total Loans}}$$

A final ratio that relates adequacy of capital is the debt-to-worth ratio:

$$\text{Debt-to-Worth Ratio} = \frac{\text{Total Loans}}{\text{Net Worth}}$$

The debt-to-worth ratio relates the total debt to the net worth of the business. This ratio compares the creditor's contribution of capital, that is the total loans, to the farmer's contribution, or net worth. The debt-to-worth ratio helps evaluate the financial trend of the business. Since the goal of most farmers and ranchers is to eventually operate a debt-free business, a continual lowering of the debt-to-worth ratio is a step in the right direction.

Financial ratios that help determine profitability of the farm business include the net-income-to-gross-income ratio:

$$\text{Net-Income-to-Gross-Income Ratio} = \frac{\text{Net Farm Income}}{\text{Gross Farm Income}}$$

This ratio determines the amount of net income left from the gross income after expenses are paid. Farm businesses that purchase large amounts of feed from off the farm may not find this ratio to be an appropriate indicator. Instead, these farms may need to subtract feed purchases in addition to livestock purchases from total sales and arrive at a measure called *value of farm production* to replace gross farm income in the ratio.

One must keep in mind that the interpretation of one ratio may be altered by other ratios of the same business. A specific ratio concentrates attention upon specific details of a business. For this reason, financial ratios are best interpreted as a group, rather than making judgments based on individual ratios. Instead, individual ratios can be examined to detect strengths and weaknesses within the farm business.

The objective in using financial ratios is to analyze the farm business situation as a unit. Calculating all the various possible ratios is a tool toward reaching a valid conclusion about the financial status of the farm. Basically, it is a good idea to limit current liabilities to a one-to-one ratio. That is, current liabilities would be no greater than current assets. Naturally, it would be even better if current assets exceeded current liabilities. However, especially for a farmer just starting out, the ideal is rarely possible. Because beginning cattle producers have had a very short time to build up net worth, they often must go deeper into debt than would normally be desirable.

Generally a good measure used to determine the advisability of making a loan to a farm business is the debt-to-worth ratio, comparing total liabilities to net worth. The ideal relationship would limit the debt-to-worth ratio to a one-to-one ratio. For the beginning cattle producer, however, lending institutions would take other factors into consideration such as health and the ability of the operator, the dependability of the project, and the successful experience of the operator.

Although a bank or other lending institution will be able to advise a cattle producer about the wisdom of making a loan, it is good management for the farmer to know as much about the financial phases of the operation as possible. This would include determining how much debt the operation could carry without endangering the financial stability of the farm or ranch.

HOW MUCH DEBT?

There are two basic types of farm or ranch loans. The first type of loan is for specialized buildings, facilities, machinery, or land. Usually this type debt must be repaid from net income. The second type of loan is for the purpose of buying something, such as feeder cattle, that will be resold later. The loan could then be repaid from gross sales. The latter type of loan often is referred to as a *self-liquidating loan*.

There are some important considerations to be made when determining how much one can borrow to finance land, machinery, and buildings. Where payments must be made from net income, one must realize that family living expenses must first be met from net income before even one payment on the debt could be made. Even though the new investment might be expected to produce additional income, one must realize that it often takes longer than expected to get a new or larger project operating at a level that generates additional profit.

Also important in determining whether an operation can afford to incur a loan is the length of time allowed for repayment and the rate of interest. The longer the time allotted for repayment and the lower the rate of interest, the greater will be the debt that can be carried by any certain level of net income.

The interest rate is of far less importance on short-term loans than on long-term loans. On any loan, however, it pays to shop around and obtain the most favorable loan rate available.

An additional factor to consider when obtaining loans is the skill and experience of the operator. Good management of all phases of the farm or ranch is imperative for prompt loan repayment. For example, if an experienced rancher produces even one additional calf each year over the period of a loan through reduced death losses, higher conception rates, or other management successes, he is that much more able to repay a loan than the inexperienced rancher.

COST OF CREDIT

Most farmers and ranchers use credit in their operation to enable them to continue expanding their business even though all of their personal funds already are invested in the farm business.

All banks and other lending institutions charge interest for the use of their money. Interest rates go up and down based on the current cost of money in the money market, the cost of servicing the loan, including making it, handling it, collecting it, and keeping records on the loan, and finally, the risk associated with a particular loan.

There are two basic types of interest—*straight* and *discount*. Straight interest means paying the interest on the principal at the end of the period for which the interest is being calculated. Discount interest, on the other hand, means charging for the interest in advance and reducing the principal by the amount of the interest.

With straight interest, the rate of interest is paid on the original amount of the loan. For example, if $1,000 was borrowed for 1 year at 8 percent, the total interest charge would be $80. ($1,000 $\times$ 8%). If the $1,000 were borrowed for 2 years at the same rate, the interest charge would be $160. Straight interest may also be charged on the unpaid balance of a loan. For instance, if the $1,000 was borrowed for 1 one year at 8 percent annual interest rate on the unpaid balance, and $500 principal paid at the end of 6 months, the total interest paid would be $60:

$1,000 × 8% = $80; $80/2 = $40
$ 500 × 8% = $40; $40/2 = $20
$60 Total interest

Discount interest is taken in advance rather than at the end of the period. If $1,000 was borrowed at 8 percent annual interest and was discounted, the borrower would receive only $920. The $920 is the original loan of $1,000 less the $80 interest. When using this method, the interest rate is, in reality, higher than the same rate of interest in the form of simple interest. In this example the actual rate of interest is 8.9 percent since the interest is paid on $1,000 but the borrower actually receives only $920.

By law, lenders must disclose the actual interest rate on any loan contract. The true interest rate is called *annual percentage rate*, and by virtue of the Truth-in-Lending Law, will be found on every loan contract.

INCOME STATEMENT

An income statement, also referred to as a profit-and-loss statement, tells the farm business owner whether or not the business is financially stable. The income statement shows income earned during the year, the expenses incurred during the year, and the difference between the two, or the net income. Usually farm businesses run on a calendar-year basis, although they may be run on a fiscal-year basis, if desired.

To compile an income statement accurately, the farm owner must gather together information on all income, all expenses, and calculate depreciation and changes in inventory value. (*See* Table 1-B overleaf.)

Income is one of the easier pieces of information to obtain. Usually farm income will come from the sale of livestock, milk, grain, and other farm products. Additional income may come from participation in government programs, dividend and interest from bank accounts and investments, and from special projects, such as feeding cattle for an absent owner.

Expenses, too, are easily determined. Operating expenses are those whose benefit expires within a year. For instance, hired labor, repairs, feed, taxes, and insurance are all farm operating expenses.

Purchases of equipment and buildings that will last more than a year cannot be deducted as expenses. Rather, they must be considered as capital expenditures and depreciated over a period of years. Depreciation represents the annual loss in value of these assets resulting from wear and tear and obsolescence.

TABLE 1-B.   EXAMPLE OF INCOME STATEMENT OF A FARM BUSINESS

(ACCRUAL OR INVENTORY BASIS)

John P. Recorder
Jan. 1, 19 **77** to Dec. 31, 19 **77**

FARM BUSINESS RECEIPTS

Livestock Sales .... (1A)	₡ 80,740	
Less Livestock Purchases .... (1B)	13,065	
Net Livestock Sales .... (1)	67,675	
Crop Sales .... (2)	12,490	
Agricultural Program Payments .... (3)	4,260	
Other Receipts .... (4)	2,175	
Total Receipts (Add lines 1 thru 4) .... (5)	86,600	
Change in Inventory Value of feed, supplies, grain and livestock .... ± (6)	1,900	
GROSS FARM INCOME (Line 5 ± Line 6)......... (7)		₡ 88,500

FARM OPERATING EXPENSES

Labor Hired .... (8)	2,560	
Equipment and Machinery Repairs .... (9)	5,470	
Interest .... (10)	8,545	
Cash Rent .... (11)	3,870	
Feed Purchased .... (12)	18,800	
Crop Expense, Seed, Etc. .... (13)	2,765	
Fertilizer and Lime .... (14)	4,150	
Machine Hire .... (15)	1,285	
Livestock Expenses .... (16)	3,305	
Gasoline, Fuel and Oil .... (17)	4,460	
Real and Personal Taxes .... (18)	2,250	
General Insurance .... (19)	450	
Utilities .... (20)	540	
Conservation Expense .... (21)	680	
Farm Org. Fees, Publications, Etc. .... (22)	585	
Total Oper. Exp. (Add Lines 8 thru 22) .... (23)	₡59,715	

DEPRECIATION EXPENSES

Machinery and Equipment .... (24)	₡ 2,725	
Motorized Equipment .... (25)	3,000	
Buildings .... (26)	940	
Other Depreciation .... (27)	—	
Total Deprec. Exp. (Add lines 24 thru 27) .... (28)	6,665	
TOTAL FARM EXPENSES (Add lines 23 & 28) (29)		₡ 66,380
NET FARM INCOME (Line 7 — line 29) .... (30)		22,120

Each year as inventory changes, these changes must be accounted for in order to accurately determine the true profit picture of the farm business. For example, inventories represent products produced or purchased for resale but not yet sold such as feeder livestock. Feed would be an inventory item if it had been purchased but not yet used.

, If the inventory value is greater at the end of the business year, inventory value has increased and that increase in value should be added to the farm income. If the inventory value is less at the end of the business year, the decrease should be subtracted from the farm income when determining net income. If the total inventory value at the beginning of the period is exactly the same as it is at the end of the period, then inventories have no effect on the net income. Although this last method would be by far the simplest, inventories rarely turn out this simply. The change in inventory value must be considered in order to gain an accurate picture of net farm income.

Table 1-C shows an example of an inventory change.

TABLE 1-C.   EXAMPLE OF LINE-BY-LINE INVENTORY CHANGE

Ending inventory		
Feed (purchased and grown)	$ 5,525	(1)
Supplies	1,450	(2)
Grain	6,575	(3)
Livestock	15,165	(4)
Total ending inventory (Add Lines 1–4)	$28,715	(5)
Beginning inventory		
Feed (purchased and grown)	4,600	(6)
Supplies	1,600	(7)
Grain	3,565	(8)
Livestock	17,050	(9)
Total beginning inventory (Add Lines 6–9)	$26,815	(10)
Net change in value of feed, supplies, grain, and livestock ($\pm$) (Line 5 minus Line 10)	$ 1,900	(11)

Analyzing a farm's income statement can provide a good picture of the financial status of the operation. An even better financial picture can be obtained by looking at the income statements from preceding years to determine overall profitability.

TABLE 1-D.   EXAMPLE BALANCE SHEET OF A FARM BUSINESS

(NET WORTH STATEMENT)

NAME _____   MAJOR ENTERPRISES _____

ADDRESS _____   STATEMENT DATE _____

FARM ASSETS			FARM LOANS		
CURRENT			**CURRENT**		
Cash on Hand	(1) $	–	Notes Payable	(21) $	22,000
Cash on Deposit in Bank	(2)	2,000	Accounts Payable	(22)	–
Accounts Receivable	(3)	–	Portion of Intermediate-Term Debt Due Within 12 Months	(23)	2,000
Notes Receivable	(4)	–	Portion of Long-Term Debt Due Within 12 Months	(24)	4,000
Livestock	(5)	29,000			
Crops Held for Sale & Feed	(6)	22,000	Rent, Taxes, and Interest Due and Unpaid	(25)	–
Fertilizer & Supplies on Hand	(7)	2,000	Other Debt Due Within 12 Months	(26)	–
Other (Specify)	(8)	–	TOTAL CURRENT FARM LOANS (Add lines 21 thru 26)	(27) $	28,000
TOTAL CURRENT FARM ASSETS (Add Lines 1 thru 8)	(9) $	55,000			
INTERMEDIATE			**INTERMEDIATE**		
Autos and Trucks	(10) $	5,400	Notes Payable (Maturities from 1 to 7 years for other than seasonal needs—less portion due within 12 months)	(28) $	3,200
Machinery & Equipment	(11)	27,500			
Other (Specify)	(12)	–	Other (Specify)	(29)	–
TOTAL INTERMEDIATE FARM ASSETS (Add lines 10 thru 12)	(13) $	32,900	TOTAL INTERMEDIATE FARM LOANS (Add lines 28 and 29)	(30) $	3,200
LONG TERM			**LONG TERM**		
Farmland	(14) $	120,000	Mortgages on Farm Real Estate (Less portion applied to current)	(31) $	55,500
Farm Improvement	(15)	15,000	Mortgages on Other Real Estate (Less portion applied to current loans)	(32)	–
Other (Specify)	(16)	–			
TOTAL LONG TERM FARM ASSETS (Add lines 14 thru 16)	(17) $	135,000	Other (Specify)	(33)	–
			TOTAL LONG-TERM FARM LOANS (Add lines 31 thru 33)	(34) $	55,500
TOTAL FARM ASSETS (Add lines 9, 13 and 17)	(18) $	222,900	TOTAL FARM LOANS (Add lines 27, 30, and 34)	(35) $	86,700
TOTAL NON-FARM ASSETS	(19) $	20,000	NET FARM WORTH (Assets—Loans) (Line 18 — line 35)	(36) $	136,200
TOTAL FARM & NON-FARM ASSETS (Add lines 18 and 19)	(20) $	242,900	TOTAL FARM LOANS & NET WORTH (Add lines 35 and 36)	(37) $	222,900
			TOTAL NON-FARM LOANS	(38) $	–
			TOTAL FARM & NON-FARM LOANS (Add lines 35 and 38)	(39) $	86,700
			TOTAL FARM & NON-FARM NET WORTH (Line 20 — line 39)	(40) $	156,200
			TOTAL FARM & NON-FARM LOANS & NET WORTH (Add lines 39 and 40)	(41) $	242,900

BALANCE SHEET

The balance sheet, or net worth statement, tells the financial status of the farm business at a specific time. The balance sheet is one of the most important financial tools in a business since it shows what is owned, what is owed, and the owner's share, or net worth, of the business. The net worth of a business is often determined by comparing past balance sheets with current balance sheets and analyzing the growth or the decline of assets and loans.

Net worth is, simply, the amount resulting when loans are subtracted from assets.

In determining net worth, all assets are listed, even if they are not completely paid for. Assets would include any cash on hand, bank accounts, loans or accounts due from others to be paid to the farm business, feed supplies on hand, livestock, equipment, buildings, land, and other items.

Any unpaid accounts, notes, and mortgages are listed as loans.

The balance sheet can provide the farmer with information on how best to meet financial obligations. By listing assets and loans in terms of current, intermediate, and long-term, he or she can determine how best to meet the loans. For instance, current assets are cash or other assets that can be converted to cash quickly, that is, within a year through normal business processes. Current loans are those debts that are due and payable within a year.

Intermediate assets, on the other hand, are used primarily to support farm production. Generally this would refer to machinery and equipment, items not expected to be sold in the normal business process. Intermediate loans are those for periods of 1 to 7 years, and usually are for items like machinery and equipment that will last for several years.

Long-term assets are those needed to produce income, but which would be more difficult to convert to cash. Long-term assets include land and buildings. Likewise, long-term loans include land contracts and mortgages on land and farm improvements.

The balance sheet enables the farmer to compare total current assets with total long-term assets, allowing a determination if too much or too little capital is tied up in permanent investments. A farm business with too many long-term assets has less flexibility than one with sufficient current and intermediate assets. To be most successful, economists suggest retaining some flexibility in the farm business.

Also, the balance sheet will show when loans are due and whether current assets will be adequate to meet those obligations. If not, then other plans must be made, such as making a longer term loan, or renegotiating the same loan.

Utilizing ratios can help the cattle producer evaluate the farm's balance sheet. For example, the current ratio, the total ratio, and the debt-to-worth ratio all give important comparisons of balance sheet information in a readily understood form. The ratios are computed as follows:

$$\text{Current Ratio} = \frac{\text{Current Loans}}{\text{Current Assets}}$$

$$\text{Total Ratio} = \frac{\text{Total Loans}}{\text{Total Assets}}$$

$$\text{Debt-to-Worth Ratio} = \frac{\text{Total Loans}}{\text{Net Worth}}$$

DEPRECIATION

Any purchase with a useful life of more than a year is considered by the government to be a capital expenditure. A capital expenditure cannot be deducted as an expense for tax purposes. Instead, a reasonable allowance for the exhaustion, wear and tear, and obsolescence of property used in the farm or ranch business can be taken in the form of depreciation.

Depreciation is allowed for farm machinery, buildings, and other physical farm property. Purchased breeding livestock may be depreciated as well. No depreciation is allowed for land, or for personal property used in the home or in nonbusiness activities.

The most common method for determining depreciation is the *straight-line method*. With this method, depreciation is taken in equal annual amounts over the estimated useful life of an asset.

If the item has a salvage value, that is, if the item will have a value at the end of its period of usefulness to the taxpayer, that value must be deducted from the original cost of the item to determine the basis for depreciation.

In some cases the salvage value may be no more than junk value if the taxpayer plans to use an item for a long period of time. If assets are normally disposed of while they are still in good working order, however, the salvage value may be substantial. Salvage values will vary greatly among farm businesses depending upon the policy of the owner. If an item (other than livestock) has at least a 3-year useful life, the salvage value may be reduced up to 10 percent of its cost basis. For example, if an item costs $3,000 and the salvage value is estimated at $250, the salvage value can be disregarded and depreciation computed on the full $3,000 cost (10% of $3,000 = $300). If the estimated salvage value of a $3,000 item is $1,500, then $300 of the salvage value may be subtracted, using $1,200 as the salvage value.

Salvage value, if applicable, must be subtracted from the cost basis in calculating straight-line depreciation.

Property purchased outright without a trade, with no salvage value deduction, uses the actual cost of the item as the basis for depreciation.

Of course if an item is owned only part of a year, only part of the full year's depreciation may be claimed. To compute the partial deduction, the first full year's depreciation allowance is multiplied by the fraction of the year it is owned. For example, if something is owned for 6 months, only half of a full year's depreciation may be claimed.

With straight-line depreciation, depreciation is taken in equal amounts over the estimated useful life of the asset. If salvage value is a consideration, it is subtracted from the original cost basis of the item. This amount is then divided by the number of years of useful life of the item. This gives the amount the item may be depreciated each year until it is depreciated down to salvage value or sold. No depreciation is allowed below the estimated salvage value of any asset.

Also, any taxpayer except a trust may elect to deduct an additional 20 percent first-year depreciation. After taking the additional 20 percent depreciation, any of the regular depreciation methods may be used.

The 20 percent additional first-year depreciation may be used on new or used tangible personal property if it has a useful life of at least 6 years and it is not acquired in transactions between certain related individuals, partnerships, corporations, stockholders, or certain beneficiaries, or others. Only the difference paid is subject to additional depreciation in the case of property acquired through a trade.

Farm machinery, equipment, and purchased dairy and breeding livestock are eligible for the extra 20 percent first-year depreciation. Buildings, structures, and other farm improvements that become a part of the real estate are not eligible for this additional depreciation.

The cost of property on which the additional first-year allowance may be taken is limited to $20,000 on a joint return and $10,000 on an individual return. This limitation refers to the entire cost of all qualifying property purchased during the tax year. For corporations and partnerships, the maximum additional allowance is 20 percent of the cost of qualifying property not in excess of $10,000.

Additional first-year depreciation can be taken only in the first year for which a depreciation deduction is allowed on the property. If an item qualifies for the additional depreciation, the full 20 percent applies regardless of the time during the tax year it is purchased.

More than one depreciation method can be used on the same tax return. The choice of depreciation methods can be made on each asset individually.

The *straight-line method* usually will be the choice method of depreciation for new purchases made in years of average or below average income, whereas in years of unusually high income, the taxpayer might consider one of the accelerated methods of depreciation such as the declining balance method or the sum-of-the-years method.

The *declining balance method* allows the largest depreciation the first year and a gradually smaller allowance in each of the following years. A uniform depreciation rate up to twice the straight-line rate is used. The depreciation taken each year is subtracted from the basis of the property before figuring the next year's depreciation, so the same depreciation rate is applied to a smaller balance each year. The declining balance method may be used if the property has a useful life of 3 or more years. To figure the declining balance depreciation rate, one figures the straight-line rate and doubles it. For example, if an item with an 8-year useful life is depreciated at a straight-line rate of 12.5 percent, the declining balance rate would be twice that, or 25 percent. Exceptions to the doubled straight-line rate are used tangible personal property and new farm real property that are figured at one-and-a-half times the straight-line rate.

Table 1-E shows a comparison of the straight-line and declining balance depreciation methods.

TABLE 1-E.   DEPRECIATION METHODS*

	Annual Depreciation	
	Straight Line	Declining Balance
First-year additional depreciation	$ 0	$ 2,400
First-year regular depreciation	1,200	1,920
Total First Year Depreciation	$ 1,200	$ 4,320
Second year	1,200	1,536
Third year	1,200	1,229
Fourth year	1,200	983
Fifth year	1,200	786
Sixth year	1,200	629
Seventh year	1,200	503
Eighth year	1,200	403
Ninth year	1,200	322
Tenth year	1,200	258
Total Depreciation	$12,000	$10,969
Unrecovered cost		$ 1,031

*Assume a $12,000 basis, no salvage value considered.

The third method, the *sum-of-the-years digits method,* is another rapid depreciation method. It applies a different fraction each year to the amount to be depreciated.

The denominator of the fraction is the total of the digits representing the years of useful life of the asset. For example, if the useful life of the property is 8 years, the denominator is 36:

$$1 + 2 + 3 + 4 + 5 + 6 + 7 + 8 = 36$$

The numerator is the number of remaining years of useful life of the item. For the first year of an 8-year life, the numerator would be 8. Thus, the first-year depreciation of an item with a useful life of 8 years and a depreciation basis of $10,000 would be $2,222 (8/36 × $10,000 = $2,222). In the second year the numerator would be 7, so the depreciation would be $1,944 (7/36 × $10,000 = $1,944), and so on.

The sum-of-the-years digits method is used rarely in the normal day-to-day workings of business.

RECORDKEEPING FOR BEEF PRODUCERS

It is important for the beef producer to keep records. What records to keep often is a difficult question for the beginner. In addition to the financial records mentioned earlier in the chapter, other records must be maintained also. Such records as budgets, income and expenses, profit and loss statement, and net worth statement are important.

Annual Inventory

When producers take an inventory of their farm or ranch operation, they are listing everything that applies to their financial situation. They list the land, buildings, equipment, feed, supplies, and cash on hand. These are the *assets*. They tally *liabilities*, too. Such things as bills to be paid, mortgages, and loans would be listed.

What Records To Keep

The most efficient farm and ranch operations are run in ways similar to other successful businesses. Records are kept of anything and everything that will affect the business. For instance, it is a good idea to keep a record of all equipment—purchase price, necessary repairs, cost of repairs, and when repaired. If the operation employs workers outside the owner's immediate family, records of days worked, sick days, and vacation time must be kept. Additionally, Social Security taxes must be paid for workers who are paid more than a minimum amount in a calendar quarter.

Health Records

Keeping cattle healthy ranks as a primary goal of the successful cattle producer. Diseased and poorly conditioned animals drain profits from a potentially successful operation. One of the most important aids to maintaining a healthy herd is a good record system. By keeping records on animals, the producer has all important data at hand when they are needed. In addition, keeping reproductive records helps maintain a profitable calving interval.

The first step in record keeping is to establish a lifetime health record for each cow, including the animal's reproductive history. Mark and record each animal's identification.

The record program should begin with a series of temporary sheets on which all reproductive abnormalities and events, treatments, and routine information are recorded. At month's-end, temporary records are transferred to the pemanent record and the temporary records can be discarded.

The permanent record accumulates a lifetime health history on each animal. Information such as prebreeding heat dates, calving dates, inseminations, calving problems, infections, diseases, and treatments given should be included. Even records of deceased animals should be maintained with the permanent records to give a picture of inherited characteristics in the herd. Forms for lifetime health records generally include space for listing dates of heats, calving, name of sire, and dates of examinations, along with results and treatment.

Livestock records should indicate animals received, animals sold, and animals that have died. A health record should be established for each animal in the herd.

Keeping all these records by hand can be a time-consuming task. With the coming of the computer age, many producers have chosen to turn their record-keeping chores over to the computer.

Computers and the Cattle Producer

Small, home-size computers have become available at a price modest enough to tempt the livestock producer to buy a computer. Many people own their own personal computers and numerous others utilize computer services provided by banks, trade associations, and others. To use a computer effectively, the producer must have accurate, detailed records to feed into the computer. The information that the computer feeds back to the producer is only as good as the records provided to it.

CHOICES IN THE CATTLE INDUSTRY

The beginning producer faces not merely a decision over beef or dairy cattle production, there are additional choices to be made. For the dairy farmer, the primary product is the milk produced by the cows. He or she may make a profit selling bull calves and perhaps heifer calves as well (although the farmer will need most of the heifer calves for replacement purposes unless he or she chooses to purchase replacement heifers at a later time). The beef producer, on the other hand, has a number of options. He or she may choose the cow-calf program of production, or opt to operate a feedlot.

Cow-Calf Programs

If the cattle producer chooses the cow-calf program, there are three basic options. First, he or she might decide to produce purebred, *registered* cattle. The capital required for this first option is higher than for the other two cow-calf programs because it requires either the purchase or the production of purebred cows and requires a lot of paperwork to comply with registration requirements of most breeds. In many cases, detailed performance information must be maintained on each animal for it to be registered. This requires a large investment of time and effort as well. Purchase of a purebred bull is not required at first if the producer is willing to use artificial insemination. Eventually, though, the purebred producer's goal is to provide purebred bulls to the commercial cattle producer.

Production of *F-1 cattle* is considered to be the second basic option for beef cattle production. F-1 refers to the animal resulting from the crossbreeding of two pure breeds of cattle. F-1 refers to the first cross generation. These cattle exhibit hybrid vigor, an extra genetic boost gained from crossbreeding. (See page 168). The F-1 cattle producer may market steers for slaughter and sell heifers to other producers for use in rotational crossbreeding programs. (See Chapter 3—Selection).

The *commercial* cattle business is one of the oldest forms of cattle production in the United States. The commercial cattle producer may use various crossbreeding systems and thus become a customer for both the purebred breeder and the F-1 breeder. A commercial cattle producer normally has a herd of cattle with a recognizable color pattern—black, or red with white faces, but the cattle generally are not registered. When the new breeds first began entering the United States their owners immediately began advertising the advantages of their breeds to the commercial buyer. The commercial cattle producer can make the most profitable moves by taking advantage of hybrid vigor by selecting a purebred bull for use on his or her commercial cows. The use of a crossbred bull on commercial cows, however it might appear, is not second best. Because the crossbred bull has the advantage of hybrid vigor it generally will look like an excellent breeding prospect. Because hybrid vigor loses much of its effectiveness in the second generation, most crossbred bulls look far more promising than they turn out to be. Many cattle producers believe that half-blood bull calves should all be fed out for slaughter as steers. The commercial producer may market the cattle directly or sell them to a feeder.

Grazing Steers

Livestock producers with grass to use but with limited amounts of harvested feed may want to consider grazing steers. No crop land is needed for this program unless temporary pasture is used. Very little labor is required since management requirements are limited to health care during the first 30 days of ownership, checking during the pasture season, and marketing in the fall. There are potential risks involved because much of the success of this type of program depends on marketing opportunities at the end of the grazing period.

The steers are on grass for the entire period of ownership so only handling equipment and corrals are needed.

Steers for a grazing program usually are purchased about May 1. The steers should weigh less than 600 pounds when purchased or they will be too heavy for feedlot demand when they are taken off grass at the end of the grazing season. Sometimes steers are left on grass less than 180 days if grass becomes unpalatable. However, if protein or grain is supplemented to the steers during the latter part of the grazing season, satisfactory gains are maintained. Table 1-F shows a cost-return projection for grazing steers.

TABLE 1-F.   COST-RETURN PROJECTION: GRAZING STEERS

	Per Head	
Returns:		
Steer	_____	(1)
Less Cost of Feeder	_____	(2)
Less Death Loss (2%)	_____	(3)
Gross Returns	$_____	(4)
Variable Costs:		
Feed	_____	(5)
Pasture (summer)	_____	(6)
Veterinary and Drugs	_____	(7)
Gas, Oil, Utilities	_____	(8)
Labor (1 hour)	_____	(9)
Marketing Costs (3% of Line 1)	_____	(10)
Repairs	_____	(11)
Interest on Livestock and ½ Variable Costs at 9%	_____	(12)
(Interest calculated for 6 months)		
Total Variable Costs	$_____	(13)
Fixed Costs (Equipment & Buildings)		
Depreciation	_____	(14)
Interest, Taxes, & Insurance	_____	(15)
Total Fixed Costs	$_____	(16)
Total Costs (Line 13 plus Line 16)	$_____	(17)
Total Cost per CWT Gain	$_____	(18)
Return to Management (Line 4 minus Line 17)	_____	(19)
Return to Labor and Management (Line 19 plus Line 9)	_____	(20)

Wintering and Grazing Steers

Cattle producers who have high-quality roughage available for winter feed and grass for summer grazing may consider the winter and graze steer program as a method for backgrounding cattle. The risks involved in this program are less than for separate wintering or grazing programs. Steers are kept for about a year and the original weight is nearly doubled.

This program uses steers purchased in the fall at a weight of about 400 pounds. The steers are fed high-quality roughages and protein during the winter phase to gain about 200 pounds. Steers should weigh more than 800 pounds when they are taken off grass in the fall.

Under this program, the cattle producer needs high-quality harvested roughage such as silage and hay. During the wintering phase, each steer uses about 1.2 tons of hay or its equivalent. Feed costs can be reduced if sorghum fields and wheat pasture are used to replace part of the harvested roughage. Good summer pasture also is needed to attain desired weight. This can be native grass or tame grass such as brome or fescue. Table 1-G gives cost-return projections (*see* overleaf).

Feedlot Finishing

The finishing phase of producing beef to choice grade is a task performed by commercial feedlots and by the farmer-feeder. This program uses a large amount of feed grain, which comprises 85 to 90 percent of the ration. When steers are fed for 150 days, 50 to 55 bushels of grain, 450 pounds of hay, and 150 pounds of a protein supplement will produce about 400 pounds of grain.

Compared with other beef-producing programs, the capital required to operate a feedlot is relatively high. Building requirements consist primarily of feed storage facilities. Equipment includes feeding facilities, pens, handling equipment, watering, and manure disposal systems.

Labor requirements vary tremendously based on the size of the operation. An estimate for a midsize feedlot puts labor requirements at 2.5 labor hours per steer for the 5-month finishing phase. Large feedlots are more efficient than the estimate and small lots are less efficient. Table 1-H gives a cost-return projection form for feedlot finishing (*see* page 109).

Feedlot Contracting

Many livestock producers use the feeding services of a feedlot operator to improve production profits. It is important to consider the legal aspects of feedlot contracting before a problem arises.

When livestock is placed in a feedlot by an agreement between the producer and the feedlot operator, a legal transaction called a *bailment* takes

TABLE 1-G.   COST-RETURN PROJECTION: WINTER & GRAZING STEERS

	Per Head	
Returns:		
Steer	_____	(1)
Less Cost of Feeder	_____	(2)
Less Death Loss (2%)	_____	(3)
Gross Returns	_____	(4)
Variable Costs:		
Feed	_____	(5)
Pasture (summer)	_____	(6)
Veterinary & Drugs	_____	(7)
Gas, Oil, & Utilities	_____	(8)
Labor (4 hours)	_____	(9)
Marketing Costs (3% of Line 1)	_____	(10)
Repairs	_____	(11)
Interest on Livestock & ½ Variable Costs at 9%	_____	(12)
(Interest calculated over 12 months)		
Total Variable Costs	_____	(13)
Fixed Costs: (Equipment and Buildings)		
Depreciation (15 years)	_____	(14)
Interest, Taxes & Insurance (10%)	_____	(15)
Total Fixed Costs	_____	(16)
Total Costs (Line 16 plus Line 13)	_____	(17)
Total Cost per CWT Gain	_____	(18)
Return to Management (Line 4 minus Line 17)	_____	(19)
Return to Labor and Management (Line 19 plus Line 9)	_____	(20)

place. A bailment results when one delivers property to another and retains the right to have the same property returned at a later date, or to have the property delivered to a third-party designated by the producer. Delivery of property with no right to have it returned would be a gift or a sale. The producer, the person entrusting property with the operator, is called a *bailor.* The operator receiving the bailed property is called a *bailee.*

Feedlot feeding contracts may be oral or written. Often a written contract helps avoid misunderstandings and difficulties that may arise from an oral contract. In negotiating for feedlot feeding services, several things must

TABLE 1-H. COST-RETURN PROJECTION—FEEDLOT FINISHING PROGRAM

	Per Head	
Returns:		
Steer	_____	(1)
Cost of Feeder	_____	(2)
Less Death Loss (1%)	_____	(3)
Gross Returns	_____	(4)
Variable Costs:		
Feed	_____	(5)
Pasture (summer)	_____	(6)
Veterinary and Drugs	_____	(7)
Gas, Oil, Utilities	_____	(8)
Labor (2.5 hours)	_____	(9)
Marketing Costs (3% of Line 1)	_____	(10)
Repairs	_____	(11)
Interest on Livestock and ½ Variable Costs at 9%	_____	(12)
(Interest calculated for 5 months)		
Total Variable Costs	_____	(13)
Fixed Costs: (Equipment & Buildings)		
Depreciation	_____	(14)
Interest, Taxes & Insurance	_____	(15)
Total Fixed Costs	_____	(16)
Total Costs (Line 13 plus Line 16)	_____	(17)
Total Cost per CWT Gain	_____	(18)
Return to Management (Line 4 minus Line 17)	_____	(19)
Return to Labor and Management (Line 19 plus Line 9)	_____	(20)

be determined in advance. First, who will feed the livestock and what will they be fed? Frequently the feed is furnished by the operator. The kinds of rations furnished need to be discussed in advance. Since feed represents the largest cost in the feedlot contract, another matter to be discussed in advance is who pays for the feed and how the feed is to be paid for.

Another good topic to discuss in advance is who will assume responsibility for death losses in the feedlot. Ordinarily, under the rules of bailment, the property owner bears the loss for destruction of bailed property even when in custody of another. If, however, the loss was caused by wrongdoing or negligence of the operator, the producer would not be responsible for the loss. Insurance sometimes is taken out on the livestock. If this is done, it should be made clear who will be taking out the insurance.

If the producer wants the livestock sold at the end of the feeding period, provisions for the sale should be included in the contract. The contract should make it clear how the proceeds of the sale are to be distributed.

Other points to include in the contract are the complete description of the livestock by sex, breed, and weight. A listing of all brands, tattoos, and other descriptive markings found on the animals should also be included.

It is wise to have an attorney prepare the contract to ensure that both parties have a clear understanding in advance of all provisions of the contract.

Cow Leasing

Leasing has been used for decades as a method for gaining control of additional land, but until recently had not been used for cattle. Today, however, leasing contracts are used frequently for both dairy and beef cattle. To be of interest to both parties, a leasing arrangement must provide some benefits to both. Neither the livestock owner or the renter should find the lease unprofitable. If this were the case, neither would be interested in the leasing arrangement.

Like any contract, there are several things to be clarified before the start of the agreement. In cow leasing, first of all, costs must be determined. Then it must be decided who will contribute which major cost items. Finally, a determination of the percent of major costs contributed by each party must be made. With these factors determined, the owner and the renter would share in income in the same proportion as their contributions to the enterprise. They also would share veterinary and drugs, trucking and marketing costs, and other minor expenses in the same proportion as they contribute major costs.

Basically, two types of major costs will be incurred. Fixed costs are those related to the owning of property. Costs that fall into this category include repairs, interest, insurance, taxes, and depreciation.

The other kind of costs of an operation are variable costs like feed, labor, veterinary and drug charges, expenses of trucking and marketing, and other costs. They are sometimes referred to as operating costs.

Generally in a leasing arrangement, the owner is responsible for fixed costs of the livestock and occasionally a portion of the variable costs. The renter usually takes responsibility for the operating costs. He may furnish some of the fixed costs also.

Rental or leasing of cows can be considered for use by both dairy farmers and beef producers. Anyone entering into this type of agreement, however, must be certain that all important facets of the agreement are worked out in advance. One very important factor to consider is who will be responsible for death loss. When the owner is solely responsible for replacements in the herd, death loss usually is his or her contribution.

Whether the leasing agreement pertains to dairy or beef cattle, several items should be included in the contract. They are: specifics regarding financial terms; provision for terminating or arbitrating the contract; designation of responsibility for breeding and other livestock expenses; provision for addition or withdrawal of animals from the contract; and a complete explanation of rental payment methods and terms.

When dealing with dairy cow rental, the contract might specify bonus payments for production above a specified base production level. A bonus provision provides an added incentive for both owner and renter since each would collect additional income from higher milk production.

DAIRY FARMING

The dairy farm requires less land than the beef ranch, and many farmers find a dairy operation to be a profitable, rewarding enterprise. Many dairy farms are run on a dry-lot basis, that is, without pasture land and supplemental grazing land. With this type of arrangement, however, feed must be purchased rather than raised. Since feed is a major cost of any cattle operation, the dairy farmer may want to consider having additional land area to raise feed and provide supplemental grazing.

For years when one thought of dairy farming, one would automatically think of long hours of labor. Actually, however, labor requirements can be reduced with modern equipment. Table 1-I (*below*) gives estimates of time requirements for a modern dairy operation. Table 1-J gives a cost-return projection form. (*See* page 113.)

In a dairy, about 40 percent of the total costs of maintaining the herd are purchased inputs—mainly the cost of substituting capital for labor in the form of labor-saving devices.

TABLE 1-I. TIME REQUIREMENTS FOR DAIRYING

Herd Size (Cows)	Hours per Cow (Estimated)		
	Loose Housing and Milking Parlor	Gutter Cleaner and Pipeline	Stanchion
10–15	0	0	120
15–30	82	85	95
30–50	70	75	80
Over 50	60	65	75

In a typical dairy operation, feed costs account for about 60 percent of total costs. Raising one's own feed can reduce that amount.

The figures in Table 1-I do not include time spent in crop production, feed processing, repairs of equipment, or other activities associated with the dairy farm. (*See* previous page.)

They represent direct labor requirements such as milking, feeding, manure disposal, and other care of the animals, including replacements.

Dairy Herd Improvement Program

The National Cooperative Dairy Herd Improvement Program provides organized record-keeping plans that dairy farmers use to improve their herds. Coordinated by the Agricultural Research Service of the U.S. Department of Agriculture, it is carried out in cooperation with both the federal extension service and state extension services. A nationwide sire evaluation program has been a part of the national program since 1935.

Dairy farmers who realize that good record keeping and performance information can improve a herd may find the Dairy Herd Improvement Association a worthwile expense.

Currently there are three plans for record keeping: the standard DHIA, the Owner-Sampler, or the Weigh-a-Day-a-Month.

The standard dairy herd (DHIA) record-keeping plan is the official plan and provides records that are eligible for use in sire and cow evaluations.

The dairy farmer who signs a herd up for this program receives a herd code number for record-keeping purposes.

The association supervisor—there are local DHIA associations throughout the country—visits each herd in the association once a month. During evening milking, the supervisor weighs feed consumed and milk produced by each cow and saves a small sample of her milk. The same procedure is followed during the milking the next morning. The supervisor tests the milk samples for butterfat, or has them tested in a laboratory. The weights and tests for one day are used to calculate each cow's milk and butterfat production for the month. At the end of the year a record summary for each herd is made.

Studies have shown that yearly records based on weights and tests for one day each month are within 2 percent of the actual milk production and 3 percent of the actual butterfat production.

The supervisor makes all entries in a herd record book that the farmer keeps as a useful guide to managing his or her own herd.

The supervisor also helps keep breeding and calving records on herd cows. The records are needed to indicate the breeding worth of sires used in the herd.

When available, registration numbers are used. Nonregistered animals are ear-tagged to establish their identity. This way, a lifetime record for each cow is developed.

TABLE 1-J.   COST-RETURN PROJECTION PER DAIRY COW

Returns:

Milk ($ per cwt)	_____	(1)
Calves and cows	_____	(2)
Total Receipts	_____	(3)

Variable Costs: Per Cow Unit

Feed (includes replacements)	_____	(4)
Labor (see Table 1-H.)	_____	(5)
Livestock Expense	_____	(6)
Utilities	_____	(7)
Dues and Fees	_____	(8)
Insurance	_____	(9)
Machinery and Equipment Expense	_____	(10)
Repairs on Permanent Improvements	_____	(11)
Interest on Livestock Investment and Half Variable Costs at 9%	_____	(12)
Total Variable Costs	_____	(13)

Fixed Costs: Per Cow Unit

Depreciation (Buildings, Equipment, Fences, and Machinery)	_____	(14)
Taxes and Interest on Half Investment at 10%	_____	(15)
Total Fixed Costs	_____	(16)
Total Costs (Line 13 and Line 16)	_____	(17)
Total Costs per CWT Milk Produced	_____	(18)*
Return to Management (Line 3 minus Line 17)	_____	(19)
Return to Labor and Management (Lines 19 and 5)	_____	(20)

* Calculate Line 18 by subtracting Line 2 from Line 17, then divide by cwt of milk produced.

Frequently the supervisor can suggest the changes in feeding or management of the herd or of individual cows that the records show are needed. Each year, statistics show that cows managed carefully produce more milk than those managed haphazardly. For this reason, the DHIA program is a valuable one to many dairy farmers who would not take the time to keep the detailed records that the DHIA supervisor is required to make. Currently, average enrollment per cow is under $1.00 per month. For additional fees, other services are available. Print-outs on cull cows, breeding checks, heifer identification, and so on, are available.

In Owner-Sampler record keeping, the DHIA supervisor leaves sample bottles and record sheets at the farm each month. The farmer weighs the milk from each cow in the herd and saves a sample for testing. The supervisor picks up the milk weight records and the milk samples on the regular visit to the herd and tests the samples for butterfat content and computes records for each cow from figures provided by the farmer. The completed records of cows and herd are mailed to the farmer or delivered by the supervisor on the next visit.

The use of owner-sampler records is limited to the farmer's own herd. Because the weights and samples are not obtained by a disinterested person (the association supervisor), they are treated as private records. The records are not used for summarizing sires and are of limited use in selling surplus stock.

Owner-sampler records can be used as a guide for feeding individual cows according to production by recording the amount of grain fed each cow and the amount of forage fed to the herd, culling the low-producing cows, and selecting cows whose heifers should be raised for herd replacements.

Owner-sampler records can be used for starting an improvement program in many dairy herds. As plans for building a herd develop, however, many dairy farmers choose to move up to the standard DHIA program.

The Weigh-a-Day-a-Month record plan is the simplest of the DHIA record-keeping programs. In this plan, only the milk yield is recorded. No milk samples are taken; average butterfat production of the herd is obtained from the monthly milk check. The dairy farmer takes the milk weights of each cow in the herd—morning and evening—on the fifteenth of each month. Then these weights are recorded on a special form obtained from the computing service and the form returned for calculation of the monthly records. (The county agent has information about where the nearest computing service is located.) Completed monthly reports for individual cows and for the herd are then mailed to the dairy farmer.

As one might expect, monthly costs for the Owner-Sampler and the Weigh-a-Day-a-Month programs are lower than for the standard DHIA program. County agricultural agents and state extension dairy agents have information on how to sign up for the various programs, as well as current cost information.

Culling Unprofitable Cows

Culling the lowest producing cows and replacing them with higher producing cows will make a herd more profitable. Monthly records that show an individual's production, its value, the cost of her feed, and income over feed cost, enable a farmer to make an intelligent decision about culling.

Basically, each cow should return at least $2 for each $1 she consumes in feed. By maintaining this standard she pays for her feed, the labor expended on her, and a proportionate share of the total overhead, interest on investment, and depreciation. A cow that returns less than $2 for each $1 spent on feed should be replaced with a higher producing cow as soon as possible.

With feed and production records at hand, the farmer can determine the level of production necessary for profit. Below this level, cows must be culled to avoid financial loss and to obtain the greatest returns for capital and labor invested.

A dairy farmer can set arbitrary production levels that a cow must equal or exceed to remain in the herd. Even though a cow returns a profit, a progressive dairy farmer will remove her from the herd any time she can be replaced by a more profitable cow.

Basically, culling, feeding, breeding, and total dairy management are more successful when proper records are used to provide the dairy farmer with an accurate picture of the herd. The more information at hand, the more successful an operation will be. The DHIA was formed to give the dairy farmer some helpful management tools to use in herd evaluation.

Calving Interval

Calving interval is an important economic consideration in a cow-calf operation. To maintain a yearly calving interval, management pressure must be placed on getting cows bred as early as possible after calving.

Beef cows that are well fed and well managed will be cycling 30 to 50 days postcalving. A minimum postpartum interval is required for uterine involution and for recovery of the uterine mucosa. Many factors, including nutrition level before and after calving, calf suckling, and milk production influence the length of time from calving to conception.

Researchers at the University of Wisconsin say that conception in beef cows plateaus at approximately 50 days postpartum. With a 283-day gestation period, the cow should be rebred by 82 days postpartum or the cattle producer will not get one calf per year from the cows.

Producing a live, healthy calf is the goal of both beef producers and dairy farmers. For top breeding efficiency, it is imperative to keep records of several important facts. The dairy farmer, and the beef producer using AI, should record freshening dates, heat dates, service dates, and other general observations. These records provide the information necessary for high breeding efficiency. They help the cattle producer determine irregularities and diagnose problems.

Dry Period for the Dairy Cow

To produce at their best, cows need a rest each year. The dairy farmer needs accurate records to enable him or her to prepare properly for the dry period. After breeding each cow, the dairy farmer notes her calving date from the gestation table and makes plans to turn the cow dry about 2 months prior to her estimated calving date. The optimum dry period is 55 days, although some cows may benefit from a few extra days. Generally first and second lactation cows benefit from a few extra days and older cows can get by with 40 to 45 days. Good conditioning prior to the dry period is beneficial. USDA research found that body fat is replaced with 70 to 75 percent efficiency in late lactation, compared with 58 percent in dry cows. A cow turned dry in good flesh can be maintained at less expense during the dry period.

One of several ways to dry off a cow is to stop milking abruptly. The pressure of the milk left in the udder assists in the drying-off process.

For good management, dry cows should be removed from the milking herd. Grain and silage should be withheld for 2 to 3 days, with roughage and water provided only once a day for 1 or 2 days. At this point, milking should be stopped abruptly. After the last milking, each cow should be treated with a long-lasting antibiotic in each quarter to prevent new infections which are most numerous during the first 2 weeks of the dry period. A teat dip should follow. Dry cows should be observed daily for the first week or two after drying off, then every 2 to 3 days until calving.

Determining Pregnancy

Palpation is an accepted method for determining preganancy in cattle. With a large herd, a good method is to bring cattle through a chute, attempting the least amount of excitement to the animal as possible. The calmer the cow, the less danger to both the animal and to the palpator.

Equipment needs, besides a chute, are minimal in this process. The cattle producer should wear a rubber or plastic sleeve covering hand, arm, and shoulder. This sleeve guards against disease and eliminates irritation of the arm. A lubricant such as liquid soap is recommended. A large rubber band can be used to hold the plastic sleeve on the upper arm. Remove the band periodically if it seems to be too tight. To prevent deterioration of the rubber sleeve, dry immediately after use and sprinkle with talc. Plastic sleeves may tear after several uses and must be discarded.

Either hand can be used in palpation, with the other hand holding the cow's tail as a handle. To enter the cow, the hand should be shaped into a wedge and lubricated thoroughly. The hand is pushed through the anus into the rectum with one swift thrust. As the hand enters the rectum the fingers should be folded into a loosely formed fist. By balling the hand into a modified fist as it enters the rectum, fecal matter is pushed aside and the rectum straightened. When the fingers are inserted in a pointed position folds in the rectum do not straighten out as easily. Also, with pointed fingers, one faces the hazard of puncturing the cow's rectal wall, even though it is thick-walled and basically puncture-resistant.

TABLE 1-K. GESTATION TABLE—COWS

(DATE OF SERVICE IN UPPER LINE; FIGURE BELOW INDICATES DATE DUE TO CALVE.)

Month	1	2	3	4	5	6	7	8	9	10	11	12	13	14	15	16	17	18	19	20	21	22	23	24	25	26	27	28	29	30	31	
January	1	2	3	4	5	6	7	8	9	10	11	12	13	14	15	16	17	18	19	20	21	22	23	24	25	26	27	28	29	30	31	November
October	12	13	14	15	16	17	18	19	20	21	22	23	24	25	26	27	28	29	30	31	1	2	3	4	5	6	7	8	9	10	11	
February	1	2	3	4	5	6	7	8	9	10	11	12	13	14	15	16	17	18	19	20	21	22	23	24	25	26	27	28				December
November	12	13	14	15	16	17	18	19	20	21	22	23	24	25	26	27	28	29	30	1	2	3	4	5	6	7	8	9				
March	1	2	3	4	5	6	7	8	9	10	11	12	13	14	15	16	17	18	19	20	21	22	23	24	25	26	27	28	29	30	31	January
December	10	11	12	13	14	15	16	17	18	19	20	21	22	23	24	25	26	27	28	29	30	31	1	2	3	4	5	6	7	8	9	
April	1	2	3	4	5	6	7	8	9	10	11	12	13	14	15	16	17	18	19	20	21	22	23	24	25	26	27	28	29	30		February
January	10	11	12	13	14	15	16	17	18	19	20	21	22	23	24	25	26	27	28	29	30	31	1	2	3	4	5	6	7	8		
May	1	2	3	4	5	6	7	8	9	10	11	12	13	14	15	16	17	18	19	20	21	22	23	24	25	26	27	28	29	30	31	March
February	9	10	11	12	13	14	15	16	17	18	19	20	21	22	23	24	25	26	27	28	1	2	3	4	5	6	7	8	9	10	11	
June	1	2	3	4	5	6	7	8	9	10	11	12	13	14	15	16	17	18	19	20	21	22	23	24	25	26	27	28	29	30		April
March	12	13	14	15	16	17	18	19	20	21	22	23	24	25	26	27	28	29	30	31	1	2	3	4	5	6	7	8	9	10		
July	1	2	3	4	5	6	7	8	9	10	11	12	13	14	15	16	17	18	19	20	21	22	23	24	25	26	27	28	29	30	31	May
April	11	12	13	14	15	16	17	18	19	20	21	22	23	24	25	26	27	28	29	30	1	2	3	4	5	6	7	8	9	10	11	
August	1	2	3	4	5	6	7	8	9	10	11	12	13	14	15	16	17	18	19	20	21	22	23	24	25	26	27	28	29	30	31	June
May	12	13	14	15	16	17	18	19	20	21	22	23	24	25	26	27	28	29	30	31	1	2	3	4	5	6	7	8	9	10	11	
September	1	2	3	4	5	6	7	8	9	10	11	12	13	14	15	16	17	18	19	20	21	22	23	24	25	26	27	28	29	30		July
June	12	13	14	15	16	17	18	19	20	21	22	23	24	25	26	27	28	29	30	1	2	3	4	5	6	7	8	9	10	11		
October	1	2	3	4	5	6	7	8	9	10	11	12	13	14	15	16	17	18	19	20	21	22	23	24	25	26	27	28	29	30	31	August
July	12	13	14	15	16	17	18	19	20	21	22	23	24	25	26	27	28	29	30	31	1	2	3	4	5	6	7	8	9	10	11	
November	1	2	3	4	5	6	7	8	9	10	11	12	13	14	15	16	17	18	19	20	21	22	23	24	25	26	27	28	29	30		September
August	12	13	14	15	16	17	18	19	20	21	22	23	24	25	26	27	28	29	30	31	1	2	3	4	5	6	7	8	9	10		
December	1	2	3	4	5	6	7	8	9	10	11	12	13	14	15	16	17	18	19	20	21	22	23	24	25	26	27	28	29	30	31	October
September	11	12	13	14	15	16	17	18	19	20	21	22	23	24	25	26	27	28	29	30	1	2	3	4	5	6	7	8	9	10	11	

Source: "The Winner's Way," 1977–78, courtesy of the American Polled Hereford Association.

Usually it is not necessary to clean the cow's rectum of fecal material. On the range, however, it is best to do this since it is so dry. Also, in early stages of learning, removal of the fecal material from the rectum makes feeling a little easier.

Feeling through the rectal wall is similar to feeling through a layer or two of thin rubber. A quick thrust to the elbow is usually better than trying to put the hand into the rectum and then working forward. The cow is pushing her fecal matter and the inserted arm in the opposite direction so it is far easier to back up than to go forward.

The pelvis forms a bone cradle for the reproductive system and, in a nonpregnant animal, usually is located near the top of the pelvic cradle and is felt easily with downward pressure. As pregnancy advances, the uterus and cervix move down and into the body cavity.

Palpation, like techniques of artificial insemination, must be learned through practice. Accomplished palpators can detect pregnancy as early as 40 days after breeding. A veterinarian can demonstrate palpation techniques.

Some points to keep in mind, however, are that the longer the examination, the more resistance the cow will offer. Also, if the palpator feels something like sandpaper in the rectum—a gritty feeling—palpation should be stopped, as this is an indication of rectum damage. A small amount of bleeding, however, is not a sign of problems, and occasionally occurs during palpation. Table 1-L gives a description of pregnancy progress in cows.

Checking Dairy Cows

Cows should be checked 30 days after freshening by a veterinarian. This check allows the veterinarian a chance to catch minor problems before they develop into major ones. Older cows, that is, more than 5 years of age, will usually show heat between 40 and 70 days after calving. Younger cows, those 2 or 3 years old, will take longer to come in heat after dropping a calf. It may be 80 days past calving before one can expect 80 percent of them to show signs of estrus.

Even though cows may come into heat sooner than 40 days following calving, it is recommended that breeding be delayed until after 40 days to allow the cow's system time to recuperate.

If using artificial insemination, the cattle producer will have a record of which cows were served and when. If a cow fails to settle after three services, she should be checked by a veterinarian.

Usually, first-calf heifers are more difficult to get with calf than are older cows. Many producers choose sires with high known fertility for breeding heifers.

TABLE 1-L. PREGNANCY IN CATTLE*

Days of Gestation	Weight	Length (inches)	Identifying Characteristics
30	1/100 oz	2/5	One uterine horn slightly enlarged and thin; embryonic vesicle size of large marble. Uterus in approximate position of nonpregnant uterus. Fetal membranes may be slipped between fingers from 30 to 90 days.
45	⅛–¼ oz	1–1¼	Uterine horn somewhat enlarged, thinner walled and prominent. Embryonic vesicle size of hen's egg.
60	¼–½ oz	2½	Uterine horn size of banana; fluid filled and pulled over brim into body cavity. Fetus size of mouse.
90	3–6 oz	5–6	Both uterine horns swollen (3 to 3½" in diameter) and pulled deeply into body cavity (difficult to palpate). Fetus is size of rat. Uterine artery 1/8 to 3/16" in diameter. Cotyledons ¾ to 1" across.
120	1–2 lbs	10–12	Similar to 90-day but fetus more easily palpated. Fetus is size of small cat with head the size of a lemon. Uterine artery is ¼" in diameter. Cotyledons more noticeable and 1½" in length. Horns are 4–6" diameter.
150	4–6 lbs	12–16	Difficult to palpate fetus. Uterine horns are deep in body cavity with fetus the size of large cat. Horns are 6 to 8 in" in diameter. Uterine artery ¼ to ⅜" in diameter. Cotyledons 2 to 2½" in diameter.
180	10–16 lbs	20–24	Horns with fetus still out of reach. Fetus size of small dog. Uterine artery ⅜ to ½" in diameter. Cotyledons more enlarged. From sixth month until calving a movement of fetus may be elicited by grasping the feet, legs, or nose.
210	20–30 lbs	24–32	From 7 months until parturition, fetus may be felt. Age is largely determined by increase in fetal size. The uterine artery continues to increase in size—210 days, ½" in diameter; 240 days, ½ to ⅝" in diameter; 270 days, ½ to ¾" in diameter.
240	40–60 lbs	28–36	
270	60–100 lbs	28–38	

* From "Determining Pregnancy in Cattle" by A. M. Sorensen, Jr., and J. R. Beverly, Texas Agricultural Extension Service, The Texas A&M University System.

Raising Dairy Replacements

Each year, for maximum milk production, poor producing cows must be culled from the herd to make way for superior animals. Replacement heifers can be purchased from other dairy farmers, of course, but some farmers choose to raise their own replacements.

There are several good reasons for raising one's own herd replacements. First is the elimination of the possibility of bringing in diseases or parasites from other farms. Also, if a dairy farmer raises his or her own replacements, he or she is more likely to have cows with production potential available when they are needed. If the cattle producer has good quality cows, he or she may want to take advantage of their genetic potential for producing excellent replacement heifers. Raising replacements requires additional facilities, feed, and labor. If a dairy farmer can afford the extra expense of feeding young heifers to the age of 24 months, and has the available facilities and extra labor, the insurance of good health and good quality may be worth the investment. Of course if the dairy farmer's foundation herd is average or below, he or she may want to improve the herd faster than would be possible by raising replacements. In this case the dairy farmer is best off buying the best replacement heifers affordable.

Use Table 1-M to figure estimated costs for raising replacement heifers.

Raising Baby Calves

For farmers who are confident in their ability to minimize stress among baby calves, and therefore keep death losses to less than 5 percent, the raising of baby calves may be a profitable venture.

Before starting such a project, estimates of cash costs and potential profits should be made. A cost estimate will tell the cattle producer how much the calves should sell for in order to pay expenses and make a profit for labor invested. It is important to estimate how much time will be needed for each calf. The amount of time spent per calf will vary depending on the number of calves handled at one time and the kind of facilities. Generally, farmers will have small buildings on the farm that can be used to house the calves. The best buildings for raising calves have floors that can be cleaned and disinfected easily.

If baby calves are purchased they are subjected to more stress. Being hauled and placed with calves from other farms subjects the calves not only to stress but also to disease.

If possible, purchase all calves directly from one farm only. Sometimes this is impossible, but it does reduce the stress on the animals and lessens the chances of their exposure to disease.

In choosing calves, one should be certain that the animals are healthy and that they have had colostrum (the milk secreted by the cow the first

TABLE 1-M.   COST PROJECTION: DAIRY HERD REPLACEMENT

	Example*	Your Farm
Variable Costs per Heifer:		
Calf, purchased or owned	$100.00	_____
Feed, to 24 months of age	334.45	_____
Labor (15 hours × $3)	45.00	_____
Breeding Costs	6.50	_____
Veterinary and Drugs	3.50	_____
Machinery and Equipment		
(includes car)—gas, oil, repairs	2.75	_____
Building Repairs	2.35	_____
Transportation and Marketing Costs	0	_____
Interest on Average Investment in Heifer		
@ 6% × 2 Years	36.00	_____
Interest on ½ of Variable Costs		
@ 9% × 2 Years	44.51	_____
Fixed Costs per Replacement Heifer:		
Depreciation: Buildings, equipment, fences,		
and machinery	6.66	_____
Interest on Investment, Taxes and Insurance		
(Buildings, equipment, machinery)	3.75	_____
Total Costs	**$585.47**	_____

* Figures used in the example were taken from information compiled by economists based on actual farm operations, data from actual farm records, and other budget studies. They are not intended to represent "average" costs of production.

few days postcalving). Colostrum has antibodies against disease, is higher in solids than normal milk, and contains more vitamin A and globulin as well as energy and other proteins.

Baby calves are subject to two types of problems: scours and respiratory disorders. If these problems can be prevented, death losses can be kept to a minimum and profit can be made from raising baby calves.

Basically, scours can be caused by overeating or from an infection. Watch calves to see if they are alert, nursing vigorously, acting hungry, and having normal stools. A calf like this probably is all right. Unfortunately a calf *can* have scours and show no visual symptoms. Usually, though, scours are readily recognizable as a runny, liquid stool.

Respiratory problems such as pneumonia kill many calves each year. To avoid these difficulties, calves should be housed where they will not be bothered by drafts and moisture in the building.

Table 1-N may help in the decision-making process over raising baby calves. Actual current costs in the area where the calves will be raised should be used to determine an accurate cost estimate.

Federal Milk Marketing Orders

The basic economic principle behind supplies keeping pace with demand in an orderly manner works for some agricultural commodities but it does not quite work for milk. Since supplies of milk cannot be turned on and off easily to fit the supply of milk to current demand, marketing conditions at various times can result in widely fluctuating milk prices. Wide price changes can cause financial hardship on the dairy farmer, who depends on the sale of milk for a living, and at other times, on the consumer who buys milk for food.

To stabilize market conditions for fluid milk and make the process of buying and selling milk an orderly one, the federal government developed the Federal Milk Marketing Order Program in 1935.

Briefly, a federal milk marketing order is a regulation issued by the Secretary of Agriculture. It places two specific requirements on the handling of milk in the area covered by the order. First, it requires that handlers of milk for a marketing area pay no less than certain minimum prices established according to how the milk is used. A milk order, including the pricing provision and all other provisions, becomes effective only after approval by dairy farmers. Prices are established under the order after a public hearing that presents evidence on the supply and demand conditions for milk in the market.

Secondly, the milk marketing order requires that payments for milk be pooled and paid to individual farmers or cooperative associations of farmers on the basis of a uniform or average price.

Simply, a federal order helps dairy farmers and consumers alike. The dairy farmer gets a reasonable price for milk and the consumer is assured of a steady supply of pure and wholesome milk.

Actually, dairy farmers are not controlled in any way by the orders. They may produce and sell any amount of milk they can produce. Any dairy farmer who can find a handler (a buyer) to purchase milk is entitled to the benefits of the milk marketing order in that area.

Since economic conditions vary from place to place throughout the United States, there are a large number of marketing areas. Thus the prices paid to producers may vary, but whenever a milk handler buys milk from a dairy farmer, he or she must pay at least the minimum price established for the local milk marketing area. The federal milk marketing order does not control from whom the handler buys, nor to whom he or she sells, nor does it dictate the retail price of milk.

TABLE 1-N. BUDGET FOR RAISING CALVES BY PERIODS OF GROWTH
(FROM 3 DAYS TO 12 MONTHS)

		Estimated Cash Costs* Per Calf	Our Estimate Per Calf
THREE DAYS TO 60 DAYS:			
Calf value at 3 days		$ 30.00	$_____
Feed: 50 lbs. milk replacer, $32/cwt.	$16.00		_____
100 lbs. dry starter, $7/cwt.	7.00		_____
Veterinary and medicine	2.40		_____
Mortality, 8.75% of investment	3.85		_____
Miscellaneous: bedding, nipple pails, etc.	2.35		_____
Interest, 10% for 2 months	.74		_____
Total for period		$ 32.34	$_____
Total accumulated cost		$ 62.34	$_____

Labor estimate 5 to 7 hours _____
At two months, estimated weight of 180 lbs.
There may not be much market for a calf of this weight and age.
Anything above $35/cwt. would be return for labor, use of
  facilities, and profits. ($62.34 ÷ 180 lbs. = $34.63)
Price expected .... $_____

THREE MONTHS TO SIX MONTHS (120 DAYS):			
Feed: 400 lbs. growing ration, $6.50/cwt.	$26.00		$_____
Hay, 300 lbs., no pasture	5.25		_____
Veterinary and medicine	2.65		_____
Mortality, 0.33%	.26		_____
Miscellaneous: bedding, etc.	1.30		_____
Interest, 10% for 3 months	1.99		_____
Total for period		$ 37.45	$_____
Total accumulated cost ($62.34 + $37.45)		$ 99.79	$_____

Labor estimate 4 to 6 hours _____
At six months, estimated weight of 360 pounds.
Anything above $28/cwt. would be a return for labor, use of
  facilities, and profit. ($99.79 ÷ 360 lbs. = $27.72)
Price expected .... $_____

SEVEN MONTHS TO 12 MONTHS:			
Feed: 500 lbs. grain mix	$30.00		$_____
1 ton hay and/or pasture	35.00		_____
Veterinary and medicine	1.50		_____
Mortality, 0.33%	.45		_____
Miscellaneous: taxes, etc.	2.25		_____
Interest, 10%	6.71		_____
Total for period		$ 75.91	$_____
Total accumulated cost ($99.79 + $75.91)		$175.70	$_____

Labor estimate 3 to 4 hours _____
At 12 months, estimated weight of 625 pounds.
Anything above $28/cwt. would be a return for labor, use of
  facilities, and profit. ($175.70 ÷ 625 lbs. = $28.12)
Price expected .... $_____

*The prices used reflect conditions in the spring of 1976. Prices will vary by
 areas of the states. Use local prices when preparing your estimate.

Source: Estimates in column 1 from the University of Missouri Extension Service.

MARKETING

Successfully producing cattle for beef or for milk is only part of the work involved in maintaining a well-managed farm or ranch. Once the agricultural product has been produced, the farmer must then market that product. How well this task is performed will make a tremendous difference in the success or failure of the farm business.

Agriculture operates in a much more competitive environment than other segments of the American economy. Because of the large number of producers and the relatively easy entry into agriculture, production and prices are difficult to predict for any given time period. When prices are high, for instance, producers respond by increasing their output. Producers have traditionally not organized to restrict production and maintain high prices.

In 1976 farm families received about 80 percent as much income, on the average, as nonfarm families. At the same time they had four times as much net worth.

Some farmers and ranchers believe that if a high percentage of the consumer's food dollar is returned to the farmer, the market system is efficient and fair. Conversely, a low percentage indicates that the system is inefficient and unfair. The agricultural strikes and marches on Washington of the last few years have been based on this belief. However, a farmer's share of a consumer's dollar is more a measure of the contribution made to the final product on retailers' shelves than efficiency or inefficiency in the market system.

Required marketing services vary among products. As a result, the farmer's share of the retail price also varies. As an example, there is far less involved in getting an egg to market than in processing a farmer's wheat into a loaf of bread. A question often arises regarding the addition of unnecessary marketing services.

Things like background music in the supermarket, check cashing services, and other amenities do not add to the farmer's income, but do increase the cost of marketing. Many farmers would like to see these items eliminated, with more money going back to the farm. It is doubtful, however, that even if these items were deleted the savings would be returned to the farmer.

Some farmers believe that parity prices are the best measure of well-being for the farmer. Actually, the economic status of farmers is measured better by income than by prices. The parity ratio for individual products compares current production costs and product prices to those in the parity base period, 1910–14. There are several problems with using parity prices as a measure of economic well-being.

First, the parity ratio for individual products says nothing about volume. Net farm income is a function of both prices and volume. Even though prices of farm inputs have generally increased more than product prices, volume on most farms has multiplied several times during the past 60 years. Regardless of price relationships, net farm income has continued to rise, reaching $20 to $30 billion during the 1970's.

Secondly, technological developments have markedly changed ouput per unit of input since 1910–14. For example, a bushel of seed corn today is much more expensive than one purchased 60 years ago. At the same time, today's seed corn can be expected to yield 100 bushels or more per acre, hardly a realistic expectation before the development of hybrid corn.

Finally, parity prices ignore changes in demand. Consumers may be unwilling to pay a price equal to 100 percent of parity on every farm product. Consumer demands are not so inflexible that prices can be raised indefinitely without either reducing consumption or encouraging substitute products.

New and more appropriate measures need to be developed to deal with low farm incomes. Continued focus on prices may not be the best way to bring farm income up to the same levels as nonfarm income. An index that measures net income per farmer has been suggested by some economists and might prove more suitable.

Prices for agricultural commodities are determined primarily by two factors: the supply-demand situation for the commodity and government programs. When supplies are short and demand is high, prices are high. With surplus supplies and lowered demand, prices go down also. The cyclical demand for beef is an example of this. Throughout history, beef production has followed a typical production cycle.

Because of the high perishability of milk, the government stepped in with programs to support the price of milk at a stable level. With other commodities besides milk, the government may step in to alter prices by restricting supplies or by stimulating demand.

Foreign trade is another factor that influences supply and demand. There often is a great deal of criticism of imports, but rarely are U.S. exports criticized. Foreign trade represents a two-sided issue. If foreign countries are to have money to purchase our exports, we must buy something from them. Trying to achieve an equitable balance is a difficult task.

Group Bargaining by Farmers

In the past several years, farmers have taken an increased interest in group bargaining. Noting the disparity between the incomes of farmers and the nonfarm population, many farmers see group bargaining as a possible solution to their plight. Of course, not all farmers have low incomes. It can be assumed, however, that practically all farmers would like to see their incomes increase, whatever their present economic level.

With fewer and fewer numbers of people involved in the business of farming, farmers as a percent of the total population are becoming an increasingly small minority. Politicians tend to pay less attention to the problems of the farmer than ever before. To some farmers, group bargaining action seems a good way to offset their lack of numerical superiority and do for farmers what they feel other bargaining organizations have done for other vested interest groups.

Farmers are business people in all senses of the word. Farm wives of today take an active role in the business decisions of the family farm. Today's farmer is better educated than ever before, and has a heightened awareness of agricultural and marketing problems. It is this high level of business awareness that has caused farmers to look for effective ways to increase their incomes. To many, group bargaining holds promise of doing just that.

There are a number of factors that affect the success of bargaining efforts. First, control over production is needed by the bargaining group. If the bargaining group has little control over the market supply, their chances of bargaining successfully are greatly reduced. In addition, volume control must apply not only to present production, but also to future production, especially in the near future. If control is inadequate, new production from member-producers and nonmember-producers, along with existing production from the two groups may quickly eliminate any price increase from bargaining.

Another factor affecting the success of bargaining is the perishability of the product. If a product can be stored it can be held off or put on the market at various times to intentionally control the supply. Storage costs must be considered also in relation to possible price benefits from storage.

An informed membership in the bargaining group contributes to the success or failure of the effort. An informed group supports sound production and marketing programs that are negotiated for them. Uninformed groups are less likely to follow the lead of the group.

With some farm groups, it might be difficult to convince some producers to withhold their production. Many farmers are reluctant to cooperate in actions that deprive them of their privileges for individual decision regarding time and place for marketing their products. Changing these long-held attitudes requires an education program featuring a market program the farmer would see as a workable one.

Bargaining can be a successful tool for farmers to use to increase the prices they obtain for their products. Common sense, good judgment, and economic analysis are needed when selecting those products that are adaptable to group bargaining.

Bargaining cannot be considered as a complete answer to income problems on the farm. For one, price increases must be reasonable or they will not be accepted. An overpriced product will lose part of its potential market to substitute products. Secondly, there are necessary marketing costs involved in getting a product from the farm to the consumer. Retail prices must reflect a price that covers those marketing costs, provides income to the farmer, and yet is reasonable enough that the consumer will buy.

Defining Market Area

According to the American Angus Association, surveys show that most cattle producers drive no more than 50 miles to buy a registered bull or replacement heifers. Armed with this information, the producer knows that the best customers are within a 4- to 10-county area around the farm.

There are several things a small rancher can do to market cattle as successfully as the larger professionals.

1. Advertise. This means not only local radio, local newspapers, etc., but also by putting up a sign on the farm so that people driving by learn of the ranch too. Some breed associations offer free advertising materials and assistance to their breeders. Ask.
2. Get involved in local, state, and national cattle associations, 4-H, FFA, and other farm groups. Even volunteering to have a field day at one's own farm can be an aid to getting one's ranch known.
3. Keep the farm or ranch clean and attractive so that visitors will be impressed and not appalled when they come to look at cattle.
4. Use farm vehicles as advertisements on wheels. Trucks and trailers can be painted with the farm name and a picture of cattle, letting everyone who sees the vehicles know about the ranch.
5. Big businesses have found direct mail advertising to be a successful sales tool and farmers and ranchers can too. Whenever people inquire about cattle, get their names and addresses and file them on cards for ready reference. Any information about the person's herd should be noted also. Later, this information will comprise a valuable mailing list of potential customers.

MANAGEMENT PRACTICES

A really important part of cattle production is performing a few management practices well. For instance, a basic tool for management is identification of the animals in the herd. Branding, tattooing, use of ear tags, and so on, are important for the cattle producer. Without these important aids, one would not be able to tell one animal from another, or be able to keep important health and breeding records.

Branding

To presume that cattle rustling began and ended with the cowboys of the Old West is to lose sight of the fact that human nature being as it is, there have always been "good guys" and "bad guys" and the latter always attempt to outwit the former. Branding was devised to limit the losses.

For one reason or another even the ancient Romans found branding necessary. Virgil, in his *Georgics*, talked about branding as early as 37 B.C.:

Strait stamp their lineage with the branding fire;
Mark which you'll rear to raise another breed,
Which to consecrate the altars, which to earth
To turn its rugged soil and break the clods.

In the United States cattle rustling increased around 1971 and brought about renewed interest in branding on the part of livestock producers.

There are two kinds of livestock brands—hot-iron brands and freeze brands. A hot-iron brand usually is made of iron, steel, or stainless steel with a 30- to 38-inch handle. The face of a hot-iron brand that contacts the skin should be ¼ to ½ inch wide. For cattle the wider face is preferred. Letters or figures are usually 3 inches for calves and 4 or 5 inches for mature cattle. The same size brand is used for freeze branding.

Figure 1-1 Branding was popular as a method of identification in 1884. Note the brands on the cattle in these advertisements. *(Courtesy of The Kansas State Historical Society, Topeka)*

Figure 1-2   Cattle branding in the 1880's. *(Courtesy of The Kansas State Historical Society, Topeka)*

TABLE 1-O.   BRANDING EQUIPMENT GUIDE

Equipment	Hot-Iron Branding	Freeze Branding
Branding irons	Iron, steel, stainless steel	Heavy copper or bronze
Heat source	Wood fire or butane. Electric branding iron	None
Refrigerant	None	Dry ice, alcohol
Clippers	Electric hair clippers	Electric hair clippers
Container for coolant	None	Insulated container
Brush	Bristle—To brush way loose hair Wire—To clean irons	Bristle—To brush away loose hair
Restraining equipment (may not be needed for calves)	Squeeze chute, head chute	Squeeze chute, head chute
Oil or grease	To apply to skin after branding	None needed
Alcohol in squirt bottle	None needed	Spray on area to be branded just prior to branding

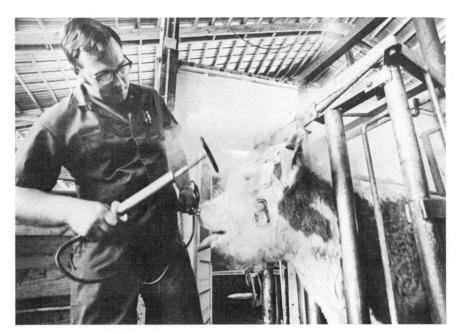

Figure 1-3 Cattle branding today—the use of chutes and restraints makes the job easier than in the "old days." *(Courtesy of the U.S. Department of Agriculture)*

A hot-iron brand produces a scar from which no hair will grow. A freeze brand destroys pigment-producing cells on the hide of the animal so that when hair grows back it is white. A freeze brand is most effective on darker coated animals.

Proponents of freeze branding claim that a freeze brand is more legible throughout most of the year than a hot-iron brand, that freeze branding is less painful to the animal, and that freeze branding damages the hide less than the hot-iron brand.

Freeze branding, however, still must be regarded as an experimental technique. Hot-iron branding has been tested and proven effective through years of use. With either method the user must follow directions closely and use proper safety methods.

The dry ice used to chill freeze-branding irons can cause severe burns. It should never be handled without gloves. When filling the container with dry ice, some of the pieces should be broken into very small segments for rapid cooling. Some large pieces will be retained for sustained cooling.

The container used for the dry ice and its accompanying alcohol solution must be insulated to keep the cold inside. Frequently used are two metal containers, one set inside the other with an insulating material in between. Also used is a bucket wrapped in insulation. Styrofoam buckets or coolers hold the temperature well, but since they are apt to break and leak, should be set inside another container. Naturally, the chosen container should be large enough to accommodate all the irons needed. When purchasing dry ice, 15 pounds is considered enough for a small herd. An additional 5 pounds should be purchased if branding is expected to take some time, or if the dry ice is to be transported more than a short distance.

When dry ice is added to the refrigerant—95 percent alcohol, either methyl, isopropyl or ethyl—it will bubble. As the solution cools it will bubble at a steady rate. The solution itself cools to its minimum temperature in about 5 minutes. When the irons are first inserted, it will take about 10 minutes for them to reach minimum temperature. After they have been used in branding it will take them only about 5 minutes to regain minimum temperature if they have been immediately replaced in the solution following branding.

There are relatively few steps involved in freeze branding. First, the irons must be chilled. While the irons are chilling, the animals should be restrained, either in head chutes or squeeze chutes. Immediately before branding, the area to be branded must be clipped with electric clippers to remove hair, then sprayed with alcohol, or a solution of ⅓ glycerine and ⅔ alcohol. Immediately following application of the alcohol solution, the

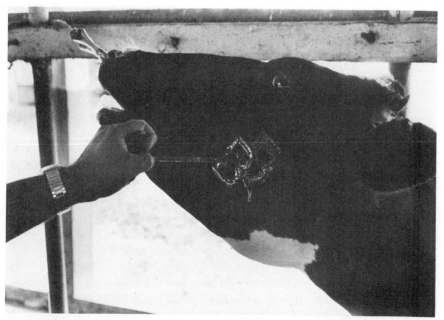

Figure 1-4 A brand should be clear and legible. *(Courtesy of the U.S. Department of Agriculture)*

branding iron should be applied to the hide. Firm pressure must be applied uniformly for a good brand to result. Generally, mature animals require a 40- to 50-second application of the iron, while calves may require as little time as 30 seconds. Time of year seems to be a factor, with fall and winter requiring longer time than spring and summer.

If the brand is left on too long the hair follicle will be killed and the area will look like a hot-iron brand. An underbrand is characterized by too little white hair when the hair grows back in. Research indicates that Herefords take a longer application than Angus.

Unlike the freeze brand, which depends on the destruction of the pigment-producing cells so that hair will grow back in white, hot-iron branding destroys the hair follicle itself so that bare skin makes up the brand.

Before heating the branding irons, the cattle producers should be sure that the irons are clean and free of rust or charred matter. Keeping a wire brush handy for cleaning irons is a good practice. Irons should be kept clean during the branding process to assure crisp, clean brands. After use, many cattle producers clean and oil the irons lightly. Others store their irons in a bucket of oil.

Heat sources for branding irons include wood, butane, and electricity. Butane is more popular than wood because it is convenient and controlled. Electric branding irons can be used with satisfactory results providing the voltage at the iron face is adequate. Inadequate wire size, either in the lead-in from the transformer or the extension cords results in improper heating and poor quality brands.

Heating the irons to an ash-gray color results in the best brand. Overheating may cause surrounding hair to burst into flame.

Cattle producers experienced in branding may or may not want to use electric hair clippers to cut the hair in the brand area. Beginners should use clippers until they get the feel of the process. For a good brand, the hair and the first layer of skin should be burned. Generally, a good application takes from 3 to 5 seconds.

After branding, a light application of oil or grease to the brand area speeds uniform healing. Cattle recently treated with an oil-base material such as insecticide, or cattle who are wet, should not be branded.

When branding, firm pressure should be applied in a rocking motion with the iron firmly against the animal.

Most states require registration of brands with the state Commissioner of Agriculture, or at the county seat. Since laws vary from state to state it is best to check with the local Extension Agent for more information. Table 1-P is a guide to branding steps. (See page 133.)

There are a number of other acceptable methods of animal identification besides branding. They include tattoos, ear tags, brisket tags, tags on neck chains, and dye or paint brands. Each has its own usefulness.

TABLE 1-P. STEP-BY-STEP GUIDE TO BRANDING

Freeze Branding	Hot-Iron Branding	Steps
X	X	Restrain animal
X	X	Clip hair at brand site
X	X	Start with clean irons
X		Chill irons. Initial chilling time—10 minutes.
	X	Heat irons to ash-gray color. Do not overheat.
X		Apply alcohol to hide, then apply freeze branding iron.
X		Apply for 40–50 seconds, 30 seconds on calves.
	X	Burn first layer of skin only
	X	Apply 3 to 5 seconds, check, may need more
	X	Remove iron. Branded area should be saddle leather color
	X	Apply light application oil or grease to promote uniform healing
X	X	Clean iron again before applying to next animal
X	X	One person should handle branding to assure uniform pressure is applied

Ear tattoos and *ear tags* are excellent for the calf. Since calves generally are not branded until weaning, the cattle producer needs a method of identification until branding time. An ear tattoo is a permanent means of identification. Of course it cannot be seen from very far away. An ear tag often is used in addition to branding for additional information the cattle producer might need on the animal, such as sire, dam, calf number, and so on.

A *brisket tag*, although easier to read from a distance, cannot be read easily when cattle are in a chute. Additionally, a brisket tag can be lost.

The primary argument against a *tag on a neck chain* is the possibility of its becoming caught on a fence or pen and choking the animal. Otherwise, it is advantageous because it is easily read from a distance.

Dye or paint brands can be used temporarily. Naturally they will wash off with rain and wear off with time, so must be used with discretion to indicate specifics about the cows so painted.

Figure 1-5 Ear tags are excellent identification, especially for calves. *(Courtesy of the U.S. Department of Agriculture)*

Tattoos

Ear tattoos are an excellent method of permanent identification for cattle. Advance planning of a tattoo system simplifies record keeping as well. For instance, the tattoo and the code on the animal's ear tag can be identical and the tattoo number can be used as part of the animal's registered name and herd number in most cases. Breed associations have specific requirements in terms of assigned numbers, so it is best to find out the procedures for numbering in advance. Also, check for specific recommendations regarding procedures.

Some cattle producers have found that using different-colored ear tags for calves from different sires aids in ready identification of their animals. The American Angus Association suggests that calves be identified at birth with an ear tag incorporating sire and dam identification either by code or by color of tag. That association has found that waiting until the calf is 3 months old for tattooing gives more satisfactory results.

Tattooing equipment can be purchased from most livestock supply dealers. Supplies needed include at least two sets of tattoo digits and letter digits, if used; a tube of fresh green tattoo paste and a toothbrush; and tattoo pliers for use with removable digits. Additionally, the cattle producer requires a chute for restraining the animal as well as alcohol and sponges for cleaning ears. Of course, herd records must be at hand for ready reference.

Since infection and disease can be spread from one animal to another by means of contaminated instruments, it is imperative that equipment be sterilized with alcohol or a disinfectant. All equipment used with cattle should be maintained in clean condition at all times. The cost to the cattle producer who allows sloppy sanitation practices will be high in terms of infection and disease.

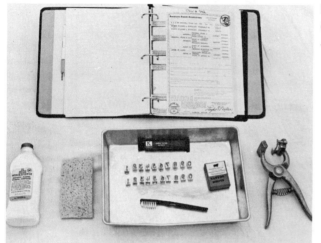

Figure 1-6 Tattooing equipment. *(Courtesy of the American Angus Association)*

Figure 1-7 Sterilize the tattoo set. *(Courtesy of the American Angus Association)*

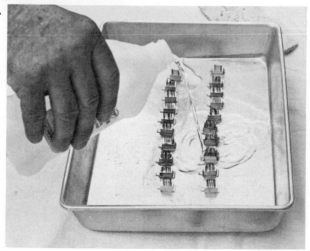

Figure 1-8 Check records to be sure the exact tattoo fits the animal to be tattooed. *(Courtesy of the American Angus Association)*

Figure 1-9 Check each tattoo on cardboard before doing the ear. *(Courtesy of the American Angus Association)*

Also important when tattooing is a careful check of herd records to be certain that the tattoo used to identify the animal matches the number in the herd record book.

Before actually beginning the tattooing process, the producer must check each tattoo by first applying it to a piece of cardboard. The letters and digits can easily be placed upside down or backwards and it is far more convenient to correct an error on cardboard than to correct records following an error with an actual tattoo.

After checking the tattoo on cardboard, dampen a sponge with alcohol and wipe the animal's ear lobe to remove any wax. Wax left in the ear prevents the tattoo paste from penetrating the skin and making a permanent mark.

Figure 1-10 Dampen sponge with alcohol to clean the ear lobe. *(Courtesy of the American Angus Association)*

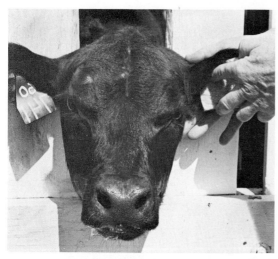

Figure 1-11 Clean the ear at the upper lobe. *(Courtesy of the American Angus Association)*

The next step involves cleaning the ear at the upper lobe where the tattoo will be applied. Green paste should be rubbed in the upper lobe before applying the tattoo. (Not all breed associations recommend green paste. Check before using.) Rubbing the paste in reduces the chances of the tattoo not "taking" since rubbing the paste in carries some of the paste into the ear as the tattoo digits are pressed into the skin.

The tattoo pliers should be applied parallel with the ear ribs and pressed firmly in place. Care should be taken to prevent the tattoo needles from penetrating the entire ear, since the penetration causes unnecessary additional bleeding.

Finally, more paste must be rubbed into the tattoo with fingers or with a toothbrush. The rubbing should be continued until all bleeding has

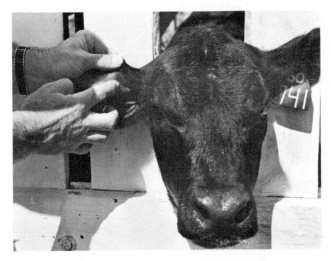

Figure 1-12 Rub green paste in upper lobe before tattooing to carry some paste into the ear with the tattoo. (*Courtesy of the American Angus Association*)

Figure 1-13 Place pliers parallel with the ear and press firmly. Needles shouldn't pierce through the entire ear. (*Courtesy of the American Angus Association*)

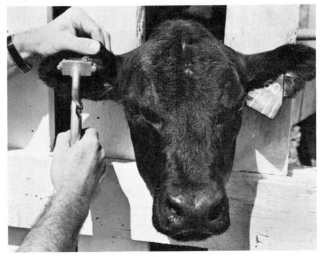

stopped and paste has filled all needle holes. Neglect of this final step will result in an illegible tattoo.

The American Angus Association suggests a number of management tips for tattooing that many producers may find helpful. First, they suggest using fresh green tattoo paste that has not been frozen. Freezing causes the paste to deteriorate. Also, the association recommends using a flashlight or spotlight for checking hard-to-read tattoos. Additionally, to be sure records match the correct animal, it is suggested that tattoos be checked at weaning and any other convenient times, but most importantly prior to delivery of an animal to a buyer.

Finally, if an animal has been tattooed incorrectly, one should contact the appropriate breed association for directions on correcting the error.

Figure 1-14 Rub paste into the needle holes to assure a legible and permanent tattoo. *(Courtesy of the American Angus Association)*

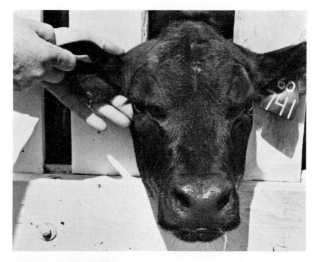

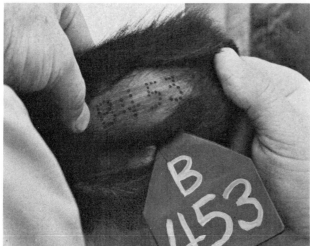

Figure 1-15 Check all tattoos. *(Courtesy of the American Angus Association)*

Dehorning

In some areas of the country cattle need their horns in order to protect themselves from predators. Many cattle producers find horns desirable in this instance. Sometimes, though, it is advisable to dehorn cattle.

Dehorning may be desirable to avoid damage among cattle caused by butting, or to prevent the animal from catching its horn on some object and causing a bleeding injury.

Good management calls for dehorning before the animal reaches 1 year of age. The younger the animal the quicker its recovery from the dehorning process. Cattle with large horn bases require more care and attention during and after dehorning than do animals with smaller horn bases. With any breed, however, the more care that is exercised during dehorning, the more successful the effort will be.

Basically there are two methods for dehorning. For some breeds, simply ringing the horn base with a sharp knife or saw and then cauterizing the wound is adequate. Other breeds may require the use of a hot iron. Generally this latter method is most effective on young calves under 6 months of age. The iron is heated to the proper temperature and then fitted over the horn button and held firmly against the head until the matrix has been destroyed. This method requires expertise to make the burn deep enough to destroy horn tissue but shallow enough to avoid causing a sore on the animal.

STUDY QUESTIONS

1. A one-person business operation is known as a _____. (Sole proprietorship)
2. To make decisions on purchases, many farmers utilize a _____ projection. (Cash-flow)
3. The objective in using financial _____ is to analyze the farm business situation as a unit. (ratios)
4. Any purchase with a useful life of more than one year can be _____. (depreciated)
5. Prices for agricultural commodities are determined primarily by two factors: government programs, and the _____ situation for the commodity. (supply-demand)
6. Good record keeping tells the farmer what level of _____ the cattle must maintain to make a profit. (production)

2

The Futures Market—
To Hedge or Not to Hedge

For the cattle producer the futures market can be an effective tool for controlling some of the risks involved in feeding cattle. Used incorrectly, it can become a money gobbling mistake. Successful cattle producers recommend using the futures market to lock in profitable hedges on livestock on feed. Most warn against the dangers of gambling in the futures market with speculative moves.

This chapter explains futures contracts and futures trading, tells how to hedge, and explains why hedging is desirable for the cattle producer.

To enter the futures market, the cattle producer needs a broker—someone who is a member of one of the livestock exchanges—to do the trading. Brokers are in the business because they make money trading and most enjoy the excitement of the futures market. Too often the cattle producer does not need to trade as often as his or her broker recommends. It is important to remember that the broker earns a living from trading. He or she earns a commission fee on each contract. The broker is interested in the success of the cattle producer, knowing his client must show a profit, but sometimes brokers may encourage speculation anyway. It is the cattle producer who must judge each trading move and decide whether the move is right or wrong at any given time.

THE FUTURES CONTRACT

Simply, a futures contract is a promise to make delivery, or accept delivery, of a commodity at a specified date, sometime in the future. The price is predetermined. A futures contract, like any other legal contract, is binding. It differs from other sales contracts in that it does not actually involve exchange of either the title or of the actual physical goods.

Standardized contracts are used. The contract specifies volume and quality as well as time of delivery, and place of delivery. For instance, a typical contract might call for 40,000 pounds of steers (volume), choice (quality), July (time of delivery), Chicago (delivery point), and price.

Because the futures contract is standardized it can be used as a negotiable instrument. Thus an individual can sell on the futures market without first buying a futures contract. Before the delivery date the seller can "offset" the earlier transaction by buying back an identical contract.

Most traders do make offsetting transactions. Only a small percentage of commodities sold by futures contracts is ever actually delivered. Open contracts are those that are still outstanding. They have not been invalidated by offsetting futures transactions or by delivery. This is referred to as *open interest.*

Figure 2-1   Most livestock futures are traded on the Chicago Mercantile Exchange. *(Courtesy of Chicago Mercantile Exchange)*

There is an instance where the livestock producer would do better to deliver the goods rather than purchase an offsetting contract. If the cash price were far below the futures price, after subtracting quality and location differences, in the delivery month, then the cattle producer might choose to deliver. In this instance it would be profitable to deliver the physical commodity to satisfy the provisions of the futures contract rather than selling livestock on the local cash market and buying back the futures contract. Because of the competitive relationship between cash and futures markets this will not happen often.

When either alternative could be selected, producers generally are better off to offset their futures position and sell their livestock on a nearby cash market. The main reason for this is that rigid specifications have to be met for livestock delivered on futures contracts.

For instance, futures contracts specify that the animals in a live beef cattle transaction must be choice quality, so most of the animals traded must be choice grade with uniform standards of weight and yield as well as quality. Steers whose weight, yield, and quality do not conform to the standards are discounted. Only a limited number of lower grade cattle can be substituted, even at the discounted rate. Even discounted animals must grade good or they cannot be used to fulfill provisions of the contract.

Contract specifications for livestock are more precise than those for grain because of the wide range of livestock possible in a single grade. For this reason livestock delivered on futures contracts often will be subject to discounts.

Most livestock producers feel that it is better to take a small loss rather than to deliver on a futures contract. The uncertainties of delivery make it an unacceptable alternative for most.

FUTURES TRADING

Futures trading in live beef cattle contracts makes it possible for cattle feeders to hedge by selling a futures contract to reduce the risk of a decline in prices during the time their cattle are on feed.

All futures trading is conducted on a commodity exchange—either the Chicago Board of Trade, the Chicago Mercantile Exchange, or the Kansas City Board of Trade. Most livestock futures are traded on the Chicago Mercantile Exchange.

The exchange establishes contract specifications, trading rules, and provides facilities for trading and for recording all transactions.

Only members of a futures exchange can operate directly in markets at the exchange. Trading by nonmembers is done through members who act as agents in return for a commission or a brokerage fee.

Trading typically is on a margin basis. A small percentage of the market value of the contract is placed on deposit in making a sale or purchase.

Futures markets exist for a wide range of commodities, including live beef cattle, steer carcass beef, boneless beef, and others.

For a commodity futures market to be successful, the contract must have speculator interest. A contract that depends only on hedging activity will never be actively traded. Speculators must be in the market for hedging to be effective. A lack of speculator interest may stem from a lack of familiarity with the product, undesirable quality and quantity specifications, or less relative importance of the product itself. If a contract experiences a lack of volume, it may be withdrawn by the exchange.

Futures trading in live beef cattle was introduced in November, 1964. Until then many believed that no perishable commodities should be traded. The argument had been that the commodity must be nonperishable so that it could be stored to meet market needs in times of scarcity.

Doubters were soon appeased, however, and futures trading in live beef cattle and other perishable livestock products has proved to be as effective as trading in established grain commodities.

To be effective, a commodity must meet the following criteria:

- It must be subject to a grading system so that separate lots of the commodity can be interchanged.
- It must not be processed to the point of being identifiable by brand name.
- Prices for the commodity must be variable and determined competitively.

One of the most tempting, and frequently most disastrous, uses of the futures market, is gambling, rather than using the futures contract as a business hedging tool.

The livestock producer must be careful to establish a futures position as nearly as possible to the same size as his or her cash position. When producers are tempted to take larger futures positions than the cash positions being offset, they are speculating on the market. Their reasoning is that if it is desirable to replace the cash pricing of a number of choice steers with one futures contract, it is even better to replace the cash position with five futures contracts.

Taking a speculative position should be done only with money the producer can afford to lose. If the move is successful, the producer can make a large profit, if not, huge amounts of money can be lost. Generally, experts recommend that the livestock producer keep separate records for hedging and speculating transactions, limiting the latter.

In the example above, where the producer buys five futures contracts when only one is needed, he or she is speculating on the four additional contracts. Positions in futures must be opposite the cash positions. If the producer is trying to establish a price for cattle on feed, he or she is holding

Figure 2-2 Excitement runs high on the trading floor. *(Courtesy of Chicago Mercantile Exchange)*

the cash commodity and therefore must sell futures. If the producer buys futures the risk increases.

A second reason for a producer's failure in the futures market is a failure to close out cash and futures positions simultaneously. Sometimes producers are reluctant to take losses on futures. For instance, if a producer has sold futures against feeder cattle and both cash and futures prices go up he or she has made money on the cash market but lost on futures. The producer may be tempted to sell the cash market and not buy back the futures at the same time, hoping that the price will go back down so that cash profits can be retained without having to offset them with futures losses. If prices continue to go up, however, the position in futures will worsen and the producer will lose even more money.

Finally, the producer should not panic when the market moves up, or try to make exorbitant profits when the market goes down. The error of trading in and out of the market too frequently causes good hedges to become nothing more than speculation. For example, if the market moves up, the producer may become concerned when his or her broker calls to request additional money for margins. He or she panics and sells. Soon the market begins a decline and the producer is caught without a hedge. The producer loses money on both the futures and on the cattle as well. While supply and demand considerations change and cause a review of hedging strategy, it is important to avoid the temptation to take a quick profit with the hope of reselling on a rally or repurchasing on a price dip. The results of actions like these invariably include financial losses.

HEDGING

Futures markets reduce price risks through hedging. For instance, a livestock producer can reduce price risk during the time cattle are on feed by selling an equivalent quantity of the commodity in the futures market. This sets the approximate selling price. In a hedge the risk of a price change is transferred from the seller to the buyer of the contract. This often is called a *short hedge.*

Producers who will need a commodity at a later date can set the approximate purchase price in advance by buying futures contracts. This is known as a *long hedge.*

Hedging cattle on feed involves selling futures contracts when the cattle go on feed equal to the expected eventual selling weight of the cattle. As in grain, the basic hedging principle is that futures and cash prices tend to move up and down together. If a price decline causes a loss on the cash market while the cattle are on feed, it can be recovered by buying back the futures contract at a lower price. On the other hand, if the cash market advances, the cattle feeder who has hedged cannot take advantage of it. Any advantage will be lost because of the higher price paid for the futures contract when it is bought back.

In practice, the difference—or basis—between the price at the delivery location and the futures contract at that location will depend upon several factors: location relative to the par delivery point for the futures contract, quality difference between the cash item and the futures contract specifications, and storage costs, if any, that are incurred in the time period prior to contract maturity.

Feeder cattle can be hedged by producers in two different ways. Generally, a rancher who sells feeder calves might prefer a short hedge, whereas a cattle feeder who buys feeders to put in the feedlot might prefer a long hedge. Futures trading in feeder cattle contracts often is characterized by a "thin" market. That is, it is sometimes difficult to offset trades because no one wants to buy when a producer wants to sell, or vice versa. The rancher and cattle feeder are affected in opposite ways when prices change. One gains only at the expense of the other.

To determine when to hedge, the producer must consider the condition of the market. A careful evaluation of the supply and demand situation must be made before placing a hedge. For example, if it appears that higher prices are coming, the producer would want to wait for a better opportunity to place the hedge at a higher price. Conversely, if it appears likely that

TABLE 2-A. PROFIT IN DOLLARS

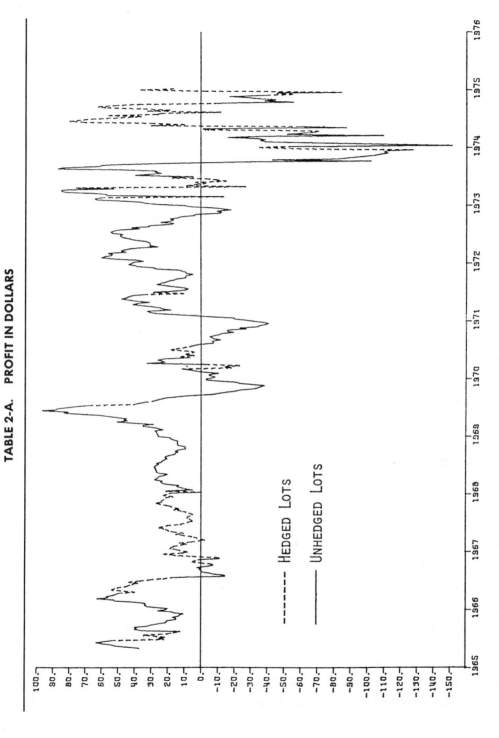

Source: *Cattle Hedging Strategies*, Bulletin 591, Agricultural Experiment Station, Kansas State University.

prices will decline, the producer will want to lock in a price on the futures market.

Hedging is a management decision that must be governed by careful decisions on the amount of profit to be set. Table 2-B compares results of each of the seven hedging strategies tested by Kansas State University in their 9½-year study of the futures market.*

Researchers at Kansas State University found that hedging all lots would reduce the variation in gains and losses. The drawback to hedging all lots was found to be an unacceptable reduction in profits. The seven programs tested were:

1. All lots fed out unhedged. This was the control group.
2. All lots routinely hedged.
3. Lots hedged only when the futures hedge price equalled or exceeded the calculated break-even price.
4. Lots hedged only when the futures hedge price equalled or exceeded the cash price for finished cattle when the feeder cattle went into the feedlot.
5. Lots hedged only when the futures hedge price equalled or exceeded both the break-even price and the current cash cattle price.
6. Lots hedged only when they finished during September, October, November, or December.
7. Sold finished cattle by contract the day feeder cattle went into the feedlot at the prices for finished cattle that day.

The hypothetical operation was patterned after a 20,000 head (one-time capacity) feedlot with feeder cattle scheduled in every week and finished cattle scheduled out every week. Costs of inputs and prices of finished cattle were based on current quotations throughout the period. A total of 505 lots of cattle was involved in the simulated analysis.

A combination of two hedging programs proved to be the most effective of all the strategies tested. The combination specified that cattle would be hedged only when the effective futures hedge price equalled or exceeded both the break-even price and the current cash price. Profits then were $14.43 per head, the highest profit of all strategies tested. If this strategy had been followed throughout the test, only 29 percent of the lots would have been hedged. Had cattle not been placed on feed when those two criteria were not met, average profits would have dropped to $7.10 per head.

Average profits on completely unhedged operations for the test period were $9.55 per head. The trend in profits was characterized by instability.

---

* *Cattle Hedging Strategies*, Bulletin 591, Agricultural Experiment Station, Kansas State Univ.

TABLE 2-B.   AVERAGE PROFITS COMPARED (IN DOLLARS), PER HEAD, FROM 7 ALTERNATIVE CATTLE HEDGING AND CONTRACTING PROGRAMS, MAY 1965–DECEMBER 1974

Alternative	1965	1966	1967	1968	1969	1970	1971	1972	1973	1974	Average 10-yr. Profits	Variance	Lots Hedged
I. Unhedged	36.30	13.68	2.97	18.67	26.77	−1.46	21.52	29.85	8.55	−53.11	9.55	1079.737	0
II. Routine Hedge	15.51	16.12	14.01	6.23	2.23	−6.98	−7.36	−1.54	−29.06	−2.67	0.18***	417.243***	505
III. Futures ≧ Break-even	19.05	17.22	14.01	16.71	18.98	−5.32	21.45	27.28	2.05	−11.31	11.81	980.095	218
IV. Futures ≧ Cash	29.89	23.48	14.01	19.36	26.10	−6.23	10.48	29.85	−10.89	−0.23	13.08*	732.439***	204
V. Futures ≧ Break-even & ≧ Cash	29.89	23.33	14.01	19.36	26.10	−4.76	21.32	29.85	2.05	−12.28	14.43**	1060.335	145
VI. Seasonal Hedged (Fall)	31.65	17.22	6.66	14.39	28.29	0.96	10.61	24.24	20.80	−44.48	10.38	907.302**	174
VII. Contract	19.69	17.43	−1.33	13.72	21.42	−0.97	2.06	21.43	−29.98	−34.38	2.41***	199.556***	0

*** Indicates that difference as compared to unhedged value is statistically significant at the 1 percent level.
** Indicates that difference as compared to unhedged value is statistically significant at the 5 percent level.
* Indicates that difference as compared to unhedged value is statistically significant at the 10 percent level.

TABLE 2-C. EFFECT ON PROFITS OF HEDGING WHEN FUTURES PRICE IS EQUAL TO OR MORE THAN BOTH THE BREAK-EVEN AND CURRENT CASH PRICE, KANSAS, MAY 1965–DECEMBER 1974

UNHEDGED			HEDGE ONLY WHEN FUTURES PRICE IS EQUAL TO OR MORE THAN BOTH BREAK-EVEN AND CURRENT CASH PRICE			
Financial Outcome	Avg. Profit or Loss per Head	No. of Lots	Financial Outcome	No. of Lots	Avg. Profit or Loss per Head	Avg. Change Due to Hedging per Head
			Profits			
			Unhedged Profits[1]	261	$ 32.29	$ ----
			Profits Increased[2]	38	29.12	18.15
			Profits Reduced[3]	40	13.92	−16.64
			Losses Changed to Profits[2]	43	25.04	54.31
Profits	$ 30.03	349	**Subtotal Profits**	382	$ 29.31	$ 6.18
			Losses			
			Unhedged Losses[1]	99	$ −35.29	$ ----
			Profits Changed to Losses[3]	10	−13.28	−51.78
			Losses Reduced[2]	13	−20.87	48.77
			Losses Increased[3]	1	−11.56	−11.20
Losses	$ −36.27	156	**Subtotal Losses**	123	$ −31.78	$ 0.85
All Lots	$ 9.55	505	**All Lots**	505	$ 14.43	$ 4.88

[1] Lots that would not have been covered by a hedge under the program considered (360 lots).
[2] Lots whose profits were increased by hedging (94 lots, average increase $38.93).
[3] Lots whose profits were reduced by hedging (51 lots, average reduction $23.42).
Source: *Cattle Hedging Statistics*, Bulletin 591, Agricultural Experiment Station, Kansas State University.

Routine hedging would have reduced profits to $0.18 per head, an unacceptable level. Routine hedging when cattle prices are on a generally increasing trend, as they were during the test years, 1965 to 1974, wipes out windfall profits.

One alternative did not use the futures market but assumed that the day the cattle went on feed they were contracted for delivery when finished at the price for finished cattle that day. Profits from this approach were $2.41 per head. This system precludes windfall profits during rising price trends.

Table 2-C shows how the profit total for the most effective method was determined (*facing page*).

THE "BASIS"

The basis in livestock futures refers to the difference between the local cash price (with adjustments for quality) and the futures price at a particular time. The basis is most important to the cattle producer during the contract month.

To ensure profits in futures hedging, the producer must calculate the basis accurately. For instance, in Table 2-D the basis was calculated at $1 per cwt. The basis was correctly calculated. Had it been less than $1 in November, the profit from all the transactions would have been increased. Had the basis been more than $1, profits would have been lower than expected. With a correctly figured basis, prices could have fluctuated either way and the producer still would have had price protection.

TABLE 2-D. HEDGING AT WORK*

Cash		Futures
June 30 Production costs calculated at $44.30 per cwt.		Sell 40,00 lbs Chicago December live beef cattle at $47.50 per cwt.
November 25 Sell 40,000 lbs cattle on cash market at $45 per cwt.		Buy 40,000 lbs Chicago December live beef cattle at $46 per cwt.
Absolute change	$0.70	$ 1.50
Hedging cost		−0.20
Net for cash and futures	$0.70	$ 1.30

* This is an example of a perfect hedge coupled with declining prices. Compiled by Agricultural Extension Economist A. L. Frederick, Kansas State University.

To determine a basis the producer can either look at past local cash-futures price relationships, or figure the actual costs to deliver the physical commodity to the contract's designated delivery point.

For example, if over the past 5 years live beef prices at the local market have averaged $1 per cwt below the October futures prices on October 1, then the basis would be $1. If prices at the local market have averaged $2 below the October futures price on October 1, then the basis would be $2, and so on. Since basis patterns stabilize over a period of years basis prediction is a fairly reliable tool. Experienced cattle producers who have followed cash and futures prices have a good idea of what their local basis will be during particular times of the year.

PRICE MARGIN

A price margin in cattle refers to the amount by which the selling price per cwt of cattle is above or below the price paid when the cattle were bought. A positive margin indicates a profit for the producer—the selling price is above the buying price. A negative margin indicates that the producer took a loss, that the cattle were sold for less than their cost. Naturally other factors affect the margin including feedlot costs, weight, sex, grade, time of purchase, and time of sale. Generally, though, if factors affecting profit are equal, the more positive or less negative a price margin, the better the position of the producer.

Figure 2-3 Selling at local cash markets usually is more profitable than satisfying provisions of a futures contract. *(Courtesy of The Kansas State Historical Society, Topeka)*

A price margin should not be confused with the term margin used in reference to futures trading wherein a small percentage of the market value of the commodity in the futures contract is placed on deposit to guarantee a sale or a purchase.

GRAIN FUTURES AND THE LIVESTOCK PRODUCER

To be able to estimate how much it will cost the livestock producer to finish a lot of cattle, he or she must have an accurate idea of the cost of feed for the feeding period. There are two options. The producer can hedge grain futures or make a contract with a grain producer for the amount of feed needed. With either of these methods the livestock producer will know how much the feed will cost and will be better able to estimate costs.

Knowing how to estimate costs for the feeding period is imperative for the livestock producer to make any profit at all. If the producer has an inaccurate idea of costs he or she may lock in an unsatisfactory profit or even a loss by hedging. Producers have found that locking in a loss is far worse than not owning the cattle in the first place.

Costs that must be considered include the cost of the livestock to be fed, the feed costs of production, any nonfeed production costs, hired labor costs, labor income for the producer, and minimum acceptable profit.

In Table 2-E, prepared by an agricultural extension economist, a hypothetical producer purchases feeder steers at 650 pounds at a cost of $50 per hundred weight (cwt). With costs at 1,050 pounds, the break-even price for the steers would be $465 divided by 1,050 pounds, or $44.29 per cwt. If hedging did not offer a potential return of $44.29 or better, the livestock producer would not hedge *at that time.* Since cattle normally stay on feed for about 120 days there are additional opportunities to hedge the cattle besides the initial opportunity when the cattle are placed on feed.

TABLE 2-E. ESTIMATING COSTS

Cost of feeder into lot (650 pound steer @ $50 per cwt)		$325.00
Estimated feed cost (400 lb. gain)		96.00
Estimated nonfeed costs		24.00
Interest on cattle investment	$7	
Equipment costs	6	
Veterinary and death costs	4	
Marketing cost	5	
Hired labor	2	
Total cost		$445.00
Labor income plus minimum profit		20.00
Estimated break-even costs		$465.00
$465 divided by 1,050 lbs steer weight = $44.29 per cwt		

When producers know their costs they operate from an advantage. When the futures market becomes more favorable, they can hedge then because they know the costs in advance. Rarely the market will not vary enough to give producers an opportunity to hedge. However, that situation would be preferable to locking in a loss on the livestock.

A cattle producer with a grass operation who will own feeders for nearly a year has even more chances to hedge effectively.

THE SPECULATOR

Cattle producers reduce their risks by hedging on the futures market. For this to be possible someone else must be willing to assume those risks. This is the role of the speculator. Speculators assume risk by agreeing to either make delivery or accept delivery at a later date at a specified price. Normally a speculator has no interest in actually obtaining the product. A speculator enters the futures market to make a profit, not to purchase goods. They are instrumental in the operations of a futures market in that, without speculators, there would be no one to buy when hedgers want to sell and no one to sell when hedgers want to buy.

Speculators make money if they can buy contracts for less than they sold, or if they can sell for more than they paid. They lose if they must sell for less than they bought or if they must buy for more than they sold.

Basically, speculating is a calculated risk—a gamble. Unfortunately most livestock producers have poor records at speculating. Even the experts do not always have success in the speculating game. In 1969 one major commission house reported the following results to Kansas State University:

Profit Accounts	*Loss Accounts*
164 Number	298 Number
$462,413 Total profit	($1,127,355) Total loss
2,819 Profit per account	(3,783) Loss per account

The net loss on the 462 accounts was $664,942. Of this total, $406,344 could be attributed to commissions. Thus, the gross loss before commissions was $258,598. Nearly twice as many people lost money as made money. Each loser, on the average, lost more than the winners made.

As in any kind of gambling, risks are great and potential winnings match the risk. However, cattle producers who gamble with their ranches and cattle herds may be risking more than they are willing to lose.

In general, cattle producers suggest that speculation be done only with money that is expendable—that can be lost without harm. Effective use of the futures market demands self-control. One estimate indicates that 90 percent of cattle producers have speculated at one time or another. Many still are recovering from their losses.

STUDY QUESTIONS

1. To enter the futures market, a cattle producer needs _____. (a broker)
2. A _____ in cattle refers to the amount by which the selling price per cwt of cattle is above or below the price paid when the cattle were bought. (price margin)
3. Someone who enters the futures market to take risks in order to make a profit is known as a _____. (speculator)
4. Most livestock futures are traded at the _____. (Chicago Mercantile Exchange)

Figure 3-1   The Texas Longhorn was allowed to develop pretty much on its own. These Longhorns were photographed in the stockyards at Abilene, Kansas, in 1886. *(Courtesy of The Kansas State Historical Society, Topeka)*

3

Selection—Choosing the Best

Some people choose a cattle breed the same way they would pick a new car —it looks good so they buy it. The problem with this mode of selection is that cattle producers do not make the most of their herds by selecting cattle that have been bred to perform well under the specific conditions at their ranches. There is, of course, no perfect breed of cattle available to fulfill all needs. For the past several hundred years, however, cattle producers have used selective breeding to develop a number of different breeds that will

Figure 3-2 For comparison, the Texas Longhorn of today photographed at the U.S. Wildlife Refuge, Cache, Oklahoma. *(Courtesy of Texas Longhorn Breeders Association)*

outperform others under specific circumstances such as adverse weather conditions (both cold and hot), making the most of poor quality forages, developing superior carcasses, producing the most milk, and so on. Today's cattle producer can choose from a number of different breeds, taking into account their advantages and their disadvantages, along with their ability to perform under specific conditions present at their ranches.

For hundreds of years, cattle producers have bred their best cow to their neighbor's best bull to develop a better animal—for draft, for milk, or for meat (or any combination of all three). Some breeds developed for the most part on their own—more a survival of the fittest than anything else. The Texas Longhorn is one of those breeds that was selected primarily by nature, and only the most hardy survived. Other breeds have been allowed to develop in a similar manner with the idea of creating a breed that could survive extreme conditions.

Each breed has its own strong points and weak points. There are advocates for every breed who claim that their breed is the best. Actually, their breed might be best for them, but no breed is best for every ranch and every condition. Obviously, if there were one best breed of cattle, everyone would raise the same breed. A total takeover by one breed appears highly unlikely and cattle producers can continue one of the most exciting facets of cattle raising—selection for better and better animals.

Selection of good breeding stock involves a lot more today than it did hundreds of years ago when about all a cattle producer could know about an animal was what he or she could see. To provide themselves with more information, cattle breeders began recording pedigrees. Knowing the pedigree is helpful, but sometimes a breeding that looks good on paper just does not work out in practice. Most helpful has been the recording of performance information. Although visual examination and study of pedigrees have their place in selection, the hard facts about how an animal, and even better, how its progeny, have performed is indisputable evidence of quality or lack of it.

PEDIGREE

A cattle producer may use a pedigree for selection if the animal involved is so young that its own performance and that of its progeny are known. Pedigrees also are useful in selecting for characteristics that are measured only as the animal ages. Factors such as longevity and resistance to cancer eye are two such traits. Pedigrees also will be used in selecting against undesirable traits such as dwarfism and double muscling. In most cases, looking at the parents and the grandparents on a pedigree is the most effective. Looking at distant relatives generally is not as useful since the most distant relatives influence the heredity of the animal in question only through the sire and the dam. By the time an animal is old enough to have its own performance information available, pedigrees become of less value. Certainly when progeny information becomes available, a pedigree becomes even less valuable.

Figure 3-3   "Shorty," a Hereford steer owned by the Crawford girls of Ellis, Kansas, in the 1950's, carried the trait for dwarfism. *(Courtesy of The Kansas State Historical Society, Topeka)*

INDIVIDUAL PERFORMANCE

Selection based on an individual's own performance will result in rapid improvement in the herd when heritabilities are high. (See page 162.) For instance, growth rate has a relatively high heritability. Using a bull with a good growth rate will quickly improve that quality in the herd.

PROGENY INFORMATION

To select accurately for carcass quality, progeny information is a must, especially when good indicators are not available in the live animal. Progeny information also is important for sex-limited traits such as mothering ability, and milk quality and quantity, and for traits with low heritabilities.

All three types of information can be used together to give the cattle producer a good, sound basis for selection: pedigree, individual performance, and progeny information.

There are several factors that affect the rate of improvement when selective breeding is employed. Heritability, selection differential, genetic association among traits, and generation interval all determine, to some extent, how much improvement can be gained from careful selection.

HERITABILITY

Heritability refers to the proportion of the differences between animals that are transmitted to the offspring. Naturally it is desirable that heritability for economically important traits be high. For this reason, selection for traits should be made for highly heritable ones, rather than for traits that are influenced mainly by environment, and will therefore have low heritability.

Some traits with high heritability include such carcass traits as area of ribeye, tenderness, and final feedlot weight. Traits with moderate to high heritability include birth weight, daily rate of gain, efficiency of gain, carcass grade, and carcass fat thickness. Traits with medium heritability include milking and mothering ability. Traits with low to medium heritability include weaning weight, pasture gain, and susceptibility to cancer eye. Fertility (calving interval) has a very low heritability.

SELECTION DIFFERENTIAL

Selection differential is the difference between the selected individuals and the average of all animals from which they were selected. Selection differential is determined by the proportion of progeny needed for replacements, the number of traits considered in selection, and the differences that exist among the animals in a herd. If the average weaning weight of a herd is 450 pounds and the individuals selected to be kept for breeding average 480 pounds, the selection differential is 30 pounds.

Most of the opportunities for selection and for real herd improvement are involved with selection of the bull since fewer bulls must be saved for replacement than cows. Also, since a bull in natural service will sire around 20 calves each year and a cow will bear only one, the bull will have a greater effect on herd improvement than the cow.

GENETIC ASSOCIATION

A genetic association among traits is the result of genes favorable for the expression of one trait tending to be either favorable or unfavorable for the expression of another. These may be either positive or negative. When the genetic association is positive, the rate of improvement is increased. When the genetic association is negative, the rate of improvement from selection is decreased. For example, a major negative genetic association has been noted when marbling (an important factor in carcass grade) has been selected. Unfortunately, when marbling is a selected trait, excessive outside fat may also result, thus decreasing the rate of improvement from selection because even though a desirable trait has increased, an undesirable trait has increased also.

GENERATION INTERVAL

The generation interval refers to the average age of all parents when their progeny are born. In most beef cattle herds, the generation interval averages about 4 to 6 years. Progress toward selection of any given trait can be greater when the generation interval is shortened. This can be accomplished by vigorous culling of cows on the basis of production. If this were done, however, the herd would contain more young cattle or cattle of a nonproductive age.

TYPES OF SELECTION

Three common types of selection are used to bring about progress in a herd. They are *tandem selection, selection based on independent culling levels,* and *selection based on an index of net merit.*

Tandem Selection

Tandem selection is based on selection for one trait at a time. When a desired level of performance is reached in the first trait, selection begins on a second, and so on. The primary drawback to this method is that by selecting for one trait at a time some animals that perform poorly in other traits will be retained as replacements. Additionally, tandem represents an extremely slow method of improving a herd. Since good performance is based on several traits, tandem usually is not the best method for herd improvement.

Independent Culling Level

Selection based on independent culling levels requires that certain performance levels be attained in each trait before an animal is retained for replacement. When using this system, some individual analysis of the animals is necessary since, if culling levels are too high, too many animals might be culled from the herd, leaving an inadequate amount for replacements. The system, strictly interpreted, does not allow for slightly substandard performance in one trait to be offset by superior performance in another. The independent culling level is generally accepted as the second most effective method of selection. It can be effective if modified with common sense and good management.

Selection Index

Most commonly accepted as the best method for selection is selection based on an index of net merit that gives weight to various traits in proportion to their economic importance and heritability, taking note of any genetic association among the traits. With this method, an animal that is excellent in one area but below average in another can be retained because his above average qualities offset any slight deficiencies in others. Increasing the number of traits considered reduces the speed of progress in any one of the traits. To get the most out of this system, major consideration should be given only to traits with economic value and relatively high heritability. About the only pitfall with this method is the temptation to include too many traits, or to select for traits with extremely low heritability. If a trait has very low heritability, little genetic improvement in that trait can be expected.

Traits that affect economic value should be considered in selection. The major traits affecting the economic efficiency of a successful beef cattle operation are fertility, mothering or nursing ability, rate of gain, efficiency of gain, longevity, and carcass merit.

Fertility is an important trait with low heritability. Most experts concur that variations among herds in reproduction are usually a result of differences in management, nutrition, herd health and other environmental factors or by heterosis (hybrid vigor) resulting from crossbreeding. (See page 168.)

Mothering or nursing ability is a basic requirement for effective cattle production. Weaning weight of the calf is used as a measure of nursing ability. Meat scientists and some producers know, for example, that a Jersey-Angus or Jersey-Hereford cross female mated to a Brown Swiss likely will produce a heavy calf at weaning because the mother has a plentiful supply of rich milk. They suspect, however, that once this offspring is moved into the

Figure 3-4   Mothering ability is basic to effective cattle production. *(Courtesy of North American South Devon Association)*

feedlot it may not do as well as other breed combinations. The calves are apt to be somewhat light muscled and carry excessive fat. There are other combinations that do better and some that would not do as well in the feedlot. Researchers are trying to develop more data on the influences of the dam on feedlot performance. Basically, each cattle producer must determine what level of nursing ability is needed for optimum performance in the herd. In most cases, the need for nursing ability will be moderated by the amount and kind of feedstuffs available to the dam.

For instance, in one study, Simmental cows proved to be a very heavy milking breed, able to wean a heavy calf. This would offer a lot of potential for a producer to use in a crossbreeding program in an area where there is an adequate supply of quality grass. The combination might not be as desirable elsewhere, with the cow giving too much milk for the limited amount of quality grass needed by the cow to provide milk production for her calf and to maintain herself and rebreed successfully. The producer in that situation might prefer to use British breeds instead.

Growth rate can be measured rather accurately by determining final weight and grade at somewhere near normal market age for a high percentage of slaughter cattle—12 to 18 months of age. Research results indicate that a reasonably high level of feeding is desirable to appraise differences in growth rate most accurately. A high percentage (perhaps 50 percent) of heifers must be kept for replacements, so one cannot put as much selection pressure on heifer replacements as on individual bull selection.

Efficiency of gain, it is currently believed, can be selected for by choosing animals with a good rate of gain, thus assuming that the fast gainers will also be efficient gainers. Efficiency of gain refers to the differences in the amount of feed required to produce an animal of a specified weight.

Longevity is valuable in a herd because it reduces the number of replacements necessary. However, longevity does reduce the opportunity for quick genetic improvement through selection since the original animals remain in the herd for a longer period of time. Selection for longevity generally is made through use of pedigree information—how long close relatives lived—and through an evaluation of the soundness of the individual animal.

Carcass merit is important to beef cattle producers because the quality of their product directly affects their economic gains from it. A number of research studies have shown that large growthy breeds have less outside fat and lower degrees of marbling but greater retail product yield than smaller early maturing breeds when compared at the same age, and particularly, at the same carcass weight. One study indicated that marbling, the distribution of fat throughout the meat, is more of an expression of how well the feedlot calves have been fed than a prediction of expected tenderness or flavor. With few exceptions, young cattle that received good nutrition most of their lives are going to produce tender, flavorful, juicy meat, even though one breed may not show as much marbling as the next. Basically, if a steer is young and has been well fed, it probably will be excellent for eating. A U.S. Department of Agriculture experiment involving more than 1,000 steers found that a taste panel evaluating beef from all breeds in the study rated tenderness, flavor, and juiciness well above minimum levels of acceptance. Small differences in tenderness between breeds were observed by the taste panel, but differences between breeds in flavor and juiciness were insignificant. At the same time, marbling differed significantly.

Although meat quality is determined primarily by marbling, the USDA study determined that increasing an animal's time on feed in order to increase the marbling of its carcass is of dubious value since, although slight increases in tenderness associated with marbling occur, they are more than offset by decreased tenderness associated with older age. Selection for marbling may also increase the tendency to put on extra fat, reducing total yield from the carcass. Studies have determined that the penalty of increased fat trim and cost of production associated with increased time on feed to meet present marbling requirements for the low choice grade are not justified in terms of improvement in eating quality.

CARCASS DATA SERVICE

A good way to obtain carcass data on progeny or siblings of a potential herd sire is to use the Carcass Data Service for beef. This is a joint effort of the U.S. Department of Agriculture and the cattle industry to help cattle producers and feeders obtain carcass data—mainly quality and yield grade factors—on important value-determining characteristics of the carcasses their cattle produce.

Specially designed ear tags are purchased from a cooperating source such as various organizations and state departments of agriculture that are participating as cooperators. Ear tags cannot be obtained directly from USDA, but USDA will provide information on sources of ear tags. (Write: Livestock Division, Agricultural Marketing Service, U.S. Department of Agriculture, Washington, D.C. 20250.)

Producers and feeders can apply the bright orange, shield-shaped, serially numbered ear tags to those cattle on which they want carcass information. When ear-tagged cattle are slaughtered, a meat inspector will remove the tag from the ear, attach it to the carcass, and notify the USDA meat grader assigned to the plant.

After the tagged carcasses have been sufficiently chilled, the meat grader evaluates the quality and yield grade factors and records the carcass data together with the ear tag serial number and slaughter date on a special carcass data form. The completed data forms are forwarded to the Carcass Data Center in Washington, D.C., where the information is processed and mailed to the cooperator, who then mails it to the ear tag owner. The ear tag owner is billed for each completed data form received.

Information on the data form includes conformation, maturity, marbling, quality grade, packer's warm carcass weight, adjusted fat thickness, ribeye area, kidney, pelvic and heart fat, and yield grade.

ULTRASONICS

A useful measuring device to determine meaty beef cattle without slaughtering them to examine their carcasses now in use is ultrasonics. Researchers have developed a portable device that can be taken out into the field to measure the fat and muscle areas of an animal. The ultrasonic instrument operates on a similar principle to sonar, the device used by submarines to detect objects under water. The ultrasonic instrument uses high-frequency sound waves and a small screen known as an oscilloscope to detect depths of tissue layers with different densities—such as fat and lean. The drawing of the loin area based on ultrasonic readings is a reasonably accurate predictor of carcass fat content.

CENTRAL TESTING STATIONS

Performance testing makes sire selection easier for the breeder interested in improving specific traits. If a breeder chooses bulls because of color, color patterns, shape of ears, etc., he or she is using random selection in the performance program. Eventually the breeder may develop a herd that is all the same color, with the same shape of ears, but herd performance will not be one pound better than the day he or she started. Selecting for traits that are highly heritable and economically important and using the bulls with the best performance gives the breeder the performance needed to compete in today's cattle business.

By using the services of a central testing station, the cattle producer can estimate the genetic differences between herds or between sire progenies in gain ability, grade, finishing ability, and carcass characteristics; determine gain ability, grade, and finishing ability of potential sires as compared with similar animals from other herds; determine gain ability, grade, and finishing ability under comparable conditions of bulls being readied for sale to commercial producers; and become acquainted with performance testing.

Central testing stations are only one phase of a complete performance evaluation program. However, they can provide the cattle producer with important information and are a valuable part of performance testing.

Some central testing stations maintain slaughter facilities to provide an additional kind of information known as cut-out data. This is useful in conjunction with such tools as ultrasonics and bull testing to evaluate a potential sire. In this test a steer, usually a half brother to the bull being tested, is taken through the testing station feeding program and slaughtered at its conclusion. The carcass data from this steer are useful as sibling data for evaluating the individual bull on test. (Full brother data would be ideal, but since most cattle are single births, and because ova transplant is not yet in widespread use, full brothers seldom go through the tests at the same time.)

Other ways to measure performance are less complicated. Breed associations and stud services provide free vest-pocket size notebooks to record important data such as date of birth, birth weight, date of first heat, breeding and calving dates. In conjunction with use of a notebook, another important measuring tool is a scale. Without a scale, the cattle producer could not accurately determine birth weights, weaning weights, or yearling weights. To provide accurate performance information, weaning weight should be adjusted based on age variation and adjusted for age of the dam. Table 3-A aids in figuring calf weaning weight to a standard 205 days of age.

The most important single weight to both the purebred and the commercial breeder would probably be the yearling 365-day weight. Yearling weight has a moderate to high heritability and there is a good genetic association between yearling weight, weaning weight, and birth weight. To evaluate bulls for replacement, bulls should be selected based on their superiority to the average performance of the herd.

Other important factors to consider in selecting a herd bull include overall health and soundness, masculinity, testes size, and docile disposition.

SELECTING A HERD BULL

Health and Soundness

Bulls should be free of obvious physical and genetic defects in conformation. Feet and legs should be inspected carefully to eliminate animals with extreme sickle hocks and crooked ankles. Pigeon-toed or splay-footed cattle should be avoided. Too much width between the toes is undesirable since feet of this kind are more subject to injuries and are susceptible to corns and other foot problems.

If the bull is being purchased or simply being selected from within one's own herd, his semen should be evaluated before turning him out to pasture. If he is infertile, money can be lost by turning him out with the cows before testing him. It could be 60 days before the cattle producer determines that the cows were not being bred, and by that time a substantial amount of money could have been lost in terms of potential calves.

Masculinity

Masculinity is an important trait for a bull. A bull that looks like a bull may have a greater sex drive and cover the cow herd more effectively. Masculinity expressed in the head and the crest on the neck of a breeding-age bull is related to the natural level of male hormone.

TABLE 3-A.   NOMOGRAPH TO USE IN FIGURING CALF WEANING WEIGHT
(TO 205 DAYS OF AGE)

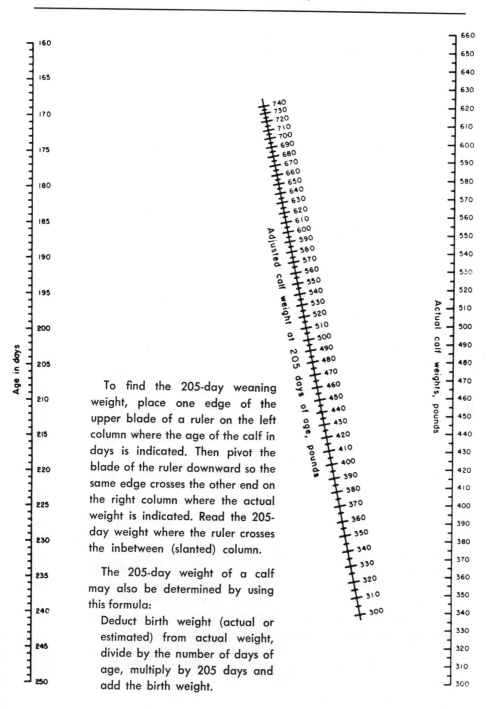

To find the 205-day weaning weight, place one edge of the upper blade of a ruler on the left column where the age of the calf in days is indicated. Then pivot the blade of the ruler downward so the same edge crosses the other end on the right column where the actual weight is indicated. Read the 205-day weight where the ruler crosses the inbetween (slanted) column.

The 205-day weight of a calf may also be determined by using this formula:

Deduct birth weight (actual or estimated) from actual weight, divide by the number of days of age, multiply by 205 days and add the birth weight.

Testes Size

If a cattle producer is choosing between two bulls with similar performance records, the bull with larger testicles often will have a greater reproductive capacity. A tape measure can be used to find the bull with the largest testicles. Selection based on testicle size alone can be done accurately at an early age.

Disposition

Disposition of bulls is important because a nervous disposition is a highly heritable trait in cattle. Wild, high-headed, skittish animals tend to produce nervous, undesirable offspring. Nervous animals fail to gain rapidly in the feedlot, are inefficient producers, and tend to disturb animals with quiet dispositions.

Horned or Polled

Generally breeders in enclosed pasture conditions prefer polled cattle for easier handling. Breeders working under range conditions where cattle are subject to native predators generally prefer horned animals.

CROSSBREEDING

One way to improve traits with low heritability is through crossbreeding. Crossbreeding of two unrelated animals results in heterosis, or hybrid vigor, that extra vigor and growth found in crosses between two genetically different strains, breeds, or even species. Increased hybrid vigor response is not obtained by selection. Also, crossbreeding should be done with the best quality animals available. The crossing of two average quality animals will not accomplish much. Too, the wider the cross, the greater the resulting hybrid vigor. It is to obtain this extra measure of hybrid vigor that breeders often cross Brahman, of the species *Bos indicus* with British breeds, of the species *Bos taurus*. The two species are totally unrelated.

What is crossbreeding? Simply, it is the mating of one unrelated animal with another unrelated animal. In practice, it may be mating top-producing bulls with commercial cows, either of one breed or crossbred. Many cattle producers believe that extra hybrid vigor results from the use of superior bulls of a third breed on crossbred cows. A good beginning for a crossbreeding program would be using superior bulls of a third breed on first-cross cows. From this point the cattle producer has a choice of several breeding choices: a terminal cross, a rotational cross, criss-cross, or, for the small herd, a three-sire breed rotation.

The crossing of two pure breeds of cattle is referred to as an F-1 cross. The cross may be between species, as in a Brahman × British breed cross, or may simply be between two distinct breeds.

Figure 3-5   Crossing species, like the Brahman *(Bos indicus)* with British breeds *(Bos taurus)* results in the greatest of hybrid vigor. *(Courtesy of the American Brahman Breeders Association)*

Rotation Systems

The simplest rotation system is a *two-breed rotation* or a criss-cross. F-1 females are bred to bulls of one of the parent breeds. This is called a back-cross. In subsequent generations, females are bred to bulls of the breed other than their sire. The system eventually stabilizes with two distinct populations. Each population contains approximately two-thirds of the breeding of the sire and one-third of the breeding of the grand sire. For this system, two breeding pastures are required unless artificial insemination is used.

A *three-breed rotation* mates the F-1 females with a sire of a third breed. Then the three-breed cross females are bred back to sires of one of the two breeds used in the first-cross stage of the rotation. Three distinct groups are eventually created. The genetic make-up of each group is about four-sevenths of the breed of the sire, two-sevenths of the breed of the dam's sire, and one-seventh of the remaining breed. Females are mated to sires of this remaining breed. Rotation of more than three breeds is possible, but is even more complex. In any rotation, cows are mated to the breed of sire to which they are least related, this scheme continuing for the life of the cow.

Figure 3-6   This Brahman-Hereford hybrid steer is a typical F-1 cross. *(Courtesy of the American Brahman Breeders Association)*

A *terminal cross* ends at some planned point. A first cross can be terminal if the system is stopped at this point, and all cattle produced are intended for sale. This would be a two-breed terminal cross.

A *three-breed terminal cross* is an extension of the two-breed program. Here, F-1 females are bred to bulls of a third breed. The genetic make-up of the offspring is half the breed of the sire and one-fourth of each of the breeds represented in the dam.

Small herds with only one breeding pasture must use a different sort of crossbreeding system. A high level of heterosis can be restored from one generation to the next by using three sire breeds in rotation and replacing sire breeds every three years. Heterosis will approach the maximum level if replacements are kept from the last two of each three calf crops produced by each sire breed used in the rotation.

The primary disadvantage to crossbreeding is the necessity for either maintaining purebred females to produce F-1 females (by use of artificial insemination), or having to purchase F-1 females. Or, if F-2 and F-3 generation replacements are used in a rotational cross, they may lose some of their hybrid vigor potential.

Termination cross

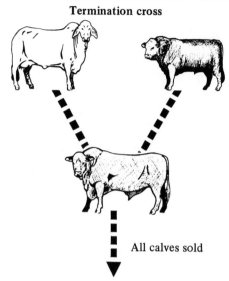

All calves sold

Figure 3-7 Examples of a 2-breed terminal cross (top) and a 3-breed rotational cross (bottom) which take advantage of hybrid vigor. *(Illustration by Tom Stallman)*

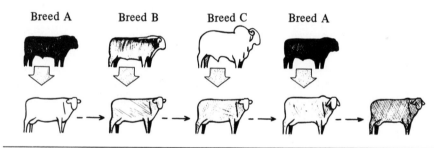

Breed A	Breed B	Breed C	Breed A

Calving Ease

Discussion of crossbreeding invariably brings up the question of calving difficulties. Sire selection is the key to calving ease in any crossbreeding program. It stands to reason that if a breeder uses one of the larger new breeds on small cows or first-calf heifers, calving problems probably will increase. This means more labor at calving time, with the possibility of a reduced calf crop, despite one's best efforts. On the other hand, sires of small mature size may be used on first-calf heifers to reduce calving problems. As noted in the section on cattle breeds, however, there is a great deal of variation in mature size within any one breed, so producers should be cautious.

Figure 3-8   Senator Harry Hays of Canada used crossbreeding of established breeds to develop a new breed, the Hays Converter. The crossing of two or more breeds to take advantage of traits of each is one reason for crossbreeding. The desire for hybrid vigor is the other reason for crossbreeding. *(Courtesy of American Breeders Service)*

Selecting Females

The cattle producer keeps cows for one purpose—to raise calves. For this reason the ability to survive and reproduce is the most important characteristic of the cow. When deciding what cows to cull and which to rebreed, there are several factors to consider. First, did the cow wean a good calf? If the calf had a good birth weight with no serious hereditary defects, the cow passes the first criteria—to get a healthy calf on the ground.

Some reasons for culling a cow include poorly attached udder, poor conformation, any inherited weaknesses such as cancer eye or prolapse of the uterus. Any cow that has a calf with a recessive genetic defect such as dwarfism should be culled. For the defect to appear the calf had to receive the recessive gene from its dam as well as from its sire.

Replacement Heifers

After culling the cow herd, the question arises as to which heifers to choose as replacements.

Replacement heifers should be from top-producing dams. Those cows who are heavy milking, regular breeding, easy calving dams are the best source of good replacement heifers. Qualities of the replacement heifer include good udders free of excessive firm connective tissue, evidence of femininity, especially as expressed in the head, good disposition, and a pedigree free from such defects as double muscling, dwarfism, prolapse of the uterus, and so on.

Figure 3-9 A good cow weans a good calf. Maine-Anjou bulls were used on half-blood Maine-Anjou × Angus and Maine-Anjou × Hereford cows to produce these calves. *(Courtesy of American Maine-Anjou Association)*

Although herd improvement can come from the sires or the dams, it is more difficult to select among the cows in the herd. Since most heifers born need to be raised as replacements, little selection of the cows to be parents of the next generation is feasible. Additionally, little selection is done when cows leave the herd for poor reproductive performance, disease, or injury.

The cattle producer in the best position to produce his or her own replacement heifers is one with high production dairy cows or top-quality beef cows; one who plans to use a good AI sire; one who is successful in raising calves and heifers; and, finally, one who has enough forage and labor to devote to raising replacements.

The producer who may want to consider purchasing replacement heifers is one who may not have enough good cows to breed for good replacements, one who wants to enlarge herd size quickly, one who has a shortage of labor, or one who has not been very successful raising calves or heifers.

When the cattle producer contracts with some other party to raise replacement heifers (this is done when the producer has limited labor and land available for raising his or her own replacements), several basic points should be considered prior to signing a contract. First and most important, a method of determining the costs involved should be settled upon. The value of the heifer calves at the beginning of the period and the age of calves at delivery should be discussed. A method of identification should be used for obvious reasons. The feed and its composition should be determined in advance also. Like all contracts, as much as possible, every point should be covered in advance to avoid misunderstandings and problems later.

Planning for replacement of the approximately 25 percent of dairy cows that leave a milking herd each year is one critical phase of proper management of a dairy farm. Similarly, a beef producer must make important decisions about the replacement of breeding cows.

The producer who hopes for increased production for the milking herd, or the beef producer who hopes to grow better beef animals, must use performance information when selecting herd sires. By looking carefully at past performance information on a sire, the producer can breed his or her own cows with more insight. Because of the tremendous advantages of comparing various sires, artificial insemination has become increasingly popular with both dairy and beef cattle producers. Some statistics cite figures of more than 70 percent of dairy cattle bred through AI each year. Although the percentage of beef cattle bred artificially is far lower, some say less than 5 percent, more beef cattle producers take advantage of AI for their herds each year.

Some cattle producers purchase replacement heifers, rather than producing them themselves. A few things to keep in mind when purchasing replacement heifers, though, are the quality of the replacements, the health of the replacements, and the added expense of buying heifers rather than producing them.

Thus, the most reliable method for improving the genetic merit of the herd is by selecting the best available sires. Using artificial insemination provides an opportunity to get a proven sire. For many producers, it offers the best opportunity for getting a quality sire as well. Each sire has demonstrated his ability to improve production in his offspring. Each stud also has a number of young sires with great potential to improve offspring.

If the cattle producer chooses natural service over AI, there are several factors to consider. The first step is to examine the bull's pedigree. The sire of any bull considered for breeding should be proved superior. Then the bull should be judged by the criteria discussed earlier in this chapter.

Choosing Dairy Sires

The dairy industry and the U.S. Department of Agriculture cooperate to produce the Dairy Herd Improvement Sire Summary, a valuable tool for selecting dairy sires to improve genetic inheritance for milk and fat production.

If a dairy farmer raises his or her own replacement heifers, about one-third of the herd 3 years later will be made up of heifers resulting from matings the first year. Four years later about two-thirds of the herd will contain cows resulting from matings the first and second years. Five years later, 80 to 90 percent of the herd will be offspring from matings made the first three years. Using genetically superior sires with predicted differences of +1,000 pounds of milk, the resulting higher quality replacement heifers will be able to increase income over feed costs substantially.

Figure 3-10 Because a rancher trusts the breeding future of at least 20 cows to a bull used for natural service breeding, that bull should be selected with care. *(Courtesy of International Braford Association)*

The DHIA Sire Summary is compiled twice a year—in February and July—by the U.S. Department of Agriculture from DHIA and DHIR records from all states.

Figure 3-11 Raising replacements offers the dairy farmer the best chance for developing a herd comprised of top-quality cows. *(Courtesy of the Holstein-Friesian Association of America)*

Predicted Difference

Predicted difference is the best available estimate of a dairy sire's ability to transmit production. It is the amount of milk and fat that a sire is expected to raise or lower in his daughter's production in comparison with herdmates at breed average levels. Predicted difference is determined by repeatability, daughter's average, adjusted herdmate average, number of herdmates, percent incomplete records, and adjustments for age, season of calving, and geographical region.

The Sire Summary is based on daughter-herdmate comparisons. Records made by the daughters of the sire summarized are compared to records of herdmates. Herdmates are other cows of the same breed, in the same herd, sired by a different bull, freshening in the same season of the year. These comparisons reduce the environmental differences that normally affect summary data.

To determine the best choice for a herd sire, the predicted difference and the percent repeatability should be considered. The sire with the highest predicted difference is usually the best transmitting sire for production. One can easily choose between the best sire and the poorest. The choice becomes more difficult between two close-ranking bulls with wide differences in repeatability.

TABLE 3-B.

Predicted Difference, Milk	Repeatability												
	15	20	25	30	35	40	45	50	60	70	80	90	95
(lb)					——— % ———								
+1000	98	98	98	98	99	—²	—	—	—	—	—	—	—
+900	96	97	97	97	98	98	99	—	—	—	—	—	—
+800	94	95	95	96	96	97	97	98	99	—	—	—	—
+700	91	92	93	93	94	95	96	96	98	99	—	—	—
+600	88	89	89	90	91	92	93	94	96	98	99	—	—
+500	84	84	85	86	87	88	89	90	92	95	98	99	—
+400	78	**79**	80	81	81	82	83	85	87	91	95	99	—
+300	72	73	73	74	75	75	77	78	80	84	89	96	99
+200	65	66	66	66	67	68	68	69	71	**74**	79	87	95
+100	58	58	58	58	59	59	59	60	61	63	66	71	79
0	50	50	50	50	50	50	50	50	50	50	50	50	50
−100	41	41	41	41	40	40	40	39	38	36	33	28	20
−200	34	33	33	33	32	31	31	30	28	25	20	12	4
−300	27	26	26	25	24	24	22	21	19	15	10	3	0
−400	21	20	19	18	18	17	16	14	12	8	4	0	0
−500	15	15	14	13	12	11	10	9	7	4	1	0	0
−600	11	10	10	9	8	7	6	5	3	1	0	0	0
−700	8	7	6	6	5	4	3	1	0	0	0	0	0

[1]Assuming standard deviation among bulls of 550 lb.
[2]Dashes indicate probability over 99%.
USDA - DHI Letter 4-68

Approximate probability that a Holstein or Brown Swiss bull[1] with a given repeatability and predicted difference has a true genetic merit above breed average.

TABLE 3-C.

Predicted Difference, Milk	Repeatability												
	15	20	25	30	35	40	45	50	60	70	80	90	95
(lb)					——— % ———								
+1000	99	—²	—	—	—	—	—	—	—	—	—	—	—
+900	99	—	—	—	—	—	—	—	—	—	—	—	—
+800	98	99	—	—	—	—	—	—	—	—	—	—	—
+700	97	97	98	98	98	99	—	—	—	—	—	—	—
+600	95	95	96	96	97	97	98	98	99	—	—	—	—
+500	91	92	92	93	94	95	95	96	98	99	—	—	—
+400	86	87	87	88	89	90	91	92	94	97	99	—	—
+300	79	80	81	81	82	83	84	85	88	91	95	99	—
+200	70	71	72	72	73	74	75	76	78	82	87	94	99
+100	60	61	61	61	62	62	63	53	65	67	71	78	87
0	50	50	50	50	50	50	50	50	50	50	50	50	50
−100	39	38	38	38	37	37	36	36	34	32	28	21	12
−200	29	28	27	27	26	25	24	23	21	17	12	5	0
−300	20	19	18	18	17	16	15	14	11	8	4	0	0
−400	13	12	12	11	10	9	8	7	5	2	0	0	0
−500	8	7	7	6	5	4	4	3	1	0	0	0	0
−600	4	4	3	3	2	2	1	1	0	0	0	0	0
−700	2	2	1	1	1	0	0	0	0	0	0	0	0

[1]Assuming the standard deviation among bulls is 400 lb.
[2]Dashes indicate probability over 99%.
USDA - DHI Letter 4-68

Approximate probability that an Ayrshire, Jersey, or Guernsey bull[1] with a given repeatability and predicted difference has a true genetic merit above breed average.

Use Tables 3-B and 3-C to make a choice between the two bulls. To use the tables, locate repeatability percentage at the top. Find the predicted difference of a bull on the left. The value where the two lines meet is the bull's probability above breed average for genetic milk production ability.

Classification/Selection for Type

An official classifier assigns a numerical score to indicate the physical characteristics of an animal. Composite score for the animal is used to determine a descriptive name for type.

Type	Description	Score
E	Excellent	90 or more
VG	Very Good	85 to 89
GP	Good Plus (desirable)	80 to 84
G	Good (acceptable)	75 to 79
F	Fair	65 to 74
P	Poor	64 or less

Type classification scores may vary for the same animal at different ages. For comparison, breed age average (BAA) scores often are used. Type information is available from dairy breed associations or AI organizations.

Using more than one young sire spreads the risk of possible disappointment and at the same time increases the chance of using a sire with truly superior inheritance.

To evaluate the success of this program, raise, milk, and test all heifers.

STUDY QUESTIONS

1. _____ are useful in selecting against undesirable hereditary characteristics. (Pedigrees)
2. A good sound basis for selection involves consideration of pedigree, progeny information and individual _____. (performance)
3. The proportion of the differences between animals that are transmitted to the offspring is known as _____. (heritability)
4. The use of _____ allows researchers to determine meaty beef cattle without slaughtering them. (ultrasonics)
5. The crossing of two _____ of cattle results in the best hybrid vigor. (species)
6. The best available estimate of a dairy sire's ability to transmit production is called _____. (predicted difference)

4

Herd Health = Producer Wealth

Preventive medicine in the form of a cow herd health program can pay off for the cattle producer in the form of reduced losses to disease and death. Unfortunately, many cattle producers are reluctant to begin a health program unless something already is wrong with the herd. In normal situations it may take years before the livestock producer can see any benefit or returns from the money and labor invested in preventive medicine.

Many farmers and ranchers get by with a minimum of problems. It is not unusual to hear a rancher say that he or she does not vaccinate for anything and has not had any problems. However, merely because a rancher has not had any trouble so far does not indicate that there will be no problems in the future. Changes in transportation and other management practices have rendered the isolation theory obsolete. It is nearly impossible to raise an animal to maturity without exposure to disease. Also, many ranchers consider survival of 80 percent of their calf crop to be adequate. "Problems" may mean different things to different people. However, loss of even one calf translates into an actual dollar loss, decreasing profits of the entire ranch.

STARTING A HEALTH PROGRAM

The time to start a health program is before disease strikes. Planning is easier when done without the added pressures of emergencies. During times of disease outbreaks ranchers and veterinarians alike may be forced to use procedures and products that are not recommended under normal conditions. Where this is the case, results tend to be poor.

A health program can be quite flexible, depending on the circumstances of each cattle operation. Each should follow some fundamental guidelines that will make it compatible with other management procedures.

- First, the health program should fill the needs of both the animals and the people involved.

- Secondly, it should be practical, low cost but not cheap.
- Third, it should prevent disease and parasite problems before they start.
- Finally, the health program must be compatible with other management practices or it will not be used.

Protected Herds

Basically, cow herds can be classified in two ways: protected herds and susceptible herds. A protected cow herd has been vaccinated for IBR, BVD, leptospirosis, and other common diseases. These animals are as nearly protected as they can be by today's standards. Protected cow herds have the advantage that calves can be vaccinated and turned back with their dams for as long as necessary, without causing abortion or the spread of other diseases. Calves born to protected cows usually receive some immunity from the cows. Processing of calves from a protected cow herd should be done at least 3 weeks prior to weaning.

Susceptible Herds

A susceptible cow herd is one that has not been vaccinated for any disease. While individuals may carry natural protection from infection, the herd's natural immunities cannot be relied upon as the base for a health program.

The Need for Vaccinations

A good health program begins with the calves. At 2 to 3 months of age calves should be vaccinated for blackleg and malignant edema. A "seven-way" vaccine is available for use in herds that have had other clostridial diseases diagnosed by a veterinarian or diagnostic laboratory. The organisms, in order of greatest danger, that may be involved are *Clostridium: chauvoei, septicum, novyi, sordelli,* and *perfringens* (types B, C and D). Calves vaccinated before 6 months of age are protected for one season only and should be revaccinated.

Some producers may vaccinate for brucellosis while others may not. Decisions on brucellosis vaccination should be made upon consultation with a veterinarian since brucellosis vaccine is not legal in some states. If vaccinating for brucellosis, Strain 19 vaccine should be given at about 3 to 7 months of age.

Procedures at Weaning

At weaning time a good health program continues by separating the calves from the cows. A common water supply and or fence line should not be used. Calves from nonprotected cows should be processed within 24 hours after weaning. Calves from protected cows should be processed 3 weeks prior to weaning.

Vaccines that should be considered at weaning include:

- IBR (Infectious Bovine Rhinotracheitis)—Every area has IBR problems in cows and calves.
- BVD (Bovine Virus Diarrhea)—Part of a health program to establish protected cows. It is doubtful that an animal can go a lifetime without some exposure to the disease.
- Leptospirosis—A vaccine should be used that fits the area. Leptopomona is the most common vaccine but other organisms are available in vaccines if needed.
- Pasteurella—Results on field trials with this vaccine are confusing, however it may be worthwhile in a protected cow herd.
- Para influenza—(PI_3) The importance of PI_3 vaccine has not been firmly established under all conditions. If used it should be given to fresh calves nursing protected cows.
- Blackleg and malignant edema—Revaccinate. This should provide lifetime protection.

Other procedures to be done at weaning time include:

- Injection of Vitamins A,D; A,D,B_{12}; or A,B_{12}. Adequate dosage.
- Control of internal parasites through individual worming.
- Control of external parasites (lice, tick, grubs).

Table 4-A lists calfhood vaccinations and injections.

TABLE 4-A.   CALFHOOD VACCINATIONS AND INJECTIONS

When Due	Repeat	What Needed
Birth		A, D, E vitamins
Birth		150 mg low molecular iron dextrin solution
2–4 weeks	6–8 months	IBR vaccine
2–4 weeks	6–8 months	PI-3
6–8 months		BVD (consult veterinarian)
2 months	4 months	Blackleg/malignant edema
2–4 months		Leptospirosis

A veterinarian can provide a vaccination program tailored to the needs of each farm or ranch, and should be consulted prior to the start of any health program.

Continuing a good health program calls for additional precautions to be taken prior to breeding. Steps which should be taken before breeding an animal include: repeat vaccinations for BVD, IBR, lepto, and a vaccination for vibriosis, which is present in most areas. Additionally, internal and external parasites should be controlled as necessary.

One disease not covered in this health program is anaplasmosis. It is impossible to give general statements that will cover anaplasmosis control on all farms and ranches. Each program must be designed for a specific ranch or farm and should be based on existing circumstances. Product choice and method for control should be worked out with the local veterinarian.

Basically, though, to prevent and control anaplasmosis, one must:

- Control the insect population.
- Use clean instruments for each animal—needles, dehorners, etc.
- Feed medicated feed during insect season.
- Vaccinate according to the program worked out with the veterinarian.
- Test any herd additions before placing with the rest of the herd.
- Eliminate carrier animals by test and slaughter.

CALVING SEASON

Several preparations should be made for calving season. They include getting calving equipment and medicine chests in order. The calf-puller should be cleaned. Emergency items to be added to the medicine chest include injectable antibiotics, hormones to stimulate labor or shrink the uterus, scour prevention pills, injectable stimulants for weak calves, and a good supply of colostrum.

If weather is a factor, the cows should be prepared to calve inside or outside. In good weather an ideal calving location is on a sunny slope of a hill on clean ground. In inclement weather an inside area should be prepared for use. If possible, the floor should be disinfected to reduce disease organisms. Several commercial disinfectants are available. Lye water is an excellent disinfectant if there is no metal that might be corroded.

At calving time heifers should be checked at least every 4 hours, especially if they are bred to large bulls. Cows should be checked almost as often as heifers. If a heifer or cow makes no progress after the first 2 hours of labor, calving problems may be developing and help will be needed.

If necessary to pull the calf, the cow should be coaxed into a chute or stanchion to restrain her. If a lariat is used, steps must be taken to prevent choking. Before pulling the calf, one's hands and arms should be disinfected, or plastic sleeves available from the veterinarian can be used.

Figure 4-1   To ensure healthy calves like this one, preparations should be made for calving in advance of the calving season. *(Courtesy of International Brangus Breeders Association)*

The normal presentation of the calf is front feet first with the head lying between the front feet. When the cow begins labor, the feet of the calf break through the placenta and release the amniotic fluid. Now the calf is ready to begin its journey down the birth canal. A normal birth averages about 30 minutes. If it appears that the cow is having a great deal of difficulty delivering the calf—taking more than 2 hours from the beginning of labor pains to deliver the calf—aid may be necessary. At this point, the producer may need to use a calf puller. There are safe and useful calf pullers, but using a truck or a tractor to pull a calf is inadvisable. Considerable damage to the cow and calf may result from excessive assistance. It is helpful to have a veterinarian check the cow in trouble in case the calf is lodged in the birth canal in a manner that makes normal delivery impossible. In this predicament the calf would need to be removed surgically. Unfortunately, the calf might die while the producer waits for the vet to arrive. In cases where the calf has its head turned to one side or another, pulling the calf would only damage the cow and the calf. The calf puller most frequently is used in cases of an extremely large calf, or with a breach birth.

While in the chute, the cow's udder should be checked to be sure her teats are open.

Once the calf is born, the navel must be disinfected with tincture of iodine. This is a good time to mark the cow so she can be identified for future evaluation. Medication should be readily available at this time in case the calf needs vitamin shots or a scour preventive.

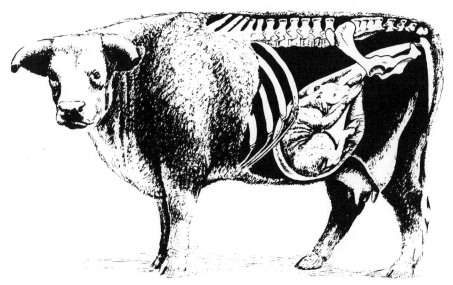

Figure 4-2   Normal presentation of a calf. *(Illustration by Tom Stallman)*

If a cow fails to claim her newborn calf, the calf should be given colostrum milk within the first 4 hours so that its resistance to disease will be built up.

The producer should observe the cow to be certain that the placenta (afterbirth) is expelled by the cow. This should occur within 2 to 6 hours after birth of the calf. Many times the cow will eat the afterbirth. It really does not matter if she does or not. If the placenta has not been expelled within 24 hours, the cattle producer should call in the veterinarian. Retained placenta can cause serious infections.

ROUTINE EXAMINATIONS

To maximize income, cows should calve every 12 to 13 months. The producer who keeps records knows when the cows last calved, when they were serviced (either naturally or by artificial insemination), and when they are due to calve again. One of the functions of a good record-keeping systems is letting the producer know when there is a problem. Cows that fail to conceive or that abort should be checked by a veterinarian. There are several other indicators calling for professional advice.

For instance, cows that have had a retained placenta should be examined. If a cow retains the placenta beyond 3 to 4 days past calving, the veterinarian should be consulted. Manual removal of the placenta is inadvisable.

Cows should be examined once or twice prior to breeding the next time to be sure the uterus remains free of infection and is returning to normal size.

A frequent problem with cows having an abnormal discharge also calls for veterinary attention. If the cow's discharge is abnormal or cloudy during heat, she should be examined and the source of infection treated. A discharge containing pus or one with a strong odor is always considered abnormal.

If a cow has an abnormal heat or abnormal heat cycle she should be examined to check for a hormonal imbalance. A normal cow comes into heat approximately every 21 days. Most cows should cycle every 18 to 24 days. Anything much shorter or much longer than the 21 day interval should be questioned.

After calving, a cow should come into heat again at 45 to 60 days postpartum. Any cow not coming into heat at this time should be examined to rule out the possibility of infection or cystic ovaries.

Finally, if a cow has been serviced two or three times and still has not conceived, she should be checked to determine the nature of the problem.

Because of the wide variety of diseases and infections that attack cattle, the livestock producer must use the services of a competent veterinarian in order to maximize profits and minimize any potential losses.

REPLACEMENT CALVES

The cattle producer who buys replacement calves for a feedlot operation or for a grass feeding program needs a health program for the new calves. First of all, records of each lot of cattle must be carefully kept to give a complete cost and health picture. Health programs will differ in various areas of the country, but there are a few basics to be considered, no matter where the location.

One very helpful item is a health record on the purchased cattle. If one is available, it can be extremely valuable in providing information on vaccinations and health problems.

If an animal looks sick, it probably is. The producer should never purchase a sick animal, or one that has been exposed to other sick cattle. To avoid the spread of possible infections, it is preferable to keep animals purchased from multiple sources separate. Isolating an infection will reduce the possibilities of an epidemic in one's herd.

When determining what size calf to buy, the producer should remember that young calves weighing 150 to 200 pounds generally are responsive to various medications should they be required, that 575 to 650 pound calves tend to be disease resistant, and that calves weighing from 300 to 450 pounds are considered high risk and must be treated carefully. Calves weighing more than 700 pounds often are moved with no problems at all.

Shipping calves creates stress. The longer the distance involved the greater the stress when time on the road exceeds 12 hours. Oddly enough, cattle hauled from 1 to 10 hours respond similarly. Studies show that calves on a truck longer than 36 hours often require extra care at time of arrival.

The University of Missouri* suggests steps to take prior to shipment to reduce stress. Their suggestions:

1. If there is any doubt about the health of the cattle, take body temperature prior to loading. It is more economical to treat feverish cattle and delay shipment.
2. Insist that cattle be assembled and held for shipment for the shortest period of time possible.
3. Avoid overcrowding cattle during hauling. Overcrowding creates excitement, slipping, and falling. Calves weighing 500 lbs should have approximately 8 square feet of floor space each. The services of a reliable, careful shipper should be secured.
4. Trucks with wooden floors should be bedded with sand or straw to help prevent slipping and falling. Straw should be used in trucks with aluminum floors to absorb excess moisture.
5. Do not use electric prods. Handle cattle as gently as possible when loading and unloading.
6. Arrange a minimum length of time as practical for transit.

When the calves arrive, check each one. Cull any that are injured or any too sick to accept. It may be advisable to treat the calves water with vitamins and antibiotics for the first few days following their arrival.

After unloading, the cattle must be fed. If they have been transported 10 hours or more, it is best to provide feed first, for about 2 hours, and then offer water. If the calves were transported less than 10 hours, the producer can provide water and hay at the same time. The cattle should be allowed a rest period of a few hours prior to worming, dipping, or other treatment.

The temperature of a calf is a reliable indicator of its health. Normal temperature falls between 100.4°F and 102.8°F. Calves with temperatures over 103°F should be treated.

Preconditioned calves may have been vaccinated. For this reason it is extremely helpful to have records of previous treatment of the purchased animals. If the animals have not been vaccinated, the veterinarian may want to vaccinate for infectious bovine rhinotracheitis, bovine virus diarrhea, leptospirosis, blackleg, and malignant edema. In some areas precautions should also be taken against *Clostridium sordelli* and *novyi*.

Newly purchased calves should be wormed and treated for grubs and lice. They should also be checked for ear ticks and treated if necessary. Castration can be done at this time also.

---

* From "Care of Newly Purchased Feeder Cattle," University of Missouri, Bonnard L. Moseley, D.V.M., and Homer B. Sewell.

Remembering that the cattle have been under stress is important when providing space for them, as well. Stressed calves need more space than healthy calves.

HEAT STRESS

Cattle suffer from the summer heat just as humans. Animals transported during periods of high temperatures may suffer muscle tremors, rapid breathing, rapid pulse, and ultimately collapse. It is harder for the animal if the truck, trailer, or other carrier remains parked than it is if the vehicle is moving down the road, since the movement allows air to circulate, causing sweat to evaporate and cool the body.

In the pasture, cows that go down while trying to calve outside during high humidity and high temperature periods are susceptible to heat stress. During this time, the symptoms of heat stress and milk fever can be confused, as they are quite similar.

To reduce heat stress situations, farmers can do several things. They include:

- Keep the air moving. Ventilation plus shade will cool, so cattle barns should be provided with fanned air or efficient air circulation through windows or the roof.
- Provide shade. Cattle are more comfortable in the shade. (This does not mean, however, that shaded cattle are the most efficient gainers.)
- Avoid movement of livestock during periods of extremely high temperatures or humidity.
- Provide an adequate source of good quality drinking water. It should be cool, not cold.
- If livestock must be moved, choose a cool day.
- Use weather reports and thermometers for an accurate gauge of how high the temperature has climbed. Often, a farmer becomes too busy to realize how hot the weather has become during the day.

VETERINARY EQUIPMENT

Most livestock producers need some veterinary equipment. The type of operation determines what equipment is needed as well as its use. Specialty tools such as calf pullers may be needed by beef and dairy farmers. In addition, basic instruments such as syringes, needles, and scalpels also may be needed.

Buying good-quality equipment represents a sizeable investment for the cattle producer, so one should be certain to buy with the amount and types of use in mind. Cattle producers who do most of their own veterinary work probably need top-quality equipment.

Some tips on selection of veterinary equipment from experts include selecting equipment and instruments with parts available locally. Although foreign-made equipment may be long-lasting and of good quality, if it does break down, parts may be difficult to locate. Another suggestion is to select equipment that fits the user. People have hands of different sizes and need equipment that best fits the hand size to make working as comfortable as possible. Finally, buying more equipment than is necessary can be an expensive mistake. For instance, an electronic thermometer is ideal for a large herd but hardly necessary for a small herd of 10 animals.

Disposable equipment has come into wide use because it is relatively inexpensive and functional at the same time. Syringes, needles, and other disposable items can be replaced for little more than the cost of sterilizing permanent equipment. Disposables save time since they are ready for use when unwrapped.

When permanent instruments are chosen over disposables, the cattle producer must take proper care of the equipment. Equipment left in water begins to rust after a time and once rust begins it can rarely be reversed. To be sure equipment does not rust, it must be dried after each use, with moveable parts lubricated properly. Storage should be in a clean, dry place.

To disinfect instruments, several methods are available. Boiling disinfects some instruments and equipment such as needles. Other equipment can be disinfected through use of chemicals. When disinfecting syringes with chemicals, one must be certain to remove all traces of chemical prior to reuse, since even small amounts left in the syringe may inactivate certain vaccines.

CHEMICAL USAGE

Chemicals represent an important part of good farm management. Using products safely makes good sense. Preventing accidents before they happen is the most economical and safe method of chemical management.

Some tips to keep in mind when using chemicals include:

1. Read and understand the label.
2. Use products for their intended use only.
3. Do not mix different products unless directions are printed on the label.
4. Separate products used on animals from those used on crops.
5. Do not store pesticides in areas used for animal feed.

6. Use on the proper age animals with recommended pressure and dosage.
7. Avoid contamination of feed or water supply.
8. Avoid use of agricultural chemicals on animals that are receiving antagonistic medication. (For example, phenothiazine and organophosphate.)
9. If a label becomes lost, discard the material in a place not accessible to livestock.
10. If an accident occurs, contact the veterinarian immediately, telling him or her the exact chemical or chemicals involved.

DISEASES

Sometimes, despite a cattle producer's best efforts, cattle will come down with a disease or a virus. It behooves the producer to determine infected animals quickly, isolate them from the rest of the herd, and begin treatment. Keeping a sharp eye out for possible problems within the herd will make early diagnosis and treatment an effective management tool, rather than simply a "hit-and-miss" operation.

If an animal goes off its feed, has a cough, diarrhea, lameness, or an unusual discharge, further investigations should be made. The first check a veterinarian will make is temperature. Anything above 103°F should be considered symptomatic of a health problem.

Figure 4-3   Sick cattle should be isolated from healthy ones to avoid the spread of infectious diseases. *(Courtesy of Dr. H. D. Anthony, Kansas State University)*

Anaplasmosis

Animals with anaplasmosis may have rapid breathing, weakness, muscle tremor, jaundice, and elevation of body temperature as high as 107°F. The disease is an infectious one and even if an animal recovers, it remains a hazard since, although it will be resistant to repeated infection, it will be a "carrier." Animals surviving an acute attack often show slow recovery, resulting in the loss of production of either milk or meat. Animals infected and not treated may die. Cattle 1 to 2 years old become acutely ill but usually respond to treatment. Mature animals have more serious infections, the mortality rate increasing with the age of the animals involved. Cattle less than a year old appear to have the mildest infections.

Anaplasmosis is transmitted by several different methods. Mosquitoes, ticks, horse flies, stable flies, and horn flies are instrumental in the transfer of the disease by moving blood from a sick animal to a healthy one. Ticks may be the worst offenders in certain areas, since the disease will live and multiply and then be transmitted by the tick at a later time. Contaminated instruments and needles may also spread anaplasmosis. Basically, anything that moves blood from one animal to another is dangerous.

The sale of carrier cattle for slaughter may be the only sure way to avoid infecting others in the herd. Control of the disease by drugs may not be practical in large herds because of the cost of the drugs and labor needed for repeated treatment.

In addition, any method of reducing or eliminating the insect pests that transmit anaplasmosis helps control the disease. Some suggested methods include dust bags, back rubbers, sprays, and dipping of cattle. Texas A&M University suggests establishing two herds, one infected and one clean, with strict isolation of the two.

The important steps to eliminate anaplasmosis include controlling the insect population; following strict sanitation standards during vaccinations or surgery; keeping needles, dehorners, an so on, spotless; testing and slaughter of infected animals if practical, or at least testing and segregating infected animals; testing new animals; treating infected animals with antibiotics; vaccinating the entire herd and all replacement animals; and feeding medicated feed during the insect season.

In some cases, especially when the disease is caught in its early stages, tetracyclines have been useful in reducing the rate of multiplication of anaplasma parasites and on the course of the disease. Whole-blood transfusions in conjunction with intravenous fluid and other supportive treatment have been of value.

When drug treatment has been chosen as the therapy, a veterinarian should monitor the progress of the animal closely. In dairy cattle, close monitoring is even more essential than in beef cattle in order to prevent drug residues in market milk.

Figure 4-4   The bloated carcass of an anthrax victim. *(Courtesy of U.S. Department of Agriculture)*

Anthrax

When an animal dies suddenly and unexpectedly, anthrax may be suspected to have invaded the herd. In most cases, animals will be found with their feet up and blood effusing from body openings. A spore-forming organism causes this disease, which is contagious to man. Unfortunately, once the spores make contact with the soil, they can survive for as long as 15 years. Generally, veterinarians presume that cattle contract the disease from drinking contaminated water or eating contaminated grass. Because of the hazards of anthrax to humans, diagnosis of the disease usually is made through smears of blood rather than through autopsy of suspected victims.

Some success has been obtained through use of vaccines to prevent the disease and with chemical disinfectants to rid the soil of spores once the disease has manifested itself.

Many animals will die without exhibiting signs of being sick beforehand. Others will give indications of illness for anywhere from 1 to 24 hours before death. Once anthrax has infested a herd, death losses usually are high.

Blackleg (Clostridium chauvaei)

Finding a dead calf may be the first clue that blackleg has invaded a herd. The disease primarily strikes young cattle between 6 months and 2 years, but age alone is no barrier to infection. Beef breeds are considered most susceptible, but dairy breeds also have been affected.

Calves younger than 6 months receive some protection from the dam. In some areas, however, this is not enough and vaccinations at a few days or weeks of age are necessary. Early vaccination lasts only one season and the animal must be revaccinated as a yearling. Best protection comes from using two vaccinations when necessary. Animals vaccinated prior to 6 months of age need a booster later in order to be fully protected. Vaccine should also protect against malignant edema.

Vaccination seems to be the only control for the disease. Treatment has not proven effective. Massive doses of broad-spectrum antibiotics are used and often cause the few animals who survive to slough off the dead tissue, ruining their value.

The blackleg organism is referred to as a *resistant spore*; that is, it can live for many years in the environment. Once soil is contaminated it will remain so for several years. The intestinal tract is the principal habitat for the blackleg spore. Although it can live in the soil it does not grow there. When an animal eats feed contaminated from contact with affected soil the spore goes through the gut wall, enters the blood, and is transported to the tissue. The disease is transmitted in other ways, also.

Some outward symptoms of blackleg include lameness, depression, and elevated temperature. Swelling in the neck, shoulders, loin, and other areas is common. However, since the disease strikes so quickly, death may follow within 12 to 48 hours following the first display of symptoms.

Figure 4-5 Cattle under four years of age are particularly susceptible to black-leg disease. *(Courtesy of U.S. Department of Agriculture)*

Bloat (Tympany)

Two cattle might graze side by side in a pasture with one developing a noticeable swelling on its left side while the other animal remains normal. The swollen animal has developed bloat, or tympany. Scientists now believe that a combination of factors work to cause the problem of bloat: the animal itself and its feed. There are two types of bloat—the free-gas type, and the gas bubble, or foaming type. Animals housed in feedlots receiving highly concentrated food, animals being fed alfalfa hay, or those grazing legume pastures tend to develop bloat more readily than animals fed differently. However, not all animals in these situations develop bloat, leading researchers to conclude that the composition of the saliva in the animal's mouth also contributes to the problem. Uncorrected, bloat can be fatal. Affected animals can be found with their legs up in positions similar to animals infected with anthrax.

Gaseous bloat can be relieved by exercising the animal, passing a tube (such as a garden hose) down the esophagus, or, if all else fails, by puncturing the rumen. The bubble type must be burst. The most effective treatment, however, is drenching cattle with 1 to 2 ounces of poloxalene and then relieving free gas with a stomach tube 10 minutes after treatment is effective. In emergencies, vegetable oils and even soap powders may be substituted.

Bovine Virus Diarrhea (BVD)

Bovine virus diarrhea is a viral disease that primarily attacks cattle of feedlot age. Often associated with the shipping-fever complex, BVD frequently develops following severe stress such as that caused by changes in feed and environment and by the excitement of loading, shipping, and unloading.

Most animals that contract BVD are not severely affected. In fact, the disease frequently is not diagnosed at the time, and knowledge that the animal had the disease at one time is indicated only by antibodies in its blood found at a later date. The disease is highly contagious. Those animals noticeably affected develop severe diarrhea, become depressed, and go off their feed. Shortly after the appearance of the diarrhea, ulcers form in the mouth along the gum line and on the muzzle. Some animals will have a nasal discharge and will drool saliva. The eyes may discharge a watery liquid that becomes encrusted on hair surrounding the eyes. The animal will have severe inflammation of the gastrointestinal tract, most acute in the lower 6 feet of the small intestine.

Some victims of the disease recover completely. Other cattle, however, will lose weight or fail to gain weight, never matching the performance of their peers. Thus, the disease can have an economic impact through higher feeding costs to bring affected cattle to market weight.

Prevention of BVD can save money. Careful handling of newly purchased animals, management techniques that keep stress to a minimum, and a good vaccination program will limit losses due to BVD.

It is recommended that vaccinated animals not be mixed with non-vaccinated animals. Additionally, the BVD vaccine sometimes produces abortions in pregnant cows. Treatment for BVD generally consists of the use of antibiotics supplied by a veterinarian to limit the spread of the disease.

Brucellosis

If a cow aborts her fetus in the final third of her pregnancy, she may have brucellosis, also known as Bang's disease. The disease also causes cows to retain their placentas. Additional symptoms of the disease include uterine infections and reduced fertility. Caused by contact with infected animals as well as contact with water and soil contaminated by infected animals, brucellosis spreads quickly through herds.

Treatment for one of the symptoms, retained placenta, consists of use of broad-spectrum antibiotics. Manual removal of a retained afterbirth is not recommended. No treatment for the disease itself has been developed. Brucellosis vaccine is required in some states and outlawed in others.

A nationwide program with state and federal authorities cooperating in an effort to eradicate the disease has reduced the number of brucellosis cases in the United States. Through blood-testing, elimination of reactors, and certification of brucellosis-free herds, the disease has been reduced considerably in this country. The effort involves testing cattle, finding animals with brucellosis, and eliminating them from the herd. Brucellosis vaccine usually is used primarily in heavily infected areas and administered to females in the breeding program.

Figure 4-6 Brucellosis control requires testing of cattle prior to shipping. *(Courtesy of U.S. Department of Agriculture)*

Figure 4-7   Blood testing identifies brucellosis reactors. *(Courtesy of U.S. Department of Agriculture)*

Calf Diphtheria

Calf diphtheria (necrobacillary stomatitis) can be fatal in young animals. It is characterized by excessive salivating and the presence of infected lesions in the gums around the teeth. For some reason the disease tends to spread further in young cattle than in older animals and an eventual result of the disease may be diarrhea. Left untreated, the animals may die.

Sulfa drugs or antibiotics are used in treatment. Good sanitation helps prevent and control calf diphtheria. Any affected animals should be separated from the herd.

Cancer Eye

Cancer eye is said to be the largest single cause of carcass condemnation in the United States. Cancer cells create a tumor that grows and spreads within the eye. An electrothermal treatment has been developed by scientists at the Los Alamos Scientific Laboratory in cooperation with the University of New Mexico. The electrothermal unit is portable, allowing on-site treatment. Heat is applied to the tumor and kills the cancer cells via high-frequency radio waves similar to those used in a microwave oven.

Figure 4-8   Fescue foot usually affects only a portion of a herd grazing tall fescue. *(Courtesy of Dr. H. D. Anthony, Kansas State University)*

Fescue Foot

Cattle grazing a tall fescue pasture may develop a noninfectious disease known as fescue foot. The cause of the disease is not known and generally only 10 to 30 percent of a herd is affected. In most instances, outbreaks of the disease are nonrecurring, however some fescue fields do have a record of repeated infections. Basically it is believed that some animals within the herd are more susceptible than others.

Symptoms usually occur within 15 days of turning cattle into a new pasture. Older cattle display a slight arching of the back, a roughened hair coat, and soreness in one or both back legs. Frequently the left rear leg is the first to be affected. Yearlings generally shift from one foot to the other, or hold a foot off the ground, displaying soreness. In both young and older stock, symptoms are most noticeable early in the morning. As the disease progresses, mild swelling and reddening of the area between the dewclaws and hooves is shown. In the final stages of the disease, the animal may lose the fleshy portion of the leg midway between the hock and dewclaws, leaving only the long bone intact. Feed intake is reduced and the animal becomes emaciated.

To control the disease, affected animals should be taken off fescue pastures at the first sign of lameness. A veterinarian should be consulted to distinguish the disease from other conditions producing similar symptoms. Animals showing signs of permanent injury should be slaughtered.

Research suggests that a fungus may play a role in the development of fescue foot. No definitive findings have been made, however.

Researchers have learned that a pasture using a mixture of fescue and legumes will give less trouble than tall fescue alone. Fescue stockpiled after July 1 appears to be less toxic than fescue accumulated for the season. Additionally, research indicates that heavy nitrogen applications for fertilizer tend to increase the chances of fescue foot.

Recommended management techniques include observation of cattle in early morning for the first few weeks on a new pasture and during cold weather. Temperatures below 60° F seem conducive to the onset of the disease.

Foot-and-Mouth Disease

Nearly every country in the world has instituted strict quarantine regulations to combat this highly contagious disease. In the mid-1940's, an outbreak of foot-and-mouth disease occurred in Mexico and resulted in a treaty between the United States, Canada, and Mexico setting up a permanent quarantine against cattle coming into any of these countries from Europe or elsewhere where the disease was known to exist. Although there have been no outbreaks in the United States since 1929, strict quarantine requirements continue in an effort to prevent the disease from entering this country again.

Water blisters in the mouth and between claws on the hooves characterize early stages of the disease. Few deaths are attributed to the disease, but foot-and-mouth disease has no cure. Some European countries vaccinate for the disease, but quarantine to locate infected animals is the primary method of prevention in the United States.

Foot Rot

Dairy farmers and feedlot operators generally see the majority of cases of foot rot. The disease appears when cattle must be maintained in wet or muddy areas. Soft tissue of the foot swells and reddens, then other parts of the foot break open. The animal becomes uncomfortable and may go lame. The cause of the condition is *Fusiformis necrophorus,* a soil organism. Scientists still are uncertain about how an animal becomes infected in the first place. It is not believed to be contagious and can be controlled with disinfectants and proper care of the infected feet.

Professional treatment might involve use of sulfonamide or antibiotics along with cleaning and disinfecting the feet.

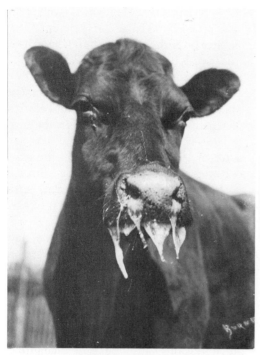

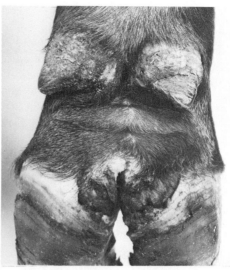

Figure 4-10   A soil organism causes foot rot. *(Courtesy of U.S. Department of Agriculture)*

Figure 4-9   Excessive salivation is a symptom of foot-and-mouth disease. *(Courtesy of U.S. Department of Agriculture)*

Goiter

Goiter in animals, like goiter in man, is an enlargement of the thyroid gland brought on by a deficiency of iodine. There are two types of goiter in cattle—nodular and diffuse. The diffuse type is by far the more common. In both types, when the animal does not receive enough iodine in its diet, the thyroid gland in the neck swells in an attempt to make up for the lack of iodine by manufacturing the body's own thyroid-stimulating hormone from the pituitary gland. When the supply of iodine to the body is adequate, the thyroid gland is able to produce the hormone thyroxine in an adequate quantity. When the iodine supply declines below necessary levels, the body compensates for the deficiency by manufacturing its own thyroxine from the pituitary gland. However, in order to accomplish this, the amount of tissue in the neck must be increased. The result is goiter. If an iodine deficiency is caught in time, the size of the goiter may be reduced. However, where the goiter has progressed to a large size, nothing can be done to reduce its size. In adult animals though, no extensive problems are caused by the presence of the goiter. It is most hazardous in terms of nutritional deficiencies to newborn calves. For this reason, great care should be taken to provide adequate nutrition for pregnant cows. Feeding iodized salt is a good preventive.

Grass Tetany

A shortage of magnesium in the blood causes grass tetany, also known as winter tetany, wheat poisoning, magnesium tetany, grass staggers, and hypomagnesemia. Most cases occur in cattle grazing lush spring pastures. Temperature and weather conditions appear to play a role in the development of the disease also. Cloudy, windy, rainy weather with temperatures during the day in the 40° to 60° F range seem to be most likely to contribute to the problem.

An additional contributing factor to a lack of magnesium in the grass is the application of potassium and nitrogen to the grass pastures. Studies have found that waiting to graze pastures that have been so treated until temperatures rise consistently above 60° F increases the amount of magnesium present in the grass.

Cool-season grasses such as fescue, orchardgrass, timothy, brome, and bluegrass contain such low levels of magnesium early in the growing season that animals consuming them would not get enough magnesium to meet their needs.

The cereal grains, wheat, rye, and oats, should be used for grazing with care since they are most prone to causing grass tetany of any forage crop.

Symptoms of grass tetany are unreliable since the same symptoms can indicate other problems as well. However, some animals may become excitable, twitch, stare wildly, and even appear to be blind. The animal may stagger and go down. In some cases the first symptom is finding a dead cow. Most frequently affected is a cow over the age of 6 which is nursing a young calf.

Quick treatment of a downed animal is imperative since an animal down for more than 13 to 24 hours may suffer muscle damage. In these cases recovery chances are slim. Generally treatment consists of an injection of magnesium sulfate (epsom salts) under the skin. Additionally, once an animal has been affected, it is more susceptible to recurrences than an animal that has never been stricken. Animals prone to the disease need magnesium supplements to maintain health.

To prevent grass tetany, where conditions are dangerous, producers should provide a magnesium supplement, making sure that each animal eats some of the supplement each day. Adding dolomitic limestone to soil low in magnesium helps to increase the level of that mineral in the grass grown in the pasture. Some state extension services recommend spraying magnesium on the pastures, treating the grass so that it may immediately be grazed, even by high-risk animals.

Crops high in magnesium include legumes or legume-grass mixtures. Additionally, red clover, ladino, and alfalfa contain high magnesium levels.

Hardware Disease

When cattle eat foreign objects such as wire, screws, or nails they may develop a disorder known as hardware disease, also called traumatic gastritis and traumatic reticulitis. Problems come about when foreign matter gets into cattle feed, or when objects are in the pasture among the grasses. Cattle eat too quickly to discriminate between feed and foreign objects that may cause them health problems. When these objects pierce the stomach wall and gain access to the heart, hardware disease results. Muscle contractions, especially abdominal movements during calving, can cause the movement of the object into the heart. Symptoms of hardware disease include a decreased appetite, depression, and reluctance to move. Additionally, cattle may show signs of indigestion and pain when defecating.

Bloat may also occur. In cases where the heart has been perforated, fluid accumulates around the heart and that infection causes abnormal heart sounds. The brisket may appear extremely flabby due to the large amount of accumulated fluid. An examination by a veterinarian with a stethoscope may spot the abnormal heart sounds. Symptoms may decrease or even disappear within a week. However, they may recur shortly.

Prevention of hardware disease is the best treatment. Keeping pastures clean and free of deteriorating fencing and machinery goes a long way toward prevention. Close monitoring of feed and good sanitation in feed processing helps. Some cattle producers administer magnets to their cattle with a stomach tube or balling gun. The magnet attracts any metal objects that might pierce the animal, and holds them together, decreasing the chance of their piercing the reticulum and gaining access to the heart.

Treatment generally consists of three options. The first prescribes elevating the forelegs 6 to 8 inches through use of a platform to halt any progressive forward movement of the hardware. With this method the limbs must be kept elevated for from 10 to 20 days. Generally the veterinarian prescribes antibiotics to stop the spread of infection. A second method is a surgical solution—a rumenotomy. If an animal has hardware disease and is not particularly valuable—neither a breeding animal or a dairy cow—the veterinarian may suggest slaughter.

From 55 to 75 percent of the cattle slaughtered in the eastern United States have been found, according to the University of Missouri, to have hardware in the reticulum. In these animals, however, no damage to or perforations of the reticulum were evident.

Infectious Bovine Rhinotracheitis (IBR)

Infectious bovine rhinotracheitis in its most severe form can cause abortions in pregnant cows. In its mildest form the disease causes high fever, drooling, a nasal discharge, breathing difficulties, and severe inflammation of the upper respiratory passages and trachea. In cows, severe vaginitis can develop. The disease is classified as a viral disease, characterized by its quick onset. Highly contagious, it can infect an entire herd in a relatively short time.

Vaccinations have proven effective against IBR. Animals should be vaccinated annually. Cows should be vaccinated at least 30 days prior to breeding so that the vaccine will not harm the fetus.

Johne's Disease

When a relatively young animal develops severe diarrhea and begins to look emaciated, Johne's disease may be the cause. From what has been learned so far about the disease, 6-month-old calves are most likely to contract this fatal and incurable disease that will bring about their deaths at about 2 years of age. Johne's disease is a member of a group of diseases that includes leprosy in humans. Like its cousin leprosy, Johne's disease is characterized by lesions. In this case the lesions appear in the intestines of the infected animals. However, severity of the lesions appears to be nonindicative of the severity of the animal's diarrhea or to its eventual wasting. No treatment or cure is known. The disease usually is fatal.

Figure 4-11   Johne's disease involves a gradual loss of condition. *(Courtesy of U.S. Department of Agriculture)*

Figure 4-12 Abortion is a frequent result of leptospirosis. *(Courtesy of U.S. Department of Agriculture)*

Leptospirosis

Leptospirosis causes reproductive problems by producing abortions in pregnant cows. The disease is one of several venereal diseases of cattle. Leptospirosis can be spread in two ways. First, when an animal drinks from a stagnant pond or puddle, it may ingest the *Lepto* microorganism deposited in the water through the urine of another infected animal. Second, an infected animal can infect another when breeding. The disease can even be transmitted by artificial insemination. For this reason, the cattle producer should be certain to buy semen from a reputable AI stud who maintains high standards of health and cleanliness.

Animals infected with leptospirosis exhibit a decreased appetite, a high fever, are anemic, and have blood in their urine. Milk may be tinged with blood. Pregnant cows, in most cases, will abort the fetus. Lactating cows may contract mastitis as a result of the venereal disease.

Vaccinations have proven effective against leptospirosis. Generally vaccination is recommended every 8 to 12 months. Sick animals should be isolated.

Listeriosis

Listeriosis also is known as circling disease because affected animals tend to walk in circles and make unusual movements. Believed to be caused by a bacterial infection, the most common source of the bacteria appears to be moldy or spoiled silage.

Affected animals should be isolated and handled only with care because people can contract the disease also.

Lumpy Jaw

When an animal eats coarse vegetation such as branches, or ingests wire or some other harsh material, it may damage its gums or mouth and allow the entry of an infection by an organism called *Actinomyces bovis*, which will attack the bones of the jaw and the nose and perhaps the soft tissue of the mouth and throat. In advanced cases the bone can become grossly enlarged and the teeth may be lost.

Sometimes lumpy jaw, also known as actinomycosis, responds to treatment with antibiotics prescribed by a veterinarian.

Malignant Edema

A wound contaminated during common management procedures like castration, tail docking, and vaccinations as well as accidental wounds, contributes to the spread of malignant edema, which is caused by the bacterium *Clostridium septicum* and is also known as gas gangrene.

First signs of the disease appear as severe swelling around the infected area. Infected animals will show an elevated temperature. Local lesions are soft swellings that pit when pressed. Lesions spread quickly and result in blackened muscles, resembling blackleg.

Results of treatment are similar to those with blackleg, basically disappointing. A vaccination program is considered most effective by preventing the disease before it strikes. The vaccination used should protect against both blackleg and malignant edema.

Mastitis

To realize the highest possible profit, the cattle producer must maximize the productive life span of each producing animal. Mastitis represents one-third of all losses due to cattle diseases each year in the United States. Mastitis lowers milk quality, cuts production, and decreases the productive life span of the cow. For these reasons, dairy farmers in particular have launched all-out campaigns to rid their herds of this menace.

Research shows that nearly 85 percent of mastitis cases result from mismanagement and improper milking machine action. Udder irritation can have numerous causes, but poor milking practices and improper machines are instrumental.

Four major classifications of organisms can cause mastitis to develop. Most of the germs are always present around the barn and cause infection only when the udder is injured, irritated, or placed under stress.

Mastitis itself is an inflammation of the udder. Its severity ranges from no obvious symptoms to severe infections. When milk from one or more quarters of the udder changes visibly, the animal has clinical mastitis. Active mastitis causes the cow to produce either watery or thick, ropy milk. At this stage the veterinarian can diagnose the disease by palpating the udder or by examining the milk. Arresting the disease before it progresses to the active stage can save money in lost profits from milk sales and prolong the active life of the cow.

To detect so-called "invisible mastitis" several paddle tests have been developed. One highly recommended test for detecting mastitis is the CMT (California Mastitis Test).* The test requires a four-compartment paddle CMT reagent and performance of the following steps:

1. Draw milk from each quarter into separate cups of paddle. Tilt paddle so that milk quantities are equal at about ½ teaspoon each.
2. Add an equal amount—½ teaspoon—of test reagent.
3. Rotate paddle to mix and observe changes in color and gel formation within 10 to 15 seconds.

After performing these steps, watch for the following results:

1. Milk from a normal quarter remains liquid and flows freely.
2. Moderate reaction is indicated when the gel that forms is fragile and breaks into small masses or clumps.
3. A strong reaction is shown by samples forming a gelatinous mass that clings together and is not broken when the paddle is rotated.
4. Milk from badly affected quarters causes a deepening of the purple color of the milk-reagent mix.

A positive test calls for further examination by a veterinarian.

---

* Data on procedures of the California Mastitis Test from "Detecting Mastitis on the Farm," by Robert T. Marshall and J. E. Edmondson, University of Missouri.

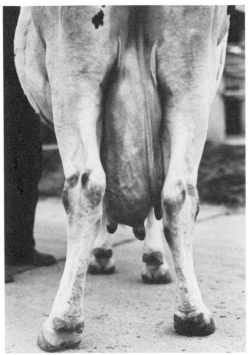

Figure 4-13 Mastitis causes a hot, very hard udder that produces lumpy milk, which is sometimes streaked with blood. *(Courtesy of U.S. Department of Agriculture)*

Individual veterinarians may prefer other tests, and can advise the producer on use and interpretation of the different testing methods. The advantages of the tests include their economy, their simplicity, and their reliability. A monthly test is advisable.

When mastitis is detected by the tests, further examination of the milk must be made to determine the type of organism causing the mastitis. Finally, sensitivity tests are done to determine which antibiotic will control the specific organism.

Treating the dry cow with antibiotics is a common practice.

Prevention of mastitis can save money, time, and effort. Proper management can reduce the chance of mastitis. First, before milking, the cow should have her udder washed and massaged with individual towels and warm water containing a sanitizing solution. If a pressure hose is not available, a bucket and water with individual towels—these can be paper—for each cow should be used.

The next step, and a very important one, is to milk out two streams of milk in a strip cup. This should be done from each quarter to check for mastitis. This step not only is an aid to the analysis of abnormal milk, but also helps in the let-down process for the cow. After about 1 minute following preparation, the milker unit should be applied. Waiting too long causes the cow to lose much of the let-down stimulation, so the milker should be applied promptly.

Cows vary, but most will milk out in 3 to 5 minutes. Machines kept on the udder after milk stops flowing will injure delicate tissues. To determine when milking is complete, each quarter should be felt by hand. Then the teat cups must be removed immediately.

A nonirritating sanitizer should be used after each milking to prevent mastitis. The extension service at the University of Missouri, Columbia, recommends a solution made from 1 gallon of clorox bleach and 1 quart of water, or a product called chlorohexidine.

Finally, it is important to keep the milking on a regular schedule. For instance, if the herd is milked at 6:30 A.M. and 5 P.M. each day, cows will produce better if the strict schedule is kept every day.

Milk Fever

Generally, milk fever is a term used to refer to a group of disorders that share a marked and sudden calcium deficiency. The problem in a cow occurs after calving when her body suddenly needs to provide a great quantity of milk to feed her calf and her own calcium reserves are not adequately mobilized to fulfill sudden demands from her offspring. Calcium injections are generally helpful as a cure. Sometimes it is difficult to prevent milk fever since an animal's need for calcium may be higher than normal and the producer may not be aware of any abnormal need for the element until the problem has occurred. Providing high levels of Vitamin D (which increases absorption of calcium) may prevent some cases, but some individuals are more likely to have milk fever than others.

Parainfluenza-3 (PI₃)

A flu-like disease apparently brought on by stress associated with shipping, parainfluenza-3 is a mild disease in itself but causes economic losses in feedlots because of the time required for animals to recover from its effects and resume full feed intake.

PI-3 symptoms include a slight fever, depression, soft cough, and nasal discharge. Symptoms last only one or two days. Unfortunately, the viral agent injures the animal's respiratory tissues and allows the entrance of bacteria. It is this bacteria, combined with the virus and stress associated with shipping, which produces pneumonia and so-called shipping fever, a cause of many losses of feedlot cattle. Deaths from PI-3 itself are uncommon.

Pinkeye

Hot summer weather usually brings a recurrence of pinkeye (also known as infectious conjunctivitis and infectious keratitis) problems for cattle producers, probably because of increased intensity of the sun, combined with such triggering agents as face flies, dust, and weed pollens. With the common bacterial form of pinkeye, eyes water and eyelids become red and swell. In severe cases, cattle may become blind. Pinkeye reduces performance of cattle and therefore warrants treatment by a veterinarian.

Contrary to some reports, vitamin A does not seem to prevent pinkeye, but does increase resistance to the disease. Vaccines for controlling pinkeye have not been successful either. Topical treatments such as sprays and powders usually produce inconsistent results. Placing the animal in a dark barn, or covering the affected eye with a patch has been an effective treatment. Controlling triggering agents such as flies, dust, and pollens also helps.

Cattle with dark pigment around the eyes tend to be more resistant to pinkeye than those animals with all-white or all-light-colored faces. Even very dark pigmented animals are not immune to the ailment, however.

Additionally, many animals diagnosed as having the common bacteria-caused pinkeye actually are suffering from IBR, the viral infection. A good health program includes vaccination for IBR and thus eliminates the chance of it cropping up in a herd.

Another alternative method for treatment of pinkeye is injection of a compound behind the eyeball. Pinkeye should not be confused with cancer eye.

Pneumonia

Pneumonia and various forms of the disease involving assorted complications, can be fatal to cattle. Normally the disease begins with a viral infection. Infected cattle wheeze, cough, vomit, and have a nasal discharge.

Shipping fever (hemorrhagic septicemia) is believed to be a form of pneumonia brought on by the stress of transit. Another form is gangrene of the lung, which is brought on by the penetration of a foreign body from the animal's reticulum and is a complication of pneumonia. A veterinarian should be consulted for specific treatment.

Generally, suggested treatment will consist of placing affected animals in a clean, quiet spot out of drafts. Feed that is easy to digest and highly nutritious should be given. The veterinarian may prescribe antibiotics and sulfonamides for most varieties of the disease.

Pseudorabies

Pseudorabies accounts for a great many deaths in hogs, but appears very rarely in cattle. Nevertheless, cattle producers must be aware of the symptoms of the virus, which vary with the stage of disease at the time of observation.

Sudden, unexplained death may be the first sign of trouble. The duration of the disease may be from 2 to 48 hours in cattle. If the animal lingers, pruritis (itching) becomes intense to the point of self-mutilation. After that, the animal will lick the infected area, which usually is located in the flank or hind leg, but can appear anywhere on the animal. Paralysis of the throat, bellowing, and convulsions will follow, with death occurring shortly thereafter.

The incubation period is believed to be 4 to 7 days, but may be longer. Transmission usually comes from rats moving from one farm to another. No direct transfer among bovines has been noted. Hogs are considered to be involved in transmission incidentally through breaks in the skin. No effective vaccine has yet been developed. Control consists of eliminating rodents and separating cattle and hogs.

Rabies

Of all farm animals, those most frequently affected by rabies are cattle. Symptoms of the disease in cattle include knuckling of the hind dewclaw, wobbling of the hindquarters, bellowing, yawning, drooling of saliva, and inability to swallow. Although symptoms seldom are constant, cattle also may appear to have foreign objects in their throats. It is during this period that exposure to humans is most likely to occur. Examination of the mouth and throat by untrained persons usually results in an exposure to the disease from infected saliva on the hands and arms.

The incubation period for rabies varies, ranging from 2 weeks to several months. The size and location of the wound generally determines the incubation period. Head and neck wounds have a shorter incubation period than wounds of the extremities.

Despite the fact that rabies is one of the oldest diseases known to man, little progress has been made toward its elimination. Knowledge of the disease and control through vaccinations has improved, but because of its continuing presence in the wild animal population, rabies represents a constant threat. Incidence of rabies cases rises in the spring and in the fall, but the disease is present all year round. Most authorities agree that the main reservoir of rabies infection in the United States rests with the wild animal population, primarily skunks.

Rabid animals transmit the disease to other animals and to humans. Infection from the diseased animal to a healthy one occurs when infected saliva contacts broken skin or abrasions. Experimental findings indicate that the virus may be airborne and that actual contact is not necessary for infection; however, airborne infections do not represent an important mode of transmission. Prevention of rabies consists of vaccination of all pet animals; control of stray dogs and cats; reduction of the wildlife reservoir population (not complete destruction); and education of the public in regard to rabies control. The use of vaccine for cattle, because of the expense, has not been justified except in areas of very high rabies concentration.

A recent experiment in a western state utilized an oral vaccine mixed with bait to effectively vaccinate wild populations of skunks, etc., around populated areas to help reduce the incidence of rabies. More programs like this can be expected in the future to help control this disease.

Red Water Disease

Cattle with bloody urine and bloody feces accompanied by fever and rapid breathing may be suffering from red water disease (bacillary hemoglobinuria). The disease is caused by a bacterium, *Clostridium homolyticum,* and can be associated with damage done by an internal parasite, the liver fluke.

The red color of urine is caused by the presence of hemoglobin in the urine, resulting from destruction of red blood cells by the parasites.

Liver fluke eggs require water to hatch and use snails as intermediate hosts. Therefore, a good preventive is to destroy snails by draining stagnant water in ponds and swampy pastures where possible. In areas of heavy infestation, vaccines may be necessary.

The disease primarily occurs during the warm months and is nearly always fatal to the animal.

Rickets

Rickets is a noninfectious disease with a nutritional basis, caused by a lack of adequate calcium and vitamin D or by a phosphorous deficiency. Rickets is more common in areas where calves are not allowed out in the sun.

Affected calves develop enlarged knee and hock joints due to the failure of their growing bones to harden properly.

In some cases dramatic improvement results when adequate levels of calcium, vitamin D, and phosphorus are supplied.

Ringworm

When cattle develop round, scaly spots on their skin, losing the hair in the affected areas, ringworm may be the cause. Ringworm is a contagious disease most generally found in cattle during the winter. Ringworm tends to attack around the head and neck or at the root of the tail. The spots itch and cause the animal discomfort.

Anti-ringworm compounds are available from veterinarians to ease the discomfort of the animal. Otherwise, a good home remedy is to remove the scabs using soap and water and then follow up by painting the wounds with tincture of iodine.

Because the disease is contagious, infected animals should be isolated from healthy ones.

Shipping Fever Complex

Animals subjected to the stress involved in being transported for long periods of time, moved to a new environment, fed new and different feed, or otherwise stressed may develop shipping fever (hemorrhagic septicemia). The

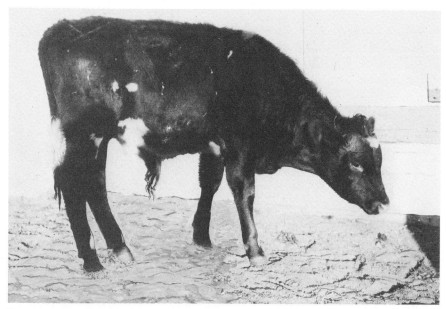

Figure 4-14 Stressed calves are targets for shipping fever. *(Courtesy of U.S. Department of Agriculture)*

disease involves high fever, discharges from the nose and eyes and a hacking cough. A virus, bacteria, and stress bring it on.

Shipping fever lasts about a week, or even less, but death losses may be high, particularly in young animals. Untreated animals may recover in some cases.

Preventive measures are recommended. Isolating newly purchased animals for at least 2 weeks prior to placing with the herd helps prevent the disease. Additionally, a fortified diet with increased amounts of vitamin A and a good mineral mix may help.

Sudden Death Syndrome (SDS)

Bovine sudden death syndrome is a fatal disease of unknown origin, chiefly affecting healthy feedlot cattle that have been on high-energy grain rations for more than 100 days. Affected animals stop eating, step back and die with no other clinical sign. Although not much is known about the disease, research currently is focusing on the role of rumen bacterial endotoxins. It is known that rumen bacteria produce endotoxins. In grain-fed cattle, a higher concentration of endotoxins has been found. It is believed that the sudden release of large quantities of endotoxin in the rumen may, in normal cattle, be absorbed and detoxified in the liver or passed on to the abomasum and

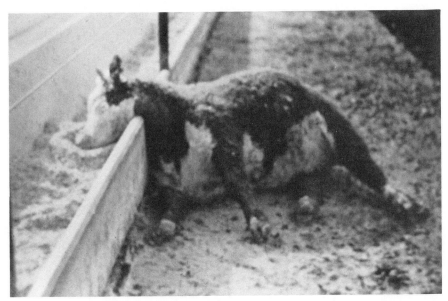

Figure 4-15   Feedlot cattle who have been eating high-energy rations may stop eating, step back and drop dead from sudden death syndrome. *(Courtesy Dr. H. D. Anthony, Kansas State University)*

small intestine where it may be inactivated by acid or enzymes or absorbed into the portal blood. In cases where the rumen lining is inflamed or damaged, however, it is believed that the same sudden release of large quantities of endotoxin in the rumen, which is harmless to some cattle, might be rapidly absorbed by a damaged rumen lining, producing endotoxic shock and sudden death of cattle.

Research continues and no preventives are available.

Tetanus

Tetanus (lockjaw) most often occurs in horses and in humans, but is seen occasionally in cattle. When an animal is wounded, a bacterium, *Clostridium tetani*, releases a toxin into the system of the animal, causing tetanus to develop. Animals with tetanus exhibit stiffness in their necks and heads. Chewing becomes a chore. Most cases result in death.

Trichomoniasis

Another veneral disease, trichomoniasis is similar to vibriosis in that symptoms of the disease may not become apparent until a fetus is aborted. Trichomoniasis also produces a slight infection in the uterus of the cow,

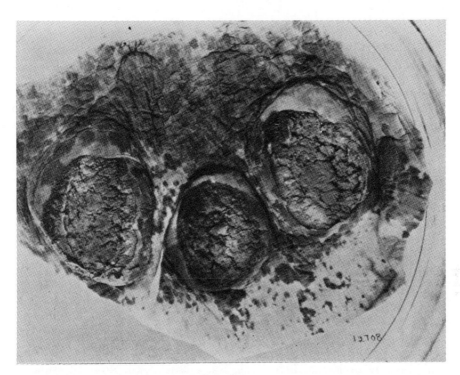

Figure 4-16 This portion of the fetal membranes, showing cotyledons, is diseased as a result of infection with an abortion organism such as trichomoniasis or vibriosis. *(Courtesy of U.S. Department of Agriculture)*

causing temporary infertility. Cows will fail to conceive, and if already pregnant may abort in the first trimester of pregnancy. No vaccine has been developed to prevent the disease. Generally the preferred treatment consists of use of broad-spectrum antibiotics and culling of bulls that are carriers.

Tuberculosis (TB)

Animals who lose weight and condition, whose joints swell, and who develop a chronic cough may be suffering from tuberculosis. On the other hand, animals may have the disease and not show any symptoms at all. In severe cases, cows may develop swollen, infected udders. There is no effective and practical method of treatment. Periodic testing for TB and removal of animals that react positively to the test is the most effective control measure.

In cattle, TB normally attacks the lungs and lymph nodes of the animal.

Good sanitation and rotation of pastures may also help in controlling the disease.

Vibriosis

When cows require several services before conceiving, vibriosis may be the cause. With this venereal disease some animals do not show any signs of sickness at all. The disease produces an infection of the uterus in cows, causing temporary infertility. In pregnant cows, vibriosis may cause an abortion. A vaccine is available to combat the disease and should be given annually to females at least 30 days prior to breeding in order to prevent damage to the fetus.

Warts

Those unsightly growths on the skin that plague both animals and humans are caused, not by touching a toad, but by a virus. In cattle, warts vary in size from very tiny to huge growths. Because warts are caused by an infectious virus, cattle with warts should be isolated from normal cattle to prevent infection of other members of the herd. Disinfectants may be used on pens, chutes, and rubbing posts to prevent spread of the virus.

Although the presence of warts does not seem to affect cattle health, the hide is damaged by their presence.

Large warts should be removed only by a veterinarian. Small warts however can be cut off with sterile scissors. The area should then be painted with tincture of iodine. Left alone, warts usually will drop off within 6 months.

EXTERNAL PARASITES

Probably the one most common menace to efficient cattle management is that of external parasites such as insects, ticks, and mites. Each year parasites may cause more losses than all infectious diseases combined. Since losses are rarely fatal, they often are only partially realized since losses from irritation, annoyance, and nutritional competition are more difficult to assess.

Generally parasites cause stunted growth, decreased production of milk, loss of edible meat, and damage to hides. Animals afflicted with parasites rarely eat properly and as a result gain poorly. Feed consumed cannot be fully utilized by the animals because parasites get their due first.

Additionally, many diseases are transmitted by parasites. Certain insects and ticks can transmit anaplasmosis, babesiasis (see page 219) and anthrax. Flies are a triggering agent for pinkeye.

Animals affected by parasites have a lower resistance to disease and lose much of their natural immunity to disease organisms, becoming more susceptible to infectious diseases.

Ideally, control of parasites would mean simply eliminating them entirely by chemical or other means. Unfortunately, eradication of parasites

Figure 4-17 Female cattle ticks in several stages of engorgement. *(Courtesy of Texas Agricultural Extension Service)*

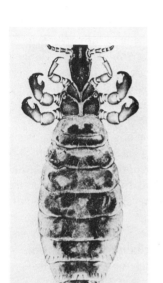

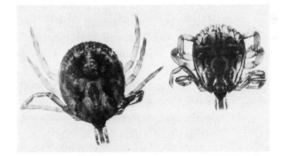

Figure 4-18 The long-nosed cattle louse. *(Courtesy of Texas Agricultural Extension Service)*

Figure 4-19 The cayenne tick—on the left, a male, and on the right, an unengorged female. *(Courtesy of Texas Agricultural Extension Service)*

is an expensive proposition. Some pests, such as the U.S. cattle tick, have been chemically eradicated. Others, such as the screwworm, have been virtually eliminated with a sterile male technique. Research continues to work on the problem of cattle parasites. In the meantime, however, the cattle producer must make use of sanitation and good herd management practices to control those pests still with us.

Ticks cause expensive economic losses each year. Heavy tick infestations cause "tick worry," manifested by a loss of condition, failure to gain properly, and a severe degree of anemia. The anemia probably results from blood removed by attached ticks. Under extremely heavy infestations, the animal becomes dull, listless, and dies. Tick bites are irritating and cause the infested animal to rub and scratch, resulting in a scabby skin condition, sometimes followed by a secondary infection. Hides of heavily infested animals are considerably reduced in value.

Lice, both bloodsucking and biting varieties, attack cattle. Sucking lice pierce the animal's skin and draw blood. Biting lice have chewing mouthparts and feed on particles of hair, scales, scab, and skin exudations. The development of both types is similar. They attach eggs (nits) to hairs and the young lice (nymphs) appear about 1 to 3 weeks later. Nymphs molt once or more before attaining adulthood. The number of molts and developmental time vary among species and according to season, humidity and other conditions. Both types begin to increase on cattle in the fall and reach a population peak in late winter or early spring. During late spring or early summer, populations decline. Lice usually cannot survive long at temperatures above 100° F. Summer skin surface temperatures may exceed 125° F. The adverse summer and fall season probably is spent in the egg stage or as adults in some protected area on the host. One species has been noted to infest the inside of the ear during the hotter seasons.

Scabies in cattle, commonly known as scab, mange, or itch, is a contagious skin disease caused by parasitic mites living on or in the skin. The four species affecting cattle are: *Psoroptes, Sarcoptes, Chorioptes,* and *Demodex*. Mites are related to ticks, spiders, and scorpions since the adults possess four pairs of legs. They resemble ticks more closely than spiders or scorpions. Mites vary in size and structure, but most species are very small. Annual loss to the American cattle industry for these four species was estimated at more than $4 million in 1964, not including money spent for control measures. Mites also transmit diseases such as scrub typhus and others to humans and animals.

Scabies is a perpetual hazard, especially with fall cattle, because that is the time when the mite is relatively inactive. As cold weather develops, the mites become more active and cause intensive itching. Often this is the first indication that purchasers of new cattle have that they have a scabies problem. The safest procedure is to dip incoming cattle for the scabies mite upon arrival.

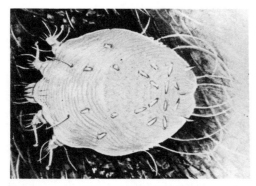

Figure 4-20 The sarcoptic mange mite. *(Courtesy of Texas Agricultural Extension Service)*

Figure 4-21 Screwworm flies—left, a male, and right, a female. *(Courtesy of Texas Agricultural Extension Service)*

Scabies must be handled by quarantine and requires stringent dipping and observation. It is against the law to move cattle under quarantine and up to the producer to report a scabies outbreak to the local veterinarian. The veterinarian must in turn report the outbreak to U.S. Department of Agriculture regulatory officials.

If scabies is suspected in a herd, a sample scraping can be taken for analysis.

The common cattle grub is the larval stage of the heel fly, *Hypoderma lineatum.* Although it occurs in all states except Alaska, it is most prevalent north of Texas. Cattle are the only important hosts of the common cattle grub. The preferred hosts appear to be yearlings, calves, and older animals in that order. Some authorities believe that cattle grubs cost the livestock industry $100 million to $300 million per year in the United States. "Gadding," the characteristic reaction of cattle fleeing fly activity, results in loss of flesh and reduced milk production since the animals are unable to graze normally. The migration and parasitism of the grubs within the animal's body cause irritation and nutritional losses. Damage to the carcass and to the hide lowers postslaughter value.

Losses due to the habits of flies and mosquitoes are important to the cattle producer since the pests cause pain and annoyance and interfere with feeding, resting, and other normal activities. Cattle lose weight, yield less milk, develop indigestion, and may suffer other disorders.

The screwworm fly has, for the most part, been controlled in much of the United States. Seasonal influxes bring the screwworm back into the country from northern Mexico. The screwworm fly is bluish-green, about twice as large as a house fly, and has three black stripes on its back between its wings, and a reddish-yellow head. The maggots are pink when they have completed feeding and are ready to leave the wound. Screwworms have been causing a lot of trouble recently.

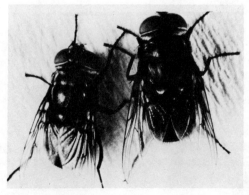

Figure 4-22 Screwworm flies—left, a male, and right, a female. *(Courtesy of Texas Agricultural Extension Service)*

To control external parasites such as lice, ticks, and grubs, there are a number of commercial products available that do an excellent job when used properly. The most effective for lice is probably dipping. However, if this does not fit in with a particular ranch management program, there are alternative methods that may be used. Spraying, pour-ons, feed additives, foggers, oilers, and dust bags also are effective when used properly. Some methods take several weeks to control the problem. Grub control usually is not difficult and, again, there are good products available. Injectable grub control may be available soon. If grub control is not necessary, cheaper products are available for lice. Table 4-B lists common external parasites of cattle.

Figure 4-23 The most effective control for lice is dipping. *(Courtesy of U.S. Department of Agriculture)*

TABLE 4-B. EXTERNAL CATTLE PARASITES

TICKS

Variety	Description	History/Habits	Damage
Lone-Star tick (*Amblyomma americanum*)	Female has one white spot on posterior of scutum; males several white spots on scutum	Three-host tick. Each parasitic stage leaves the host after blood meal and molts to next stage, or if an adult, deposits eggs on ground, or in secluded place. Larva engorges on first host, drops off and molts. The nymph seeks second host, engorges, drops off and molts. The adult engorges on third host, mates and drops off to deposit eggs.	Mouthparts cause deep, irritating wounds. Animals may become anemic from loss of blood. Transmit human diseases such as Rocky Mountain spotted fever.
Gulf Coast tick (*Amblyomma maculatum*)	Narrower in outline and more elongate than the Lone Star tick when viewed from above. Base color of both sexes is chestnut brown. Females—extensive markings on scutum; males—irregular, connected, longitudinal yellowish white lines.	Three-host tick. Usually over-winters in larval or nymphal stage. Eggs, larvae, nymphs, and adults susceptible to drying up, a factor that limits their distribution to coastal areas of high humidity, temperature, and rainfall.	Attacks head and ears. Usually attaches itself to inside the outer ear. Mouthparts produce deep, irritating wounds causing animals to rub the head and ears. Bites cause severe inflammation, swelling, cracking, and scabbing.

TABLE 4-B. (cont.)

TICKS, continued

Variety	Description	History/Habits	Damage
Winter tick (*Dermacentor albipictus*) (*D. nigrolineatus*)	Scutum has extensive white markings or is mostly white streaked with brown. Reduced or no markings on the scutum. Mouthparts on both are short and blocky.	One-host tick. Attaches itself to a host as the larva and remains on the same host to molt from the larval to the nymphal to the adult stage. The adult female leaves the host after engorgement and fertilization to deposit eggs.	Damage not as extensive as with some other pests since the total parasitic period for time spent on the host usually is 5 to 7 weeks, but may be up to 18 weeks.
Ear tick (*Otobius megnini*)	The "spinose" ear tick takes its name from the characteristic spines on the body of the nymphs. Adult bodies have no spines but have numerous pits on the upper and lower surface. The spinose second-stage nymph is the one usually observed.	Adults do not feed. Young larvae crawl on weeds, grass, or other objects to the host, then work their way up to the ears. They crawl to the inner folds of the outer ear and begin to suck blood. Upon completing engorgement, they molt to the nymphal stage in the ear.	Serious damage occurs when wounds become infected with pus-forming organisms that give rise to "canker ear" or, in serious cases, cause the animal to become deaf or even die. Not known to transmit diseases.
Black-legged tick (*Ixodes scapularis*)	Black legs.	Three-host tick. Life pattern similar to that of the Lone Star tick.	Can transmit diseases such as anaplasmosis.
American dog tick (*Dermacentor variabilis*)	Small, roundish body.	Three-host tick. Prefers high humidity. Dogs are preferred host, but will attack cattle. Life history similar to typical three-host life cycle but may require 1 to 3 years for completion.	Transmits several diseases to animals and humans. Can cause tick paralysis in young animals and children.

Variety	Description	History/Habits	Damage
Cayenne tick (*Amblyomma cajennense*)	Medium-sized tick with characteristic ornamentation on the scutum formed by reddish-brown stripes on a pale background.	Appears similar to Lone Star tick, although relatively little is known about this tick.	Attacks, cattle, humans, sheep, horses, and other animals.
Cattle tick (*Boophilus annulatus*)	Short mouthparts, no contrasting color patterns.	One-host tick. Strenuous control measures have eradicated it from the U.S. although it sometimes is reintroduced into southern Texas from Mexico.	Transmits babesiasis, or "Texas fever."
Southern cattle tick (*Boophilus microplus*)	Similar in appearance to above.		
LICE			
Cattle-biting louse (*Bovicola bovis*)	Reddish-brown, broad, blunt, flat head and yellowish-white abdomen with dark transverse bands. Small, varies in length from about 1/15 to 1/25 inch. Each of the six legs of both nymphs and adults terminates in a single claw.	During winter, biting lice group at the base of the tail, on the shoulders and along the backs of livestock. As infestations increase, the lice spread down the side and along the neck and may be found anywhere on the animal. During the summer they are mainly on the tail, head and inside the ears. This is the only biting louse that is parasitic on cattle in the United States.	With heavy infestations the skin of host animals may be raw and bleeding from the constant biting, scratching, and rubbing to relieve itching and irritation caused by the lice. When raw areas scab over they may resemble the lesions produced by scab mites.

TABLE 4-B. **(cont.)**

LICE, continued

Variety	Description	History/Habits	Damage
Short-nosed cattle louse (*Haematopinus eurysternus*)	Largest louse found on cattle. Females about 1/8 inch long and about half as wide, males slightly smaller. The head is about half as wide as the body, short and nearly as broad as long with a bluntly rounded front.	Principal breeding site in winter is the back of the neck. Secondary sites are sides of neck, dewlap, back, base of horns, and base of tail. In summer site is inside the ear near the tip, avoiding high temperatures resulting from direct sunlight.	Anemia. Loss of hair, raw skin, and bruised areas from animals rubbing and scratching against trees, fence posts, etc., to alleviate itching. (A sucking louse.)
Cattle tail louse (*Haematopinus quadripertusus*)	Resembles short-nosed cattle louse. The tail louse is larger and the head, thorax, and abdomen are dark brown.	Eggs deposited almost exclusively in the switch of the animal's tail. As the eggs hatch, the young nymphs migrate to soft-skinned areas of tail, head, and neck. Calves often heavily infested around the face as a result of sucking the dam through the rear legs and contacting the nymphs on the switch.	Facial infestations in young animals may be serious. Lice tend to feed on tender areas of the skin. (Sucking louse.)
Long-nosed cattle louse (*Linognathus vituli*)	Longer "nose" or rostrum than other lice, narrow body, giving it a slender appearance. Abdomen is bluish-black.	Occurs most often on younger animals and dairy breeds. Most common sites of infestation are dewlap and shoulders.	Same damage as short-nosed cattle louse. (Sucking louse.)
Little blue or capillate louse (*Solenopotes capillatus*)	Sometimes confused with long-nosed cattle louse but is smaller and more robust. Head short and broadly rounded. Smallest of sucking lice.	Usually clusters on the front part of the animal, especially the head and neck. Seldom survive longer than 2 or 3 days when removed from the host.	Same as from other species of sucking lice.

MANGE AND SCAB MITES

Variety	Description	History/Habits	Damage
Psoroptic (or) common scab mite (*Psoroptes equi, var. bovis*)	Small clear mites, 1/40 to 1/50 inch. Body is oval, with tapering mouthparts. Four pairs of legs rather long. First two pairs are close together and separated from third and fourth pairs which also are close together.	Most prevalent during fall, winter, and spring. Mites may spread to noninfested animals by direct contact. Rubbing objects used by infested animal also a source of contact. Complete entire life cycle on one host.	Common cattle scab can become serious if left untreated. Mites attack any part of the animal that is covered with thick hair. Mites cause itching, irritation, and cause animals to lick themselves and rub against objects for relief.
Sarcoptic mange mite (*Sarcoptes scabei, var. bovis*)	Smaller than common scab mites, with a round, rather than an oval body. Females about 1/50 inch and males about 1/60. Mouthparts are bluntly rounded and as broad as long.	Very susceptible to drying, cannot survive long periods off the host. Fertilized female burrows into upper layers of skin and deposits her eggs. Highest incidence in late fall and early spring.	Weight loss, increased death rate, functional disturbances. Milk production curtailed. Large areas of skin may be left bare from damage.
Chorioptic or symbiotic scab mite (*Chorioptes bovis*)	Oval body, slightly longer than wide. Mouthparts are rather short and blunt. More active than psoroptic mites.	Pasterns of the hind feet most important sites of infestation, though heavy infestations may spread all over the body.	Chorioptic scab, or "barn itch" milder than psoroptic scab, usually does not spread over entire body.
Demodectic or follicular mange mite (*Demodex bovis*)	Adults visible only with a microscope. Bodies are elongated and are separated into three divisions. Legs are three-segmented, short and stubby, and terminate in a pair of claws.	Live in hair follicles and glands of the skin. Can survive several days off the host in moist surroundings.	Lesions often not visible. Damage to hides. Most cases reported in old cows of dairy breeds.

TABLE 4-B. (cont.)

COMMON CATTLE GRUB

Variety	Description	History/Habits	Damage
Common cattle grub (Hypoderma lineatum)	Larval stage of the heel fly.	Common cattle grub adults usually attach their eggs to hairs on the udder, legs, belly or side. No pain is involved for the animal with this egg laying activity.	Animals run from flies and thus lose weight, and cannot graze in normal fashion. Warbles, holes made by the grubs in the skin, decrease value of the hide.

BLOOD-SUCKING FLIES

Variety	Description	History/Habits	Damage
Horn fly (Haemotobia irritans)	About half the size of the common house fly and about the same color. Piercing-sucking mouthparts.	Develop only in fresh droppings of cattle. Manure loses its attraction within 5 to 10 minutes after passing from the animal. Roost on bodies of cattle both day and night.	Serious pest. Causes pain, annoyance, loss of weight, indigestion, and other disorders.
Stable fly (Stomoxys calcitrans)	Brownish-gray with a greenish-yellow sheen, checked abdomen and piercing mouthparts.	Abundant during fall and summer. Outdoor, day-biting fly. Deposits eggs in manure or straw, or other debris.	Annoy animals and interfere with feeding activity. Flies usually attack on lower legs and cattle may stand in water to avoid them. Important in transmission of anthrax, infectious anemia, and anaplasmosis.

Tabanids (horse flies and deer flies)	Robust, measuring from ⅓ inch to 1½ inch for larger species. Various colors, usually gray, splattered with brown or black.	Eggs deposited in masses on vegetation growing in or over-hanging swampy areas, ponds, or sewerage areas.	These flies consume a great deal of blood from the host animal. Inflict a large, deep, and painful wound. Transmit diseases.
Black flies or buffalo gnats (Family Simulidae)	Small, 1/25 to 1/5 inch in length with varying colors of orange, brown, and black. Arched or humped prothorax, thus the name, buffalo gnats.	Eggs usually deposited in masses on some object in or near the edge of flowing water. Some species deposit eggs singly.	Vicious biters and serve as inter-mediate hosts for causal agents of diseases. Animals may start to die within 4 hours of an attack by large numbers. Death usually occurs as a result of acute toxemia caused by a vast number of bites or as result of anaphylactic shock.
Biting midges (Family Ceratopogonidae)	Small, 1/25 to 1/5 inch slender gnats, wings may be clear or spotted. No dense hairs or scales.	Larvae are small and wormlike. Females are the blood-suckers. When the outside temperature drops to 55° F., adult activity stops. Seldom bite in presence of even small air currents.	Transmits diseases.
Mosquitoes (Family Culicidae)	Small, two-winged flies with mouthparts produced into a long proboscis used for piercing and blood-sucking by females.	Require water to produce their young.	Painful bites. Transmit diseases, cause general unthriftiness.

TABLE 4-B.   (cont.)

BLOOD-SUCKING FLIES, continued

Variety	Description	History/Habits	Damage
Screwworm (*Cochliomyia hominivorax*)	The screwworm fly is bluish-green, about twice the size of the comon house fly, has three black stripes on the back between the wings and a reddish-yellow head.	Screwworms attack only when there is a wound or diseased body opening to attract the egg-laying female. Wounds from dehorning and castrating are frequent attractors for female screwworms. The sterile male technique has virtually eliminated the screwworm from the U.S. Farmer cooperation and the fact that the female usually mates only once have contributed to success.	Infestations in the eyes or nasal passages or following dehorning sometimes precede meningitis, killing the animal; around the navel of a newborn calf frequently result in peritonitis and death. Screwworms are flesh-eaters, cause anemia, weight loss, and alterations of body temperature.
House Fly (*Musca domestica*)	Small, black fly. Common everywhere.	Prefer to deposit eggs in animal manure. Larvae live only in moist masses of organic matter warm enough to promote their growth.	Annoy animals, causing nervousness, restlessness, reduced feed intake and efficiency. Carry human and animal disease organisms.

INTERNAL PARASITES

Because of the tremendous number of internal parasites, it is not uncommon for cattle to become infested with one or several types of worms or flukes. The life cycles of internal parasites lend themselves to ease of entrance into cattle hosts. Cattle grazing on pastures where infected cattle have voided their feces containing parasite eggs are ready targets for infestation.

Symptoms of infection by internal parasites include loss of weight and condition, anemia, diarrhea, and some damage in the area of infestation, and in some cases, render the meat unfit for human consumption.

Authorities disagree on exactly how much of an economic loss ranchers and dairy farmers suffer each year due to internal parasites, but all agree that the cost is high. For this reason, it behooves cattle producers to make an effort to control internal parasites as much as possible. The first step in control is determining which parasite is causing the problem. Next in cooperation with a veterinarian, plan a control program based on eliminating the pest at the least possible cost. Because new products are becoming available all the time, no specific products will be recommended for control. Parasites do become immune to any chemical after a while, so it is a good practice to rotate the chemicals used. Also, since so many parasites live in cattle feces, the rotation of pastures is an excellent practice where possible, based on the life cycle of the parasite involved. Table 4-C discusses some of the most common internal parasites of cattle. (*See* page 226.)

Another problem with allowing the presence of internal parasites in cattle is that damaged tissue may become the breeding ground for other disorders. For instance, the liver fluke damages and kills tissues of the liver. These damaged and dead tissues provide an ideal medium for the growth of *Clostridium novyi,* a bacteria. Other *Clostridium* varieties are responsible for such disorders as blackleg and malignant edema. Because of the tremendous potential for serious damage to the cattle, an infestation of internal parasites should be corrected as quickly and effectively as possible.

TABLE 4-C.   INTERNAL PARASITES

Parasite	Symptoms	Problems Involved with Eradication	Control
Coccidia	Diarrhea, bloody feces, weakness	Oocysts resist freezing and some disinfectants	Feed and water may become contaminated with protozoa that cause coccidiosis, parasitic disease.
Grubs (maggot stage of heel fly)	Infestations of grubs causes swelling in place of infestation and damages carcass	Eradication requires cooperation of all in a given area.	Sprays, dips, pour-ons may help.
Liver fluke	Reduction of meat & milk; lowered reproduction & resistance; livers made unsuitable for human consumption	Cattle become infected by eating forage-bearing cysts. Flukes feed on tissue rather than on blood.	Cattle final agents for the flukes, spreading eggs over the pastures by excreting them in feces. Snails used as intermediate hosts and require water to hatch.
Lungworms	Coughing; mucous discharge from nose and mouth	Can cause verminous pneumonia in young animals.	Prefer lush pastures with lots of moisture. Susceptible to cold weather.
Screwworms	Maggots grow in open wounds of cattle	Prefer warm areas of the country.	Sterile-male technique has been used effectively against the screwworm fly, but it still is a major pest.
Tapeworms	Diarrhea; weight loss; itching in anal area as tapeworms crawl from area	Cattle are intermediate hosts. Cattle become infected when they come in contact with human feces infested with the tapeworm.	Sludge from sewage plants used as fertilizer on pastures is a source of tapeworm eggs to cattle grazing those pastures.

Parasite			
Whipworms	Diarrhea	Not common in cattle, but feed on blood.	Whipworms prefer cold weather. Eggs hatch in the intestine after being swallowed. They develop without migration into the tissues.
Gapeworms	Swelling, pneumonia, hemorrhages	Damage lungs. Worms suck blood from mucus in the trachea.	
Genital tract worms	Abortion and sterility in cows, retained fetus	Introduced to females by natural service breeding with infected bulls.	Bulls remain parasitized permanently so must be removed from breeding for effective control.
Intestinal worms	Occur in small intestines of cattle. Cause anemia, diarrhea, loss of condition	Eggs excreted in cattle feces. Soil mites are intermediate hosts—crawl over pasture as cattle graze and eat eggs from cattle feces.	Grazing cattle swallow mites and thus continue the life cycle.
Stomach worms	Diarrhea, loss of condition, anemia	Barber pole stomach worms and Brown stomach worms are two types. The former is a voracious blood-sucker, the latter a parasite of the abomasum.	Drenching with phenothiazine may help.
Nodular worms	Causes bleeding, leakage of protein from the mucosa into the intestinal lumen, causing hypo-protein anemia	Infection occurs when cattle swallow forage infested with the larvae of these worms.	Rotating pastures may help in control.
Bile duct fluke Blood fluke Rumen fluke	Diarrhea, loss of condition	Flukes migrate to a specific area of the body, depending upon what type fluke they are.	Eggs voided with feces

STUDY QUESTIONS

1. A "protected" herd is one that has been _____. (vaccinated)
2. Newborn calves get _____ milk from their dams. (colostrum)
3. Sudden, unexpected deaths, with animals found with their feet up, blood effusing from body openings, suggest _____. (anthrax)
4. When cattle develop swelling and reddening of the area between the dewclaws and hooves, _____ can be suspected when cattle are grazing a tall fescue pasture. (fescue foot)
5. A deficiency of iodine brings on a condition known as _____. (goiter)
6. _____ manifests itself with signs of lumpy milk and swollen udders. (Mastitis)

5

Cattle Are What They Eat

To live and grow, cattle need food. Certain combinations of rations have proved more effective for various purposes than others. To keep the body functioning, an animal needs water, protein, carbohydrates, fats, minerals, and vitamins.

NUTRIENT NECESSITIES

After only a few days without *water*, cattle will die. Water comprises up to 80 percent of body weight in young cattle and allows cows to produce milk. Without adequate water a cow cannot consistently produce her maximum amount of milk. Water performs other functions in the body as well. It carries waste products through the system and even works with the blood to regulate temperature. When an animal fails to obtain adequate water it can become dehydrated and eventually die. Water should be provided at all times for cattle. Dairy cows, especially, need adequate water to produce at their best. Milk is 88 percent water. Without adequate water intake a cow never will produce at her potential.

Protein is needed by the body for use in muscle and other tissues. A deficiency of protein causes a sharp decline in production, slow growth, and a tendency for cows to fatten rather than produce milk.

Carbohydrates provide the energy necessary for life. Cattle fed a ration deficient in energy suffer a loss of weight, lowered production, slow growth, and other production-related problems.

Fats provide another source of energy for cattle. Fats are usually added to cattle feed to encourage the animals to eat the feed more readily and to increase the energy level.

Fat percentage in milk is closely related to the amount of crude fiber eaten by the cow. Chemically, crude fiber is the residue that remains after a feed sample is boiled in acid and alkali. It is commonly associated with the bulky or fill part of a diet and is the reason why high-producing animals sometimes cannot eat enough forage to meet their nutrient requirements.

Regardless of the fiber content of a ration, if the length of particles is short (less than ⅝ inch for forages) the percent fiber may be misleading. If cut extremely fine, the fat percentage of milk is reduced, and digestive problems may occur even if the ration has 20 to 25 percent crude fiber. Ground hay and recut silage are examples. Dairy farmers waste energy when they grind high-fiber materials into fine particles less than ⅝ inch and may cause the fat percentage of milk to drop.

A good way to select feeds is on the basis of cost per therm of energy. Also, the dairy farmer can use the effective fiber content of the ration to check against a fiber minimum (16 to 18 percent crude fiber) to prevent depressed fat tests and digestive upsets.

When using a high-fiber concentrate ration, it is a good idea to be sure it contains a readily digested fiber such as soybean hulls or corn cobs if an adequate supply is available.

Minerals are needed in varying concentrations for normal bodily functions. The necessary minerals are:

- *Calcium*—Builds strong bones. A deficiency of available calcium may cause milk fever, weak bones, and low blood calcium levels.
- *Phosphorus*—Builds strong bones and teeth, regulates enzyme activity, and helps maintain vital pressure balances between cells. Phosphorus is the only mineral known to affect significantly the eating quality of beef. A lack of phosphorus results in an increased need for vitamin D, a depraved appetite (chewing bones, wood, dirt, etc.), failure to show signs of heat, poor conception, lower production, loss of appetite, milk fever, and higher incidence of bloat.
- *Potassium*—Required for normal nutrition and is linked with calcium and phosphorus in bone-building processes. Affects feed efficiency by aiding rumen bacterial growth and proper cell pressure for nutrient utilization. Muscles and nerves need potassium for proper maintenance. Lack of potassium results in loss of appetite, chewing bones and wood, loss of hair glossiness, and decreased pliability of skin.
- *Salt*—Lack of salt results in a craving for salt, loss of appetite, haggard appearance, and a rough hair coat.
- *Magnesium*—Improves calcium and phosphorus metabolism and calcification of bone. About 70 percent of the magnesium in the body is in bones, combined with calcium and phosphorus. Muscles contain more magnesium than calcium and magnesium is present in the blood, organs, and tissue fluids of the body. Magnesium deficiency in the blood may cause grass tetany, loss of appetite, irritability, frothing at the mouth, muscle tremors, irregular gait or shifting lameness, and weak pasterns.

- *Iodine*—About half the iodine in the body is located in the thyroid gland that produces important hormones, such as thyroxin, which have a regulating effect on body metabolism. Thyroxin, which contains 65 percent iodine, is also concerned with growth, development and reproductive processes. A lack of iodine in the system can result in calves born dead, or dying soon after birth; abortion at any stage; irregular or suppressed heat or sterility; lumpy jaw; or goiter.
- *Cobalt*—Helps rumen bacteria synthesize vitamin B-12. Deficiency of cobalt results in a loss of appetite, retarded growth or loss of weight, anemia, pale mucous membrane, muscular incoordination, stumbling gait, rough hair coat, decline in milk production, and high mortality rate among calves.
- *Copper*—Work with iron to form hemoglobin in the blood. Deficiencies cause severe diarrhea, rapid loss of weight, abnormal appetite, bleached or graying hair coat, and anemia.
- *Zinc*—Helps to increase feed efficiency. Deficiencies cause poor hair coat with bald spots, poor feed efficiency, lesions of the skin, with calves developing swollen feet with open scaly lesions and a general dermatitis most severe on the legs, neck, head, and around the nostrils.
- *Sulfur*—Symptoms of sulfur deficiency are similar to those of protein deficiency, including poor production and slow growth. Necessary for the life of animals, sulfur is an essential part of most proteins. Aids in production of healthy hair coats and hooves.
- *Manganese*—Affects the metabolism of calcium and carbohydrates. Deficiencies result in the necessity for more services per conception, birth of calves with enlarged joints, stiffness, physical weakness, and twisted legs. Also results in lowered milk flow. In some cases tendons or muscles in the animal become deformed.
- *Iron*—Functions with copper to form hemoglobin in the blood. Deficiencies cause anemia, most likely to occur in calves because little iron passes across fetal membranes when cow is anemic, calves born weak or dead. An excess of iron interferes with phosphorus absorption.
- *Molybdenum*—Small amount needed for digestion of fiber. Toxicity causes problems with poor milk production, stiff joints, lameness, nervousness, including fighting cows and a pacing gait. Deficiencies rarely occur.
- *Selenium*—Works with vitamin E to prevent white muscle disease in calves (muscular dystrophy). Deficiency can also lead to heart failure, paralysis varying in severity from slight lameness to complete inability to stand. Usually affects young animals.

Vitamins are needed to support life. Vitamins A, D, and E are the three most important vitamins in animal nutrition. Cattle need the B vitamins and vitamin K also. The beauty of the ruminant digestive system is that these vitamins can be manufactured by rumen microflora for use by the host. Vitamin D is the "sunshine vitamin." It prevents rickets and is essential for proper bone growth and consistent reproduction. It is linked with calcium-phosphorus utilization. Animals get vitamin D from sunlight, so animals housed indoors, or those housed outside during long periods of cloudy weather may need vitamin D supplements. A vitamin D deficiency may cause joints and hocks to swell and stiffen.

Vitamin A maintains the skin and the linings of the digestive, respiratory, and reproductive tracts. Vitamin A is needed for normal sight and to prevent night blindness. Colostrum is high in vitamin A. A deficiency of vitamin A results in severe diarrhea in young calves, redness and swelling around dewclaws, stiffness in hock and knee joints and swelling in the brisket, loss of appetite, and nasal discharge, coughing, scouring, watering eyes due to drying and hardening of the mucous membranes that line the lungs, throat, eyes, and intestines. An increased incidence of mastitis and other udder problems due to drying and hardening of the mucous membranes of the udder is attributed to a deficiency of vitamin A.

Vitamin E works with selenium. A deficiency of this vitamin may cause white muscle disease (muscular dystrophy), heart failure, poor reproduction, and even paralysis varying in severity from slight lameness to complete inability to stand. Usually young animals are affected most severely.

DIGESTIVE SYSTEM

Cattle are ruminants. That is, they chew a cud, and have a complicated digestive tract. For instance, the horse and the pig have a simple stomach—it contains only a single compartment. A ruminant has a compound stomach with four distinct compartments. Of these, the first and by far the largest is the paunch or rumen. The second is the honeycomb or reticulum. The third is the manyplies or omasum, and the fourth is the abomasum, or so-called true stomach.

The four-fold stomach of a large full-grown cow may hold more than 200 quarts, while the simple stomach of a horse holds only 12 to 19 quarts. Cattle owe their ability to use large amounts of roughage to the large capacity of their stomachs and the digestive processes that take place inside.

When a ruminant, specifically a cow, bull, or steer, eats grass or other feed, it swallows the feed with very little chewing beforehand. The feed travels down the esophagus to the rumen, a small, complex chemical factory. Here fermentation takes places and microorganisms multiply and grow in order to digest and utilize feedstuffs.

From the rumen, or paunch, food is regurgitated by the animal, back up the esophagus to the mouth. The animal is then said to be chewing its cud. When the food is thoroughly chewed, the animal swallows it a final time and it settles to the bottom of the rumen-reticulum. Eventually, the finely divided digesta moves to the omasum, or manyplies, which vigorously moves and kneads the food mass, aiding in the breaking down of food particles and exposing more surface to further bacterial action. Much of the water is removed from the food in this compartment.

The food then moves on to the abomasum, or true stomach, which secretes enzymes and gastric juices to aid digestion further. The abomasum functions most like the simple stomach of other animals.

The final phase of digestion is accomplished in the small intestine. Here the protoplasm and nutrients are absorbed for the nourishment of the host ruminant animal.

Finally, any food which has not been digested moves on to the cecum and large intestine and is excreted as feces through the anus.

Ruminants do not directly digest all the food they eat. Organisms in the rumen feed on the food eaten by the animal, break it down to simpler forms, assimilate it into their own bodies in forms more digestible and available to the animal and then are themselves digested by the animal.

The length of time from the swallowing of the food by the ruminant animal until the digestive process is fully underway is referred to as the lag phase. The few bacteria available to start digestion in a given food must become numerous enough to complete efficient digestion, as food will move out of the rumen within a certain time, leaving digestion incomplete. Some rations are formulated with the goal of decreasing the time necessary for multiplication of microorganisms. Specifically, when a protein supplement is added to a ration, the microorganisms have a more readily available source of nitrogen, which is essential to their rapid growth. They digest the ration more quickly and enhance the digestive process.

There are several factors to be considered in planning a nutrition program. The stage of production for cows is of critical importance: pregnant or nonpregnant, lactating or not. The age of the animal, the condition of the animal, its weight, the weather, the breed of cattle, and any specific nutrient deficiency, based on the findings of a feed analysis test, all are important to consider when formulating a ration.

For the beef cow, one of the most critical times of the year nutritionally is the 82-day period immediately after calving. Calving problems caused by inadequate nutrition may be the first sign that rebreeding problems are on the way. Adequate energy, protein, and phosphorus must be supplied in the postcalving period to allow the cow to breed back successfully. Often, in a spring calving situation, beef cows are out on pasture in which the new grass is adequate in protein, but has a high moisture content and the cow cannot consume enough to meet her energy requirements.

Inadequate nutrition during this period will affect milk production, calf growth, heat cycles, and conception rates. If a cow misses one heat period it will cost about 38 pounds in weaned calf. At 80 cents per pound, that is $32 per calf that could have been present at weaning time.

For optimum efficiency, cattle producers should attempt to shorten the calving period as much as possible. When cows calve over an extended

Figure 5-1   After calving, a cow needs good nutrition to enable her to rebreed successfully.

period of time, it is not only difficult to plan a sound nutrition program, but also an uneven calf crop results and late calves are especially lightweight at weaning. A 60-day calving season is a guideline. Recommendations are for as short a calving season as possible. There are variations among producers.

Bred heifers should be fed separately if facilities permit because they have higher protein requirements than cows and need to gain weight up until they produce their first calf. Also, after calving, first-calf heifers should be fed separately to allow them to be in top condition for rebreeding.

RATION FORMULATION

Rations for beef and dairy cattle are calculated in much the same way, based on two factors: requirements for maintenance and requirements for production. No one ration can suffice for all herds. A ration is calculated from five steps: Daily requirements for nutrients, nutrients supplied by forage, nutrients needed from concentrates, pounds of milking ration required (for dairy cattle and lactating beef cows), and percent protein of the milking ration. The National Research Council publications are used as guides in formulating rations for each species of farm animal. Also, local extension service personnel are available to help the cattle producer formulate a ration tailored to each herd.

CROP RESIDUES

Crop residues are a good roughage for feeding to beef cows. For many cattle operations grazing during the fall and early winter months with some harvested residue saved to be fed later in the winter makes maximum use of crop residues.

If feeding crop residues, however, it is important to feed test and determine the amount of phosphorus that must be added to the ration. Dry grass and crop residues tend to be low in phosphorus, so most producers feed mineral supplements through the winter. Also, vitamin A is generally quite high in forages during early lush growth. However, as the forage weathers and matures, vitamin A levels decline. Supplemental vitamin A and phosphorus should be provided starting at least one month prior to calving and continuing through the breeding season. One key to proper feeding of phosphorus is to make sure the cattle eat some of the phosphorus supplement. To do that, many producers mix their high-phosphorus mineral with salt.

Animal nutritionists recommend mixing a supplemental phosphorus and calcium source half and half with salt. It is important to examine all labels closely to determine the phosphorus content. Feeding trials have concluded that cows with adequate phosphorus levels conceive more quickly, and at a higher percentage than cows with minimal or possibly deficient levels of phosphorus. And, after all, the goal of every producer is the production of a live, healthy calf. If the producer can get a calf from each cow in the herd every 365 days, he or she has come a long way toward efficient, effective herd management.

SELECTING FEED TO REDUCE COSTS

Good management demands economy in feeding programs. That is why feed analysis is so important. Feeding the right quantities of the right nutrients is economical and makes good sense. The most economical ration uses least-cost nutrients.

If it is necessary to buy hay or grain, one should opt for the least-cost ration that satisfies the requirements of the animals in the herd. Different feeds furnish different proportions of net energy and protein. Protein usually is the most expensive nutrient, so protein plays a major role in figuring the ration cost. The dollar value of a feed depends on the cost of protein and other nutrients in the available feed. Table 5-A can be used to compare feed prices. Contributions of net energy and protein for each feed are considered in the scale. Thus, a medium-high protein feed is more valuable when protein is expensive.

TABLE 5-A. COST OF FEEDS [Prices in dollars per ton are marked on the

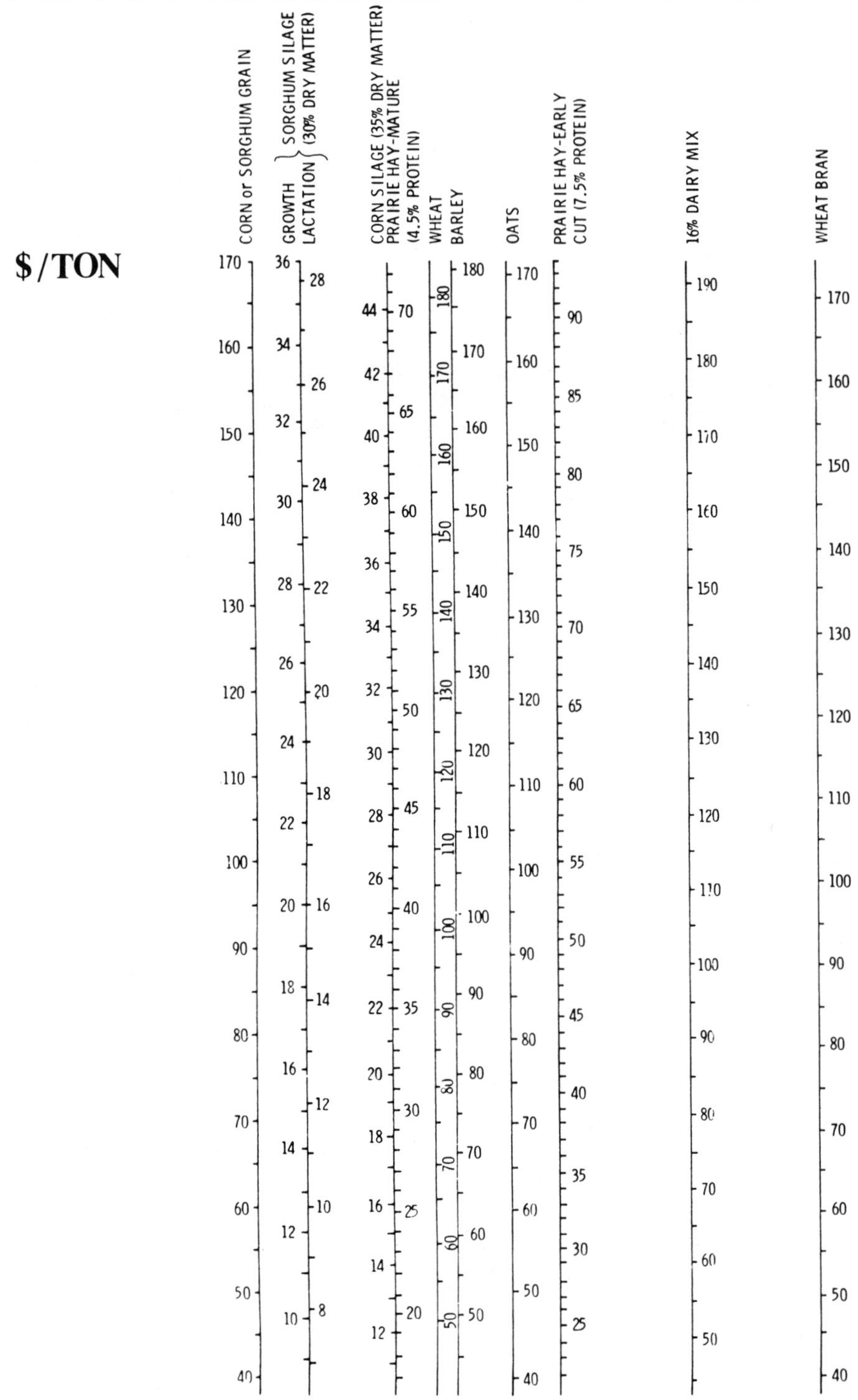
$/TON
CORN or SORGHUM GRAIN
GROWTH
LACTATION
SORGHUM SILAGE (30% DRY MATTER)
CORN SILAGE (35% DRY MATTER)
PRAIRIE HAY-MATURE (4.5% PROTEIN)
WHEAT
BARLEY
OATS
PRAIRIE HAY-EARLY CUT (7.5% PROTEIN)
16% DAIRY MIX
WHEAT BRAN

graduated scales; instructions for use of this table are on page 238.]

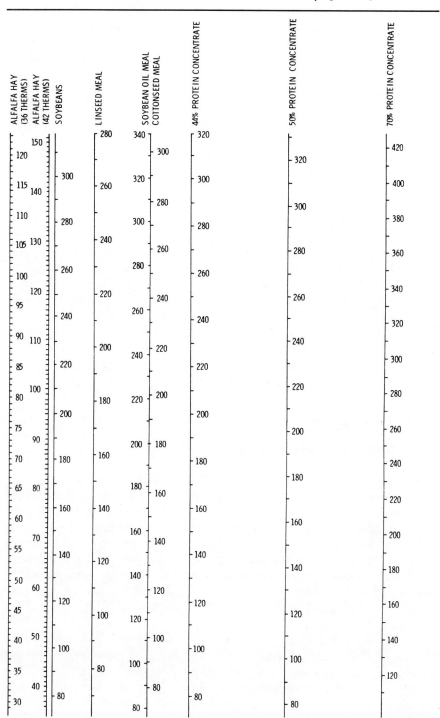

To use Table 5-A, take a ruler in hand. Suppose corn is $80 per ton and soybean oil meal is $150 per ton. To determine how much to pay for oats, place the ruler from $80 on the corn scale to $150 on the soybean scale. Then read the comparable price on the oats scale. In this example it is just below $80 per ton. At the same time, 42-therm alfalfa hay would be worth $68 per ton. But the value of alfalfa hay in excess of that required for protein would be considerably less. In this instance, worth about $33 per ton for net energy alone.

Any feed whose price is below the line of the rule is a better buy than either of the two used to form the line. For example, if 42-therm alfalfa hay were available at $40, it should be used to the limit within ration restrictions to reduce the protein supplement required.

When making a comparison, one must use prices of two feeds, one toward the right of the scale and one near the left. The feeds near the right side are major contributors of protein; those on the left are major contributions of energy.

Net energy is measured in therms, a unit of heat. The net energy content of hay can be estimated from crude fiber analysis. Excellent quality, early-cut alfalfa hay would provide about 42 therms per 100 pounds, while overmature, stemmy alfalfa hay would have around 36 therms. Feed only the amount of protein required. Any excess protein is worth only the value based upon net energy provided. Also, feed preparation costs should be included in prices. If one feed requires grinding and another does not, the grinding cost should be appropriately included or omitted. Table 5-B shows how to convert prices per ton to prices per bushel in order to compare costs.

FEED SUPPLEMENTS

Liquid Feed Supplements

Most liquid feed supplements are composed mainly of molasses (usually cane or blackstrap), urea, and a phosphorus source. These supplements are available from a number of manufacturers and are used in several ways. They can be mixed with processed grain and other feedstuffs, used as a top dressing poured or sprayed over feed, free choice by means of lick tanks, or added to the water supply, although the latter has not proved practical.

Urea in liquid feed supplements is a nonprotein nitrogen source. Urea was first discovered by Rovelle in 1773. It was the first organic compound ever synthesized in a laboratory by Wohler in 1828, and opened the door to a new field of organic chemistry.

Ideally, liquid feed supplements provide a readily digestible source of energy to be combined with the free amino groups from urea to prevent toxicity. As pasture grasses and crop stubbles go into late fall and winter months they decrease markedly in digestible energy. To maintain growth, animals need other sources of energy during these periods.

TABLE 5-B. CONVERSION TO PRICE PER BUSHEL*

	lb./bu.	bu./ton
Barley	48	41.7
Corn	56	35.7
Oats	32	62.5
Sorghum grain (milo)	56	35.7
Soybeans	60	33.3
Wheat	60	33.3

* Divide the price per ton by the number of bushels per ton to determine price per bushel.

Advantages of liquid feed supplements include improved feed palatability and masking of urea flavor, high phosphorus availability, improved feed texture, less waste in range feeding, convenience, and animal accessibility to supplement.

Problems that occur in conjunction with liquid feed supplements include difficulties with overconsumption by hungry animals during snow or sleet cover, settling out of calcium, cold weather causing the supplement to gel, equipment cost and depreciation, and above-normal water consumption by animals resulting in increased urine excretion.

Sometimes cattle producers rely too heavily on liquid feed supplements and provide too little forage. The result is poor performance from the animals. Feedstuffs must provide enough energy to allow the animals to utilize fully the nonprotein nitrogen source.

When using either liquid or dry supplements, most animal nutritionists recommend that salt and mineral supplement be available free choice to the animals in addition to the amounts supplied in the supplement itself. Free-choice minerals may not be needed in feedlots when the ration is known to be adequate in minerals. Unlimited drinking water should always be readily available and at a reasonable distance from the feeding area.

Rumensin

Rumensin* is a feed additive used to improve feed efficiency of feedlot cattle and to increase gain of beef cattle on pasture.

Research at several universities indicates that Rumensin exerts a protein-sparing effect by producing more product per unit of protein fed. It appears that the protein spared is equivalent to about 10 percent with most feedlot rations, which is the amount of improvement in feed efficiency normally associated with the use of this additive.

---

* Brand names, when used in this book, are for identification purposes only and do not imply endorsement.

Rumensin can be fed in several different ways, mixed and fed with grain on a daily basis, such as in a feedlot; mixed with minerals; mixed with a liquid supplement; or given on a self-fed basis, using a limiter such as salt to control intake. Beef researchers suggest the latter as the most practical method for cattle on pasture.

Researchers say that between 100 and 300 milligrams daily is the optimum amount of Rumensin to feed cattle on grass. Cattle fed at that rate showed a 12 to 20 percent improvement in daily gain. The Food and Drug Administration-approved level is 200 milligrams daily.

Implants

The use of hormonal and nonhormonal implants can stimulate weight gain in cattle and thus improve feed efficiency. Many cattle producers still do not use implants in their beef cattle and are missing out on a potentially profitable management practice. A criticism of using implants has been extra cost of labor required to handle the cattle. This need not be a problem because research has shown that the best time to implant is while working and before turning cattle onto grass. Breeding stock should not be implanted.

Currently, two implants are available: Ralgro and Synovex. Ralgro is a nonhormonal implant cleared for use at the rate of 36 milligrams for both steers and heifers regardless of weight. The other implant, Synovex, comes in two types—Synovex S for steers and Synovex H for heifers. It is a hormonal implant that can be administered at the same level regardless of weight.

Studies in Michigan and Nevada indicate improved average daily gains of approximately 22 and 26 percent over nonimplanted calves. Many times cattle producers question results of studies conducted under research conditions, so the Kansas Agricultural Experiment Station in cooperation with state livestock specialists conducted on-farm tests and the results were similar to those from the research stations.

If a producer considers the economics of implanting, it would be hard to decide not to implant yearling cattle. For every dollar invested in implants, approximately $10 are returned. For example, if a livestock producer assumes an increase in summer gains of 20 pounds per calf and an average of 200 pounds for each 10 implants used, there would be enough extra gain to equal owning another animal.

More recent research indicates that it may be profitable to reimplant yearlings during the summer. Some studies have shown that the life span of an implant is 80 to 100 days. Where cattle are grazed for 150 to 180 days it could pay to reimplant provided the extra cost of stress on the cattle is offset. More research is necessary before guidelines will be available on this.

Producers should know the proper way to implant and avoid crushing the pellets. Recommended location for Ralgro is within an inch from the base of the ear, while Synovex should be placed 1½ to 2 inches from the base of the ear. The implant should be placed between the skin and cartilage, not embedded in the skin, or poor absorption may occur.

Also, the pellets should not be crushed during implanting or the pellets may be absorbed too rapidly and cause poor response to the implant. To ensure that the pellets are not crushed, the needle should be inserted under the skin and then pulled back ¼ inch, creating a pocket; then as the implant is being inserted, the implant gun should be pulled back, allowing a slight spacing of the pellets and preventing crushing.

Before implanting, producers should be sure that Ralgro is implanted more than 65 days prior to slaughter, and Synovex S and H implanted more than 60 days prior to slaughter.

A few points to keep in mind when implanting are use a sharp needle, select the proper implant site, angle the needle under the skin and above the cartilage when inserting, back the needle off slightly before pulling the trigger, keep the trigger depressed as the needle is removed from the ear. Implanting near the tip of the ear, in the cartilage, or in the blood vessels may alter absorption and reduce potential gains.

Feeding Young Bulls

Because of the controversy surrounding hormones and other drugs used to promote growth in beef cattle, scientists are attempting to discover ways to achieve carcass quality and quick growth rates without synthetic growth promotants. In experiments comparing feeding bulls with steers, if steers have not been implanted, steer performance is penalized. Steers would be expected to respond to implants whereas implants have not improved bull growth rates.

In studies comparing implanted steers with bulls it was found that bulls will gain faster and more efficiently than implanted steers. Where emphasis is on high cutability and choice grade is not necessary, feeding bulls offers an attractive alternative. However, as long as market price is based on USDA quality grade, feeding bulls is not economically feasible. Feeding young bulls is an economical way to produce lean beef where choice grade is not imperative.

NITRATES AND CYANIDES

When problems arise, it is a good idea to check the feed for nitrates and cyanides. Sometimes they may be the cause of difficulties. Cyanides, if present, usually will be found in the standing forage. To check for nitrates, test all feeds that could be suspected as well as the water. Two or three tests should be run on each feed.

If nitrates are found in either the feed or the water, several precautions should be taken. First, phosphorus, iodine, and vitamin A should be provided for the cattle since nitrates increase the need for these substances.

Secondly, the energy value of the ration should be increased, since extra energy is required to convert nitrates to ammonia. Third, low-protein roughage such as corncobs, grass, hay, and corn stalks should be fed in liberal amounts to reduce the nitrogen content of the ration. Finally, the feed or water found to be high in nitrates should be diluted or discontinued.

Nitrates in feed and water can affect livestock production with lowered reproductive performance and loss of milk production. Nitrates occur naturally in most soils. It is a form of nitrogen formed when plant residues, animal manures, and human wastes decompose. It may be added to soil directly as a nitrogen fertilizer.

Symptoms of nitrate toxicity in animals include watery eyes, a rough hair coat, reduced appetite, reduced milk production, weight loss, or in acute cases, cyanosis (blue membranes, mouth, vulva), shortness of breath, and a staggering gait.

Nitrates can accumulate in water due to poor location of the water supply or poor construction of wells. Toxic nitrate levels have been found in ponds, streams, temporary puddles, and in wells.

Unfortunately there are a number of conditions that favor nitrate accumulation in plants. Drought, high temperatures, weed sprays, extended periods of cloudy weather, and frost cause immature plants and seeds to accumulate nitrates. Plants that accumulate nitrates are numerous as well. In broadleaf plants nitrates accumulate in new growth and leaves, or in stems of mature plants. In grasses nitrates can accumulate in the stems of mature plants and in new growth.

For pasture land, the best preventive action is proper management in crop production and fertilization with an attempt at maintaining the soil nutrient balance. Avoiding a high nitrogen content and a low potassium and/or phosphorus content will be instrumental in avoiding the accumulation of nitrates.

If problems do arise, the county extension service or the local veterinarian should be consulted for assistance.

FEED ANALYSIS

Taking the guesswork out of feeding cattle can pay off in lowered feed costs and higher meat and milk production. Having feed analyzed at least once a year gives the cattle producer an excellent management tool for keeping costs down and production up. When feed is analyzed by an independent laboratory, the cattle producer learns exactly how much protein to add to the ration, and the energy level, the nitrogen content, the amount of carbohydrates and fats, as well as the ash and mineral content. This information helps the good manager balance the ration to produce meat or milk economically.

Representatives of the laboratory will provide specific directions on taking samples to be analyzed. Most important, however, is taking a composite sampling of several different bales of hay, for instance, or, if sampling stored feed, taking samples from different areas and levels. This ensures that the samples are accurate representations of the total feed supply.

Dairy farmers who have had their feed analyzed find they are able to increase the production of their cattle because they no longer underfeed energy and overfeed protein. Feed analysis takes the guesswork out of cattle feeding and increases profitability on the farm and ranch.

FEEDING OPTIONS

Alfalfa—Dairy farmers have used alfalfa for many years as an ingredient in rations for dairy cattle. The value of alfalfa as a palatable source of protein, vitamins, and minerals is unexcelled by any other forage. Good-quality alfalfa is usually one of the most economical sources of natural protein. Depending on its quality, alfalfa hay contains from 12 to 22 percent crude protein. Good-quality hay contains about 16 percent crude protein and is actually a protein supplement since it replaces some of the protein needed in the concentrates.

The protein content of alfalfa haylage varies depending on its moisture content. Since protein is usually the most expensive nutrient in dairy rations, the costs of concentrates can be much lower when alfalfa is the forage fed. The cost of concentrates tends to decrease as the amount of alfalfa fed increases.

The economic value of alfalfa in dairy rations is determined by its effect on the total feed cost. Its value is influenced most by the price of soybean oil meal and somewhat less by the value of the silage or other forages it replaces.

The value of any alfalfa fed to cattle depends on its quality. High-quality alfalfa naturally contains more protein than low-quality alfalfa. Generally, early cutting is the most important thing that can be done to assure high quality.

Net energy of alfalfa is reduced by advancing maturity. Each day alfalfa matures its net energy content decreases more than a half therm per 100 pounds dry matter. Cutting alfalfa at about one-tenth bloom is recommended for highest yields of top quality alfalfa. At this stage a more palatable soft-stemmed forage is produced that results in highest protein and energy consumption.

Forage testing of alfalfa is important to assure an economical feed balance. A forage test should include an analysis for crude protein and crude fiber, plus moisture when testing silage or haylage.

TABLE 5-C.   SUGGESTED CONCENTRATES WITH DIFFERENT FORAGES

Ration A. No legume hay. All silage **or** late season native pasture **or** all native grass hay **or** combinations of these roughages.

Milo or shelled corn*	1430 lb.		Milo or shelled corn*	1560 lb.	
Soybean oil meal	520		Soybean oil meal	370	
Dicalcium phosphate***	40		Urea	20	
Trace mineral salt****	10		Dicalcium phosphate***	40	
	2000**		Trace mineral salt****	10	
				2000**	

Crude protein	18%		Crude protein	18%
Est. net energy	78 Therms		Est. net energy	78 Therms
Calcium	.61%		Calcium	.59%
Phosphorus	.76%		Phosphorus	.73%

Ration B. Light alfalfa program (10 lb./day) + heavy silage **or** midseason pasture **or** heavy feeding of native hay.

Milo or shelled corn*	1530 lb.		Milo or shelled corn*	1680 lb.	
Soybean oil meal	420		Soybean oil meal	250	
Monacalcium phosphate***	40		Urea	20	
Trace mineral salt****	10		Monacalcium phosphate***	40	
	2000**		Trace mineral salt****	10	
				2000**	

Crude protein	16%		Crude protein	16%
Est. net energy	78 Therms		Est. net energy	77 Therms
Calcium	.50%		Calcium	.48%
Phosphorus	.71%		Phosphorus	.67%

Ration C. ½ alfalfa—½ grass or silage program.

½ alfalfa—½ grass or silage program.

Milo or shelled corn*	1840 lbs.		Milo or shelled corn*	1740 lb.	
Soybean oil meal	100		Soybean oil meal	220	
Urea	20		Monacalcium phosphate	10	
Monacalcium phosphate	10		Monosodium phosphate***	20	
Monosodium phosphate***	20		Trace mineral salt****	10	
Trace mineral salt****	10			2000**	
	2000**				

Crude protein	13%		Crude protein	13%
Est. net energy	78 Therms		Est. net energy	78 Therms
Calcium	.15%		Calcium	.16%
Phosphorus	.63%		Phosphorus	.65%

Ration D. All alfalfa program, liberal feeding.

Milo or shelled corn	1960 lb.		Crude protein	9%
Monsodium phosphate***	30		Est. net energy	78 Therms
Trace mineral salt****	10		Calcium	.03%
	2000**		Phosphorus	.65%

* Wheat or barley may be substituted up to one-third of grain mixture.
** Supplementing 4,000,000 units Vitamins **A** and **D** per ton is recommended.
*** Monosodium phosphate, trace mineralized salt and bonemeal or dicalcium phosphate should be fed free-choice also.
**** A trace mineral supplement may be substituted at the rate of two to three lb. for trace mineralized salt.

Excess amounts of alfalfa may predispose cattle to scours.

Corn—The advantage of harvesting before cold weather and recent energy cost increases have made high-moisture corn an attractive winter feed for finishing steers.

Researchers studying feedlot performance of steers using five different methods of storing high-moisture corn found no significant difference in rate of gain among dry rolled corn, aqueous ammonia-treated corn, ground corn stored in a concrete bunker or rolled corn stored in a concrete bunker. Best performance occurred with animals feeding on high-moisture corn stored in an airtight structure.

Highest feed intake was observed with rolled high moisture corn in the concrete bunker. This treatment, however, required 1.7 percent more feed per unit of gain than did dry rolled corn. The lowest feed intake, but best efficiency (5.5 percent better than for dry rolled corn) was obtained with high-moisture corn stored in the oxygen-limiting bin.

No significant differences were observed among carcass characteristics in all of the treatments. Dressing percentages were higher for cattle fed rolled high-moisture corn stored in a bunker and ensiled ground snapped corn.

Data on the performance of the animals using the mixture with aqueous ammonia in the feedlot trial offer encouragement to cattle feeders who might want to use ammonia-treated corn in the future.

In one study, rate of gain, feed consumption, and feed efficiency with aqueous ammonia-treated corn were comparable or somewhat better than with the dry rolled corn.

The use of ammonia-treated corn would allow the cattle producer to increase the crude protein content by 2½ to 3 percent (raising it from about 10 to about 13 percent on a dry matter basis). If this can be accomplished with consistency, it would be possible to prepare a ration for high-moisture corn where supplemental protein would not have to be added, particularly for finishing out cattle. In the past a problem has existed with stabilizing the ammonia in the corn.

The most common method for storing high-moisture corn in areas where large numbers of feedlot cattle are fed is the grinding or rolling process, then storing it in large concrete bunker silos. Often more spoilage is found with the rolling method, probably because of the difficulty of packing the material into the silo. The animals performed poorest when high-moisture corn was rolled prior to being placed in the concrete bunkers.

Wheat—Feeding wheat to cattle should be undertaken with care. Although the advantages are many, there are drawbacks. The advantages of feeding wheat relate to its normally higher protein content over other feed grains, its overall quality, and easy processing. Because wheat is such a rich, quickly digested feed, feeding it requires more care than other grains. If an animal unaccustomed to grain eats too much wheat, it may die from rumen acidosis, which results from large amounts of wheat rapidly fermented in the forestomach.

Since wheat is usually higher in protein than other feed grains, the protein supplement in a ration can be reduced ⅛ pound for each pound of wheat in the ration. A small amount of wheat in a beef cattle ration tends to improve the animal's use of nonprotein nitrogen.

Also, feed intake averages about 10 percent less when a finishing ration contains 30 to 50 percent wheat. Cattle should be gaining the same as when eating 10 percent more of a ration containing no wheat. The reduced intake provides a savings on the feed bill provided wheat is equivalent in cost to the other feed grains.

Some management points to keep in mind when feeding wheat to cattle include: take care to feed limited amounts of wheat to cattle on pasture or stalk fields because individual intakes among cattle may vary tremendously; feed more roughage than usual; grind wheat coarsely; keep feed before cattle at all times when on a finishing ration; be certain ration is completely mixed; limit wheat to 40 percent of the total ration in most cases; take at least 35 days to put cattle on "full feed"; and do not use wheat for creep feeding calves.

The beef producer who uses wheat in the cattle ration need not invest in expensive processing facilities. Simple rolling is a satisfactory way to process wheat. Commercial feedlots with heat-treating facilities may want to consider heat processing for the wheat they use because recent research shows that wheat for beef cattle can be improved about 5 percent by heat processing.

Formaldehyde-treated wheat—The past few years formaldehyde has been effectively used to protect nutrients from ruminal fermentation. If a high-quality protein escapes microbial degradation and is digested directly in the abomasum and intestine, the animal absorbs a more favorable amino acid balance. Formaldehyde also may be used to prevent ruminal micoorganisms from saturating dietary fat and thereby changing the composition of fat in meat and milk.

Wheat and Barley Silages—Wheat and barley silages are excellent forages for growing cattle. Research has shown that cereals harvested and fed as silage produce more beef per acre than grain. Yearling steers can be expected to gain 1.5 to 2.5 pounds per day when fed rations containing 85 percent good-quality wheat or barley silage, supplemented with appropriate protein, mineral, and vitamin components.

Wheat silage may be a viable alternative to other silages as a roughage source for feedlot rations. Steers fed corn silage gain only slightly more tenths of pounds per day than those fed wheat silage.

Harvesting cereal for silage rather than as grain may mean increased dollar returns per acre. Cereal silages represent more total nutrient yield per acre than do cereal grains and, when fed to beef cattle, result in increased beef production. Basically, the net return from beef produced per acre from cereal silage compared with that from grain tells a farmer whether to harvest cereals as silage or as grain. Harvesting wheat, barley, or oats for silage has several advantages. Early summer crops like wheat and barley can be used with fall-harvested crops in a year-round forage program. That allows greater use of existing silage facilities during the summer.

Making silage, however, has some disadvantages. The farmer must invest in harvesting and storage equipment, must expend more labor than is required for grain production, and merchandise silage through cattle; thus silage is not as liquid an asset as grain.

Silage is produced by controlled anaerobic fermentation of green forage. Ensiling forage allows a minimal loss of nutrients. Bacteria produce organic acids (notably lactic acid) that serve as the agents of preservation. The acids formed in the ensiled forage lower the pH of the forage, slow enzyme action, and stop fermentation. Ideally, this results in a desirable silage with a pleasant odor, good palatability, and little nutrient loss.

If excess fermentation occurs, the silage loses nutrients and is less acceptable to livestock. Generally this problem is attributed to an insufficient production of lactic acids in the forage. The pH of the forage is not lowered enough to slow enzyme action and stop fermentation.

Wheat straw—Many producers bale their straw right after wheat harvest, while others allow the weeds to grow for a month and then swath and bale everything. Either way, wheat straw is a good, low-cost feed. While straw has definite value as a feedstuff it also has some distinct deficiencies. When a producer feeds a straight straw ration it is hard to start and keep cows eating it. For this reason, it helps to blend with alfalfa, red clover, lespedeza, or some other better quality roughage.

Straw is low in protein and extremely bulky. Its bulkiness can be an advantage on cold January days, but may cause problems by preventing constant passage of feed through a cow's digestive system. Blending straw with a more laxative roughage will help solve those problems. Also, straw must be supplemented to make up for its deficiencies in phosphorus and vitamin A.

Research indicates that the best use for straw is for pregnant cows during the middle part of gestation when their nutrient needs are lowest. As cows get closer to calving, and following calving, they need a higher quality roughage.

Some producers feed approximately 5 to 10 percent straw in their growing and feedlot rations. That seems to keep cattle on a uniform feed intake pattern that is particularly helpful in high-wheat and high-moisture rations. Producers have accepted wheat straw as a substitute feed. To what extent they use it depends on how badly they want, or need, to cut feed costs.

Experiments have been conducted adding aqueous ammonia to straw and results have been good, the only drawback being high rate of evaporation of the ammonia. However, wheat straw treated with ammonia increased daily gains 3.9 percent and improved feed efficiency 8.5 percent compared to rations containing dry wheat straw. Enough ammonia was applied to raise the protein level fivefold, but by the time the wheat straw reached the feed bunks, evaporation had reduced the protein level to about half the initial amount.

TABLE 5-D.   FEEDING WHEAT TO CATTLE*

	Backgrounding (Percentage of each ingredient)	Finishing	
		Winter	Summer
Silage	89.0	34	28
Rolled wheat	6.5	29	32
Rolled milo		32	34
40% protein supplement	3.3	2.9	3.6
Dehydrated alfalfa	1.0	1.5	1.7
Ground limestone	0.2	0.6	0.7
	100.0	100.0	100.0

* These rations were successfully used by Kansas Agricultural Experiment Station in feeding trials.

FEEDING FOR SPECIAL CONDITIONS

Environmental Conditions—Researchers have found that beef cattle producers could cut 2 to 3 cents off the cost of every pound of grain by feeding for environmental conditions. Cattle first begin to feel cold at 30° F. From that point, as temperatures get colder, the energy requirements of the cattle go up. Basically there are two ways to handle cold stress. The first is simply to feed cattle more during cold weather. The second is to provide shelter for the cattle to protect them from the cold conditions. Shelter can be in the form of windbreaks, open-front buildings, or even total confinement facilities.

If using shelter, it is a must to figure costs closely when deciding on the construction of additional housing.

All cattle have a 10 to 15° (centigrade) temperature range, or thermoneutral zone, where efficiency is maximal. When temperatures drop below this comfort zone, energy requirements for maintenance go up. How much the energy requirements increase depends on two factors, the size of the cattle and how much insulation they have.

With mature cattle, the size range is narrow enough that it need not be considered. The thickness of the hair coat is definitely important, however. Coats can be grouped into four categories: summer hair coat or a wet hair coat, fall, winter, and heavy winter hair coats. Cattle with each of these hair coats have their own comfort zones. If temperatures drop below that zone, the cattle are cold. Energy requirements go up a certain percent for each degree of temperature drop.

Figure 5-2 Energy requirements increase as the weather gets colder. *(Courtesy of the American Maine-Anjou Association)*

For example, if an 1,100-pound cow is in winter coat, she might require 13,600 kilocalories of energy, according to National Research Council requirements. She will need an additional 1 percent or 136 kilocalories for each degree Fahrenheit of cold below her comfort zone. Table 5-E shows estimates of additional energy required during cold weather for an average-sized beef cow. In the example above, if the temperature outside is 5° F, each cow experiences 25 degrees of cold stress. (Table 5-F, page 250.) That means she needs 3,400 or 25 times 136 additional kilocalories of energy. That additional energy could be supplied with 2.3 pounds of corn or 3.4 pounds of alfalfa hay.

TABLE 5-E. ESTIMATES OF ADDITIONAL ENERGY REQUIRED DURING COLD

Beef Cows (900 to 1,300 pounds)	Percent Energy Increase per °F Below Base Temp.
Summer coat or wet	2.0%
Fall coat	1.3%
Winter coat	1.0%
Heavy winter coat	0.8%

TABLE 5-F.   THERMAL NEUTRAL OR BASE TEMPERATURE

Summer coat or wet	60° F
Fall coat	45° F
Winter coat	30° F
Heavy winter coat	20° F

Wet cows get cold faster or at a higher temperature because a wet hair coat provides no insulation regardless of how thick it is. If a cow is wet and the temperature is 30° F, she is 30° cold. She would be even colder at 30° wet than at 5° dry.

Under range conditions, cattle tend to put on more weight in the summer than they need. In the winter they lose the fat by using it to meet their increased energy requirements. Putting on fat and taking it off is an inefficient process, however, because it takes energy both to put on fat or stored energy and to take it off. In other cases, range cattle are left out on pastures too long so they come in with less fat than they need that winter. Since most cows calve either in the fall or the spring, the cows may end up short on energy during the most critical time of the year.

Pregnant and lactating cows need extra energy for their young and also to keep warm. Even feeding according to National Research Council recommendations will not provide adequately for animals subjected to cold stress. Feeding recommendations generally are formulated for optimal weather conditions. If cattle are placed in less than ideal conditions, their rations must be adjusted to provide for any extra energy requirements.

From a practical standpoint, rations might be adjusted on a month-by-month basis. Although one might not know exactly what the weather will be like on any given day, it is safe to assume that the weather will be colder in January than in October and to feed accordingly.

During periods of extreme cold, the cattle producer can provide poor-quality roughages such as wheat straw or other crop residues such as corn and milo stalks (stover) for the cow. The internal fermentation process in the cow will convert that roughage to calories that will provide warmth or energy.

Pregnant Cows—Two-thirds of the weight on the fetus, or calf, is developed during the last third of the cow's pregnancy. Excessive feeding of the dam, however, can cause problems after calving. Excessive milk flow or calf scours may result. For this reason it is a good idea to increase feeding levels slowly several weeks before calving to prevent milk fever, as there is a tremendous drain on the cow's body toward the end of the gestation period.

During the gestation period, cows may be fed approximately 1 pound of total digestible nutrients per 100 pounds of body weight and 0.9 pounds crude protein per head daily for maintenance. After calving, however, a cow's

TABLE 5-G.   WIND CHILL INDEX FOR CATTLE—WINTER COAT

Wind Speed (mph)	−10	−5	0	5	10	15	20	25	30	35	40	45	50
Calm	−10	−5	0	5	10	15	20	25	30	35	40	45	50
5	−16	−11	−6	−1	3	8	13	18	23	28	33	38	43
10	−21	−16	−11	−6	−1	3	8	13	18	23	28	33	38
15	−25	−20	−15	−10	−5	0	4	9	14	19	24	29	34
20	−30	−25	−20	−15	−10	−5	0	4	9	14	19	24	29
25	−37	−32	−27	−22	−17	−12	−7	−2	2	7	12	17	22
30	−46	−41	−36	−31	−26	−21	−16	−11	−6	−1	3	8	13
35	−60	−55	−50	−45	−40	−35	−30	−25	−20	−15	−10	−5	0
40	−78	−73	−68	−63	−58	−53	−48	−43	−38	−33	−28	−23	−18

Temperature (°F)

Data provided by Dave Ames, livestock physiologist at Kansas State University.

requirements nearly double. Calcium, phosphorus, and vitamin A requirements also double for the cow after calving.

Mineral requirements may be met by self-feeding a loose mixture of 50 percent trace mineralized salt and 50 percent dicalcium phosphate before and after calving. If good-quality alfalfa hay is fed, vitamin A requirements will be met.

Calves and Colostrum—Every newborn calf needs colostrum (the first milk of its mother). It is important as the first feed to condition the digestive tract and to give the calf resistance to disease. Disease resistance is provided by the presence of immunoglobulins in the first milk of the dam and the ability of the calf to absorb these antibodies during the early hours of its life. This ability declines and disappears about 24 hours after birth. Consequently, the earlier the calf receives colostrum the greater the benefits it will receive.

A calf should receive colostrum in an amount equivalent to 3 to 5 percent of its body weight within 4 hours following birth. If it cannot nurse its dam it should be fed by nipple bottle or pail. Following this feeding, the calf should receive no more than 4 percent of its body weight per feeding twice daily, preferably for 36 to 72 hours.

If milk from the dam is not available, colostrum from another cow freshening at the same time, or fresh, frozen colostrum stored for such an eventuality may be used.

TABLE 5-H.   COLOSTRUM VS. WHOLE MILK

| | Percentages compared | | | |
	Water	Protein	Fat	Ash
Colostrum	74.5	17.6	3.6	1.7
Whole Milk	87.0	3.3	4.0	0.7

MANAGEMENT OF GRAZING LAND

Overgrazing can be a real problem for cattle producers. Cattle are creatures of habit and tend to overuse some areas of most range units and underuse others. Unfortunately, the first place of any size that is overgrazed determines the capacity of the whole range. Overuse and underuse are either injurious or wasteful and both are costly. Keeping every area grazed uniformly and properly may be difficult, but this proper management increases the grazing capacity of any land.

There are some effective ways to encourage proper grazing by cattle. For instance, fencing to separate cool-season grasses such as western wheatgrass from warm-season species on upland sites can help. Grazing animals seasonally select easily accessible areas and grasses that they prefer. Fence off separate vegetation types and allow the cool-season species to be grazed early when they should be, then later move livestock to the warm-season range when it is time to graze there.

Small economical ponds dozed into a hillside to catch water for live-stock make underused areas more attractive to cattle.

Salting locations are among the easiest and cheapest ways of regulating grazing distribution. Too often salt is located near water, doing nothing to improve grazing distribution. Repeated observations of livestock usually show that they salt in the early morning or late evening and that they resume grazing after visiting the salt box even if water is available. Locating the salt near undergrazed areas may increase use of that site. Whenever a salting location is moved, however, cattle should be driven to the new location so they will know where it is.

Also, rotation grazing may be used to improve grazing distribution by crowding cattle into a range unit and grazing it heavily for a short period of time before moving to the next location. Cattle graze less selectively as grazing pressure is increased, resulting in areas being grazed more uniformly. Rotation grazing may have a disadvantage in reduced steer gains per head if they are moved too often, but usually has no detrimental effect on calf weaning weights. Three or more range units of approximately equal size, close together, are necessary before rotation grazing can be effective.

Riding and drifting cattle into undergrazed areas is still a very effective method of more uniform grazing distribution if cattle can be kept in the new location. This means having sufficient water and salt available for the amount of grass that is present. Drift fencing can be used to break cattle movement patterns to force them into areas not previously used. This may be a short fence of only 200 to 300 yards in length that forces cattle to climb out of a normal path in a valley up to an unused area above.

Cattle will not graze an area without adequate water. Watering locations should be no more than 1 to 5 miles apart, the latter an absolute maximum.

SOIL SURVEYS

The Soil Conservation Service of the U.S. Department of Agriculture publishes soil surveys of counties throughout the United States. Each soil survey contains detailed maps and descriptions of soils in the area surveyed.

Soil surveys can help cattle producers determine range land potential and aid in management decisions for the grazing potential of ranch land.

For instance, the soil in an area of brush or mesquite may have such low potential productivity that the cost of chaining or chemical removal may not be worth the ultimate yield in forage. On the other hand, there may be rocky areas or hillsides where the soils are capable of producing more forage if properly managed. A soil survey can help the cattle producer determine such natural differences in productivity.

Soil surveys help in grazing management too. If a range is overgrazed, desirable plants decrease and less desirable plants may take over the site. A soil survey can help identify soils that are producing at less than their potential. Each soil survey names the main species of desirable and undesirable range plants that grow on the soils and provides estimates of forage yields that can be expected under favorable and unfavorable conditions.

If the farmer needs to grow more winter feed or establish more pasture, a soil survey rates soil suitability for hay and pasture plants so that it can be determined which areas will be most productive for this use.

To determine whether a soil survey of a specific area is available, call the local office of the Soil Conservation Service, or the county extension agent. Published soil surveys can be purchased from the Superintendent of Documents, Government Printing Office, Washington, D.C. 20402.

Many libraries also maintain copies of soil surveys. In any event, the local soil conservationist or soil scientist can discuss conservation management of soils. Soil surveys are primarily intended to help farmers provide for the nation's agricultural future. With the assistance of accurate soil information, farmers and ranchers can get maximum utilization from the land.

STUDY QUESTIONS

1. Cattle can go for a longer period without _____ than they can without _____. (food, water)
2. Cattle have a _____ digestive system. (ruminant)
3. The length of time from the swallowing of the food by the cow until the digestive process is fully underway is known as the _____. (lag phase)
4. _____ stimulate weight gain, improving feed efficiency. (Implants)
5. Watery eyes, a rough hair coat, reduced appetite, shortness of breath, and a staggering gait are symptoms of _____. (nitrate toxicity)
6. An effective way to determine the quality of the feed one is giving cattle is through _____. (feed analysis)

6

Artificial Insemination—How and Why

Always looking for new ways to improve their herds, cattle producers found that they could breed their cows to the top bulls in the country at a nominal cost per cow, improving their genetics and increasing their profit potential. Artificial insemination became the key to better herds for many cattle producers. Artificial insemination was first developed for commercial use in 1938 and early proponents of the method had a difficult time countering objections from registry associations. At first, many breed associations frowned on the use of AI even to the extent of refusing to register animals conceived this way. As the effective results of artificial breeding became obvious, however, attitudes changed. Perhaps because of relative ease of heat detection, dairy farmers accepted the process more readily than beef producers. Today, artificial insemination is accepted almost universally, although dairy farmers continue to breed far greater numbers of their cows artificially than do beef breeders. One primary requirement for registration of progeny from AI breedings is the keeping of proper records.

Figure 6-1 Cows should be checked for signs of heat in early morning, at noon, and again in the evening after milking or feeding. (*Courtesy American Normande Association*)

RECORD KEEPING

Proper record keeping can be as simple as identifying one's cows and knowing which have been bred and which are open. For the commercial farmer, this often is enough. Of course, the purebred breeder must maintain more detailed records.

In addition, by using semen from proven bulls, the cattle producer can compare the performance records of several sires and match his or her cows with the most effective bulls. The opportunity to purchase small amounts of semen from several proven sires assures the breeder that the best bulls are being selected for the herd. To aid the breeder in sire selection, the professional AI stud services publish sire directories, or "Bull Books," listing their studs along with performance data on each sire. Some breed associations publish listings of their sires with the same performance information. With this data in hand, the producer can compare progeny statistics from one sire to another and improve herd performance in desirable characteristics.

To register purebred progeny, the breeder must maintain a precise record of breeding and calving dates, record which cows were served by which bulls, and list the method used—natural service or AI. In addition, in order to satisfy the performance record requirements of many breed associations, data such as birth weight, weaning weight, and yearling weight must be recorded.

The standard breeding receipt shown on the opposite page is typical of the sort provided by AI breeder services. Such a receipt gives the producer valuable information for his management records.

With so many record-keeping requirements, the potential AI breeder might wonder if the process is worth the extra time required for herd management alone. Actually, though, the improved record keeping has its own benefits by providing the cattle producer with vital information about the herd. Artificial insemination has additional benefits as well.

To understand why many producers are so enthusiastic about AI, one must look carefully at the benefits of breeding artificially. Most obvious, of course, is the opportunity to use top bulls that are too expensive to be used in natural service. Proven, genetically superior sires can service 50,000 cows or more each, per year. Shipping semen costs far less than shipping a live animal and requires less care during transport. Storing semen for months or even years requires only the minor expense of liquid nitrogen and a small investment in equipment. Compare that to the cost of feeding, housing, and caring for a top bull. Also, producers gain a safety aspect by using AI and eliminating a bull from their herds. This is especially true with dairy bulls.

Most everyone has heard horror stories about cattle producers who have to pull all their calves with a calf puller. If true, these cattle producers caused some of their own problems through poor sire selection and inadequate herd management. Cattle producers beginning an upgrading program

TABLE 6-A.   SAMPLE STANDARD BREEDING RECEIPT

* **CSS** APPROVED

Date of   Breed   Serv.
Breeding .... of Cow .... No. ....
Name of Cow ....
.... Reg. No. ....
Owner No. .... Tattoo or Tag ....
Owner ....
Address .... Fee ....
Name of Bull ....
.... Reg. No. ....
Semen Collection No. .... Bull Code ....
SFB or SPB Code on Inseminating Unit ....

Date of Previous   Bull Registry
Service (if any) .... No. ....
Tech. ID No. .... Bull Code ....

"I hereby certify that I am duly authorized to issue this receipt which is given as evidence of service rendered and also a certification of date of service and identity of semen used for service of animal identified hereon."

....
(Inseminator's Signature)   ID No.

The original copy of this receipt should be given to owner at time of service.

For Optional Identification of
Animal bred or Resulting offspring

Tattoo .... Ear Tag ....

Birth date .... Sex ....
IF THE ABOVE IS USED IN A BREED · IDENTI-FICATION PROGRAM I certify that the animal described carries the permanent identification as shown and resulted from the mating on the reverse side of this form.

Signed ....
        Owner of dam at time of calving

* Certified Semen Services, Inc., a subsidiary of the National Association of Animal Breeders.

must, above all, consider their own cows when selecting a herd sire. Common sense indicates that a small cow would have calving difficulties bred to a bull known to produce large calves. Both calves and dams can be lost when the cattle producer fails to consider progeny data when selecting a stud. Progeny birth weight is the important indicator of calving ease passed on by any sire.

If available, progeny carcass and cutability data provide information on future profit prospects of beef cattle. Milk production of daughters provides dairy farmers with an indication of a sire's economic potential.

For beef cattle producers, progeny yearling weight offers valuable performance data. However, weaning weight often reflects mothering ability as much as it does sire performance.

DISEASE CONTROL

Another reason artificial breeding has become popular is its role in disease prevention. Reputable AI studs maintain a high degree of sanitation; test bulls frequently for tuberculosis, brucellosis, leptospirosis, and trichomoniasis; and add antibiotics to semen for control of vibriosis. Since venereal diseases are spread by natural-service breeding with infected bulls, AI can prevent this contact and assure disease-free semen. AI studs make a tremendous effort to assure the safety of their semen. High sanitation standards make sense economically for both the professional AI studs and for the cattle producer–consumer. The AI stud reaps the economic rewards of repeat business from a satisfied customer. The producer keeps his or her herd disease-free and eliminates losses from venereal diseases. The diseases spread by natural-service breeding with infected bulls include vibriosis, trichomoniasis, leptospirosis, brucellosis, and IBR.

Vaccines are available against vibriosis, leptospirosis, brucellosis, and IBR, although brucellosis vaccine is illegal in some states. To be safe it is best to vaccinate open cows and heifers no later than 30 days before breeding. Then, good management calls for continuing a planned vaccination program. Brucellosis, in particular, is devastating economically since the retained afterbirth affects the cow's future fertility adversely.

Additional ways to prevent disease include maintaining clean, dry pastures for calving, ascertaining that all equipment used in the cattle operation is clean for each use, and preventing cows from calving in the same area over a long period of time.

HEAT SYNCHRONIZATION

If cows could begin their heats at the convenience of the livestock producer, the entire process of artificial insemination would be a great deal easier. Labor could be saved because someone would not have to spend valuable time watching cattle three times a day for signs of heat. Calf births could be planned for a few days or a couple of weeks sometime during the calving season. Proceeds from the sale of the calf crop could be increased by calving in January or February those animals to be sold in late summer. Using every management tool possible makes good sense for the livestock producer. He or she needs to impregnate as many cows on first service as possible. If a cow fails to conceive, the producer loses 21 days until her next cycle comes. Assuming that a calf gains 2 pounds a day, and that gain is worth 60 cents a pound, $24 is lost because of the cow's failure to conceive. If 100 of the cows fail to conceive during one month, the potential loss is $2400. Research on heat synchronization has shown that through the use of various compounds, cows that are cycling can be brought into heat at the livestock producer's discretion. Heat synchronization will not get 100 percent of a cow herd to go into heat but it can cause most females to show heat when the producer wants them to.

Several chemicals have been developed for use in heat synchronization. Some of them are listed in Table 6-B.

TABLE 6-B. CHEMICALS USED FOR HEAT SYNCHRONIZATION

Trade Name	Compound	Producer
Lutalyse	Prostaglandin F_2 alpha (PGF$_2$ alpha)	Upjohn Co.
Estrumate	PGF$_2$ alpha Analogue (ICI 80996 or Colprostenol)	Imperial Chemical Ind.
Syncro-Mate B	Norgestomet Implant (SC21009) and Estradiaol Valerate Injection	G. D. Searle Co.
PRID Vaginal Coil	Progesterone	Abbott Laboratories

Prostaglandin F_2alpha is a potent compound for use in synchronization. Prostaglandin itself is an unsaturated fatty acid with a cyclopentyl ring that has the basic skeleton of prostanoic acid. That is, prostaglandin may be produced in all body cells, but its richest source is in the sexual tract—the uterus, placenta, and seminal vesicles. It can be used to depress progesterone production. Progesterone is a hormone that prevents heat and ovulation.

Prostaglandin F_2alpha also might remedy some female problems in cattle such as retained corpora lutea, luteal follicular cysts, silent ovulations, and others. It is produced under the trade names Lutalyse and Estrumate.

Syncro-mate B treatment for estrus or heat synchronization involves placing a 6-milligram norgestomet implant in the ear of the cow for 9 days. The cow or heifer is injected intramuscularly with 5 milligrams of estradiol valerate and 3 milligrams of norgestomet at the time of implantation. The estradiol-norgestomet injection places the cow in a stage of her cycle where she is capable of coming in heat once the implant is removed. The nor-gestomet implant holds the cow out of heat until the implant is removed 9 days later. Removing suckling calves at the time the implant is removed speeds up and more closely synchronizes heat in lactating cows. With this procedure calves usually are put back with the cows at breeding 48 hours after implant removal. Syncro-Mate B is effective in inducing heat in non-cycling cattle; however, fertility after induced heat appears to vary from good to low.

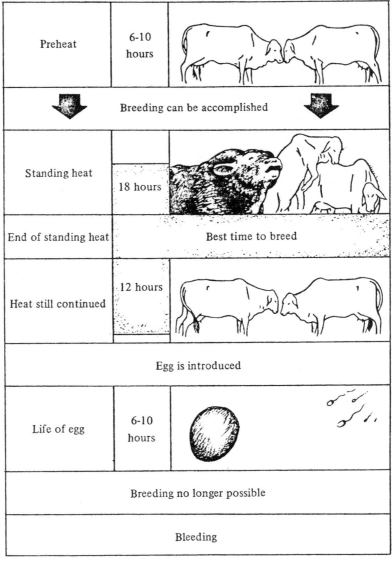

Preheat	6-10 hours	
	Breeding can be accomplished	
Standing heat	18 hours	
End of standing heat		Best time to breed
Heat still continued	12 hours	
	Egg is introduced	
Life of egg	6-10 hours	
	Breeding no longer possible	
	Bleeding	

Figure 6-2   The breeding sequence. *(Illustration by Tom Stallman)*

The first attempts at synchronizing heat were made with progesterone. Progesterone is normally produced by the corpus luteum, a structure that forms on the ovary after ovulation and prevents heat and ovulation. Both natural progesterone and orally active progestogens such as melengesterol acetate are effective in synchronizing heat in cycling animals by preventing heat and ovulation until all animals are in the physiological state that occurs just prior to the onset of heat. When the foreign progesterone is removed, animals tend to show heat at the same time. Conception rates after progesterone treatments have been disappointing at the first synchronized heat.

Interest in progesterone treatment for heat synchronization was revived in the early 1970's by Abbott Laboratories with the invention of the progesterone-releasing intravaginal device called PRID. Although some favorable results were obtained by this method of progesterone administration, testing of the PRID has been suspended in the United States.

Basically, the number of cows that settle during a synchronization period, or at an appointed breeding time, is dependent on the number of cows properly cycling at the time the synchronization tool was used.

Only cows that are cycling will respond to prostaglandin, and likewise, any cow that has shown heat within the preceding 5 days prior to treatment will not respond to prostaglandin.

HEAT DETECTION

It has been said that an alert cattle producer can detect heat just about as efficiently as a bull. The cattle producer watches for the one reliable sign of heat—the cow stands to be mounted by other animals. Her vulva becomes swollen, reddish, and moist with a clear mucous discharge. When the discharge becomes bloody, heat is over. The cattle producer must act quickly when standing heat is witnessed. Standing to be mounted by other cattle is the one most reliable sign of heat in the cow. Cows in heat generally exhibit these signs:

1. Cow stands to be mounted by other animals (*most reliable*)
2. Cow attempts to mount other cows
3. Cow has clear, mucous discharge on her tail or pin bones
4. Cow has smeared or ruffled pin-bones and rump
5. Cow bawls, is restless, walks excessively, or goes off feed
6. Other cows show restlessness

To be most efficient as a heat detector, the cattle producer should check cows in early morning, at noon, and again in the evening after milking or feeding. The heat detector stands unobtrusively in a spot near the place where cattle normally congregate at these times and observes the herd.

For effective results, locate the observation post at a spot near a cattle gathering point, for water or salt, for example. Observation should be done when no other activity is going on.

One reason beef cattle producers have been slower to accept artificial breeding than have dairy farmers is the inconvenience involved in heat detection. Some beef producers tried observing their cows during feeding. It did not work. Cows with weak heat signs will not be detected if observation is done simultaneously with other activities. For beef cattle, experts suggest building AI facilities out in the pastures to make observation and breeding easier. The difficulties involved in rounding up beef cattle and bringing them in to AI facilities for breeding have so far limited the number of beef cattle bred artificially to less than 5 percent, compared with 65 to 70 percent of dairy cattle bred artificially each year. Building AI facilities out in the pastures lessens the inconvenience for the cattle producer and decreases the amount of stress placed on the cow, since being driven to a holding pen does cause stress. Making AI more convenient would enable beef producers to obtain the same advantages from artificial insemination that dairy farmers have found so valuable.

HEAT DETECTION AIDS

A number of heat detection aids are used to make the job a little easier. Most frequently a Gomer bull is used to locate cows in heat. Generally the bull is equipped with a chin-ball marking device. When a cow stands to be mounted by the Gomer bull, the chin-ball marker makes a distinctive stripe on her back. Gomer bulls, however, have some disadvantages. If the bull can achieve penetration he is a potential source of disease and infection. Bulls fitted with a Pen-O-Block or a similar device, or those which have been surgically altered are much safer. Unfortunately, the Gomer bull may not find all the cows in heat. Depending on his libido, he may get lazy before his work is done.

Choosing a detector bull from within one's own herd certainly decreases chances of infection and disease being introduced. However, one of the major complaints against Gomer bulls has been the expense involved in having them surgically altered with vasectomies, sterilizations, penectomies, or penal blocks.

Researchers at Kansas State University and at Michigan State University developed a cheaper heat detector for the producer who prefers not to deal with Gomer bulls at all. Their alternative calls for injecting old cows with hormones and using them as heat detectors. The chief advantage of using a teaser cow over a Gomer bull is economic. The cow is injected with testosterone proprionate and takes on male characteristics and behavior, including a crested neck, deep voice, and coarse hair. The chemical itself is inexpensive and can be injected by the producer. When the cow has finished her usefulness at the end of the breeding season she can be sent on to market. The teaser cow would be equipped with a chin-ball marker, and like the

Gomer bull, would identify cows in heat with a characteristic marking on the cow's back. Select teaser cows that are in good condition and free of lameness.

Before a teaser cow can begin work it must be given a warm-up period:

1. Every other day, for 21 days, inject each cow with 8 cubic centimeters (200 milligrams) testosterone proprionate*
2. Injections total 10.
3. During breeding season when cows are marking, give each a booster shot of testosterone proprionate once a week.

Other aids to heat detection include use of a heat-mount detector. For example, the KaMaR heat-mount detector pad is attached to the rump of a cow with a special cement. The cow in heat stands to be mounted by other animals and when the heat-mount detector is pressed for a sufficient amount of time, the detector turns red.

A heat-mount detector consists of a white fabric base and a white transparent capsule attached to the fabric. The capsule contains red dye. The tube is constructed so that the dye is released slowly by moderate pressure. Thus, a cow not in heat will usually not allow herself to be mounted long enough to turn the detector red.

Using heat detection aids may help to make the job of heat detection a little easier. But aids are helpers, not substitutes for observation. To use artificial insemination effectively, the producer must make close, frequent observations to determine which cows are in heat.

HEAT

The anterior section of the pituitary regulates the reproductive cycle of the cow. The pituitary is located in the skull just below the brain, well protected by bone and flesh. The anterior pituitary secretes three hormones that directly influence reproduction. These are the follicle-stimulating hormone, FSH; the luteinizing hormone, LH; and prolactin. FSH causes the growth of the follicle on the ovary. LH acts on the ovary to cause ovulation and the formation of corpus luteum or yellow body. Prolactin causes the corpus luteum to secrete the hormone progesterone.

Then, in a chain reaction, the developing follicle as part of the ovary, produces estrogen that stimulates the growth and motility of the reproductive tract. It also acts on the central nervous system to bring about the physical symptoms that characterize estrus, or heat. As the follicle develops, estrogen is produced in sufficient quantity to stimulate the production of

---

*Testosterone proprionate available from veterinarians.

LH by the pituitary. The interaction of FSH and LH cause ovulation. LH also stimulates the formation of the corpus luteum.

After ovulation the cells of the corpus luteum secrete progesterone, which prepares the uterus for the fertilized ovum. It also helps in maintenance of the pregnancy.

The length of the monthly cycle in the cow normally is 21 to 22 days. The interval between heat periods can vary even in a normal cow from 18 to 24 days. Fortunately for those planning to use AI, each cow tends to repeat her own pattern. If she has a heat cycle shorter or longer than average, the cattle breeder can expect her to repeat that interval with subsequent cycles.

Pennsylvania research indicates that about 50 percent of cows have estrus (heat) from 8 to 16 hours and the other 50 percent have heat cycles from 24 to 32 hours. Taking the middle interval, about 92 percent of cows have heat periods varying from 16 to 24 hours in length. Cows coming in heat in the morning had an average heat duration of 16 hours, while those first observed in heat in the afternoon averaged 20 hours. For heifers the duration was slightly shorter than for cows, an average of 14 to 17 hours. In determining when cows come into heat it was found that there was very little difference in the time of day when heat began. Approximately a third of the cows tested came into heat between midnight and 8:00 A.M., another third between 8:00 A.M. and 4:00 P.M., and one third between 4:00 P.M. and midnight.

Ovulation normally occurs 10 to 14 hours after heat has ended. This can vary from 2 to 26 hours in some cows. Heifers may ovulate sooner than cows.

The best time for artificial insemination is in the final stages of standing heat. It takes only a few minutes for sperm cells to travel the entire length of the female reproductive tract and the egg is not released until the cow has been out of standing heat 10 to 12 hours.

When to Breed

Cows spotted in standing heat in the morning should be bred in the evening for best results. Cows observed in heat in the evening should be bred the next morning. Studies have shown these intervals to be the most effective. The egg will live a few hours, perhaps 6 to 10, following ovulation. Sperm life usually exceeds 24 hours, but sperm must be in the reproductive tract 4 to 6 hours before they are capable of fertilizing the egg. Having the sperm in the reproductive tract and ready to fertilize at or shortly following ovulation results in highest conception rates.

Cows that fail to conceive within the normal time intervals may need to be bred slightly earlier or slightly later than the norm. If conception occurs by breeding earlier or later than normal, a record should be kept of these data, since the cow is likely to perform similarly in subsequent years.

Figure 6-3   An AI technician prepares to inseminate a cow. *(Courtesy of Kansas Artificial Breeding Service Unit)*

WHO SHOULD INSEMINATE?

In many states, because of a shortage of trained AI technicians, many cattle producers inseminate their own cattle. In areas where there is a high concentration of cattle in a relatively small area, professional inseminators do most of the work. Whether or not the cattle producer needs to learn how to perform insemination will depend largely upon the area of the country. For instance, in states like Minnesota and Wisconsin, professional inseminators have plenty of work to keep them busy and to provide a profitable living. In Western and Midwestern states, where cattle ranches are far apart, there is not enough work in a manageable area so cattle producers must do their own inseminating. Where this is the case, it is vital to attend a short course on artificial insemination in order to learn proper techniques. Many AI studs provide free instruction in AI techniques to purchasers of their semen. The time and money saved by preventing mistakes in breeding makes the effort involved in learning proper methods worthwhile.

The following is a listing of the responsibilities of an inseminator:*

1. Use the best semen possible and handle it in a manner to prevent deterioration in quality.
2. Keep herd records accurately, and record data that may help to improve techniques.
3. Follow approved techniques in inseminating cows and caring for equipment.
4. Maintain cleanliness of clothing and equipment at all times.
5. Keep a record of all heats.
6. Handle cattle in a quiet, easy manner—harsh, rough treatment and AI do not go hand in hand.

Semen is sold in ampules, straws, and pipettes. Each unit inseminates one cow. Although the units contain varying amounts of liquid, they contain the same number of spermatazoa. Extender is used to fill the larger units. Ampules and straws are labeled on their ends, while pipettes are labeled on their sides.

To estimate the amount of semen needed for a herd, one unit per cow should be ordered if breeding each open cow during one heat period. If planning to breed through two heat periods, the order should call for one and a half times the number of cows and heifers expected to be open for for breeding. Generally, in a well-managed herd, it takes an average of 1.5 to 1.6 services per conception. Goals established by the National Association of Animal Breeders rate 65 percent of cows pregnant after 24 days of AI as Acceptable. A total of 70 percent cows pregnant is rated as Good; 80 percent —Better; 90 percent as Excellent; and, of course, 100 percent is Optimum.

The NAAB points out that in order to get 60 percent of the cows in a herd pregnant on first service in a 24-day inseminating program at least 80 percent of those cows must come into heat during the 24-day period. At least 75 percent of the cows must settle on the first service. With older cows it may be a problem getting them to come into heat soon enough after calving to be rebred in the first 24 days of the AI program. Nutrition can help with this problem but will not solve it completely.

Cows that do not settle on the first service must be rebred. Repeat inseminations on cows coming into heat *other than with their regular cycles* should be inseminated in the vagina, not in the cervix or horn of the uterus in case the cow is pregnant and having a false heat. The chance of a cow

---

* Adapted from Kansas Artificial Breeding Service Unit handbook.

being pregnant and appearing to cycle at her regular interval is very rare. False heats occur only 3 to 4 percent of the time. Mainly false heats occur around midpregnancy. Some AI technicians suggest that, since false heats so rarely occur at the normal 21-day cycle interval, inseminating in the normal manner should be done even with repeat inseminations in every instance where the cycle appears normal. If the timing of the cycle differs from the norm, repeat inseminations should be made in the vagina to guard against abortions.

Semen Handling

All semen produced in this country is shipped and stored in liquid nitrogen refrigerators. Semen freezing was successfully performed for the first time in England in 1952, but it was the development of liquid nitrogen refrigerators in the United States that really opened up the market for shipping and freezing semen.

Liquid nitrogen, or cryogenic, refrigerators are available from semen producers. The refrigerators are actually tanks that vary in price, size, and capacity. Tanks can be purchased for prices ranging upwards of $300. New developments in the technology of constructing tanks has resulted in the availability of tanks that weigh as little as 67 pounds when filled with semen units and liquid nitrogen, compared to a similar capacity older unit weighing 125 pounds when filled. Availability and prices of various tanks vary according to area, of course.

After obtaining a tank, the most important factor in maintaining the quality of the semen involves checking the level of the liquid nitrogen at least weekly to be sure it has not evaporated. An adequate level of liquid nitrogen must be maintained in the tank at all times. An easy way to check the level of LN is with a metal ruler. Dip the metal ruler into the liquid nitrogen, hold it there for about 10 seconds, and then remove. When the ruler is waved in the air, frost forms to the level of the liquid nitrogen.

Several precautions must be taken with the liquid nitrogen. It is dangerous to handle and can burn so it must be handled carefully. The tank should be stored in a cool location out of the elements. Semen removal must be accomplished within 10 seconds or less and other units must be reimmersed immediately. The liquid nitrogen is maintained at $-320°$ F. If the temperature of the semen itself rises above $-176°$ F it is useless.

Semen Testing

Although owners of AI studs go to great lengths to test their semen for motility, percent abnormal sperm cells, number of sperm cells per milliliter, and stress, some producers like to have their own tests run to be certain that the semen purchased meets their own standards of quality. Veterinarians most generally are called upon to make semen tests on behalf of the cattle

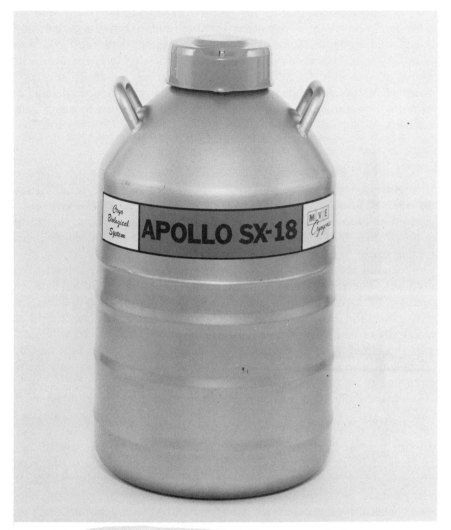

Figure 6-4 Cattle producers can purchase their own tanks for storing semen. *(Courtesy of Minnesota Valley Engineering)*

producer. The stress test, for example, involves one of the simpler testing methods. The semen is allowed to sit out, exposed to the air for varying lengths of time, and deterioration of quality is compared. Naturally there will be deterioration of quality with any semen. How much deterioration is acceptable is open to individual determination.

When a veterinarian examines sperm from a semen supplier, he or she allows it to thaw and then conducts the normal tests for evaluating fertility by looking at the initial spermatozoal motility and spermatozoal morphology. That is, the form and structure of individual sperm cells are

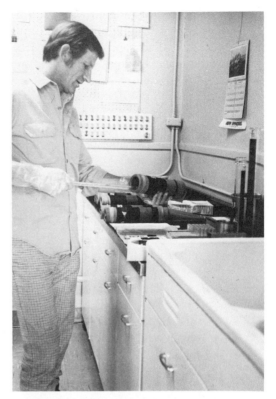

Figure 6-5   Semen suppliers use a microscope to evaluate and rate semen for motility, percent abnormal sperm cells, and other factors.

Figure 6-6   An AI technician readies an artificial vagina for use in semen collection.

examined. If the sperm fail to measure up to acceptable quality standards, the supplier should be notified.

The recommendations for handling semen vary with each semen supplier. Because it is imperative that semen be handled carefully and correctly, the rancher should follow supplier instructions carefully. A few general precautions apply to all frozen semen, however. For instance, all semen is delicate and must be protected from the elements. Heat, cold, wind, and rain can damage quality semen. For this reason, preparation of the insemination gun should be done in a protected area. Insemination should be done in a protected area, and extra semen should be stored out of the elements.

Appendix B supplies names, addresses, and telephone numbers of AI suppliers.

Taking care to handle frozen semen properly pays off in higher conception rates. Semen is delicate and must be protected from rain, wind, and thawing. Cleanliness is imperative because dirt and germs will kill sperm.

Before inseminating, it is a good idea to read the directions provided by the stud service that supplied the semen.

Each unit of semen is labeled with the name of the bull and his code number. Double check to be sure that the correct cow is bred with semen from the intended bull. Most semen suppliers use a color-coded tab to indicate bull breed, as suggested by the National Association of Animal Breeders.

Next, assemble the tools necessary for AI. Most inseminators use disposable plastic gloves. The technician also will need an inseminator's breeding gun, catheter, or syringe to hold the semen unit and deposit the semen into the cow. With these items ready, and the cow restrained in some manner, the semen should be thawed.

Thawing Semen

There are three ways to thaw ampules: in ice water, in warm water, and in hot water.

To thaw in ice water, the water temperature should be in the range of 34° to 40° F. This can be accomplished by either putting ice cubes (one or more depending on the size of the thaw box) in water or by placing the thaw box in a refrigerator. Semen should be removed from the tank exposing only the units to be removed. The semen should then be promptly placed in the ice water, with no more than five thawed together at one time. Be sure that the ampules do not stick to either the ice or to each other. Sticking together would cause them to thaw at an improper rate. Thaw in ice water for 7 to 10 minutes.

Once the semen is thawed, identify the semen and it is ready to use. Precautions should be taken to avoid exposing thawed semen to subfreezing or extremely high temperatures. When inseminating in cold weather, place catheter or other loaded inseminating instrument inside clothing, leaving it there until ready to inseminate the cow.

To thaw in warm water, remove the semen carefully from the tank, exposing only those units to be used immediately. Place semen in thaw box filled with 95° F water. Semen can be used immediately after thawing, or within 15 minutes. Semen that has been thawed out more than 15 minutes should not be used. Special care should be taken to avoid letting the temperature of the semen drop. If inseminating when temperature in the breeding area is below 60° F, the catheter or inseminating instrument should be carried inside the technician's clothing to keep it warm. Semen should be identified as soon as it is thawed.

To thaw semen in hot water, carefully remove the semen, exposing only the units needed for immediate use. Hold semen in a 150° F water bath until frozen semen in the ampule has turned to a liquid. Immediately remove the unit from the water bath, identify the semen, and use. Again, if

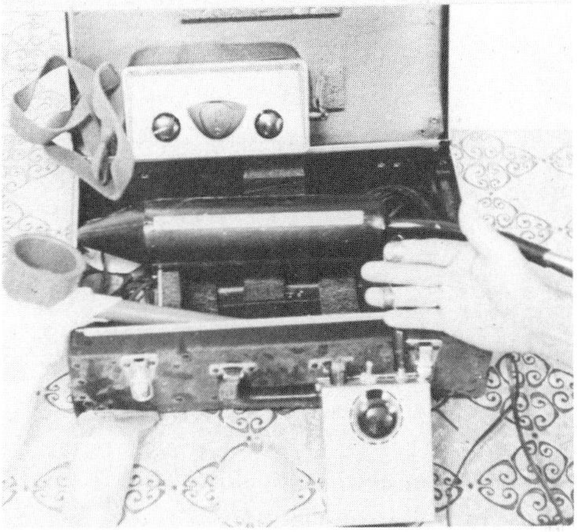

Figure 6-8   An artificial vagina has a heavy rubber, metal, or plastic outer layer, and an inner lining of thin rubber. The space between is filled with warm water and air.

Figure 6-7   Some semen suppliers use steers as "jump stock" for semen collection.

the weather is cold, the semen should be protected by carrying it inside a person's clothing.

There are five ways to thaw semen stored in straws: ice water; in the pocket; in warm water; in the cow; and in hot water.

To thaw in ice water, remove semen from the tank with tweezers, being careful not to overexpose the semen remaining in the tank. Place no more than five straws at a time in an ice water bath—temperature 34° to 40° F. Allow 3 to 5 minutes for thawing. Semen should be identified and used immediately, or, at worst, within 15 minutes. Precautions should be used to prevent a temperature drop after semen has thawed by warming the syringe or breeding gun and keeping both the inseminating instrument and the semen inside the technician's clothing until the semen is placed in the cow.

To thaw semen in a pocket, remove semen from the tank, one at a time with tweezers and place the straw in a shirt pocket. In the winter, an inside pocket is best. When semen is thawed, 5 to 7 minutes later, identify the unit and use immediately. Protect semen from temperature drop by keeping equipment and semen inside clothing until use.

Figure 6-9   An electroejaculator can be used to stimulate the bull to ejaculation.

Figure 6-10   Semen suppliers store semen in huge tanks filled with liquid nitrogen.

To thaw in warm water, remove semen from the tank taking care not to expose the remaining semen. Place the semen in a warm (95° F) water bath until thawed. Semen can be used immediately or within 15 minutes. If semen is not used as soon as it becomes liquid, it must be protected from cool temperatures by being placed inside the clothing of the technician until it is needed. Identify the semen and use.

To thaw in the cow, remove semen from the tank, with care not to expose the other semen units. Identify the straw at this time. Place the straw in the barrel of the syringe or breeding gun, cotton plug in first. Roll the sealed end of the straw between the fingers to warm it up enough so that it will not split when the end is cut off. Then cover it with the sheath and get it in the cow immediately. It will thaw in a minute or less.

To thaw in hot water (150° F), remove semen from the tank with tweezers, being careful not to overexpose the remaining semen. Still holding the unit with tweezers, place it in 150° F water. Watch the straw closely and remove it from the water when the frozen semen turns to liquid. Be careful not to leave it in the hot water too long. Usually 7 seconds is enough. Once the semen is thawed and identified it is ready to use immediately. Take precautions to prevent the temperature of the semen from dropping.

Pipettes are rarely used by semen suppliers, so chances are that most cattle producers will not have occasion to use them. However, there are two basic methods for thawing the pipette. In winter, the preferred method is to thaw in the cow. The rest of the year, a pocket thaw works well.

Directions for thawing frozen semen will vary slightly with each semen supplier. Where directions are available from the supplier, they should be followed exactly. A few general rules do apply, however. Semen must be protected from overexposure. Semen units can be ruined simply because care was not taken in removing semen from the tank. When taking semen from the tank, be careful to expose only those units that will be used immediately. Once semen has thawed, it must not be allowed to get cold. For this reason, in cold weather, it should be carried under one's coat or jacket. Water will kill semen. All units should be dried completely before using, except when thawing in the cow.

Inseminating

To inseminate cattle, remove semen from the tank and thaw. If using a breeding gun, withdraw the plunger of the gun and place the straw into the chamber, the cotton plug end first. Use a sharp scissors or knife to cut off the sealed end. Make a square cut through the air space just below the seal, cutting at a right angle to the straw. Loosen the "O" ring from the tapered end of the barrel. Place a sheath over the straw and barrel of the gun, passing it through the "O" ring. Gently pull the sheath into place so the small end of the sheath fits against the cut end of the straw. Be certain that a good seal has formed. Next, secure the sheath to the barrel by tightening the "O" ring. Push the plunger gently until the semen reaches the tip of the gun.

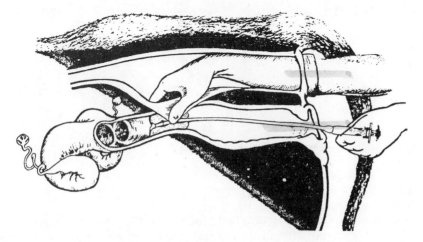

Figure 6-11 The proper technique for AI. *(Illustration by Tom Stallman)*

Keep the gun and semen warm by placing it inside a jacket or shirt while the technician puts on plastic gloves. Insert the semen into the cow. Some inseminators place the semen into the horn of the uterus while others feel that placing the semen inside the cervix is sufficient. If there is a possibility that the cow might be pregnant, repeat inseminations should be made in the vagina to avoid the possibility of an abortion.

A catheter is used to deposit ampules of semen into the reproductive tract of the cow. Figure 6-11 shows proper use of a catheter in insemination. While the left hand of the inseminator is inserting the semen, the right hand should be placed in the cow's rectum. (Thus the need for a sterile, lubricated glove). Through the rectal wall, the technician can palpate (feel) the cervix and the horn of the uterus and thus direct the semen to the exact spot where it is to be deposited. (Right-handed individuals may want to insert the semen with the right hand and place the left hand in the cow's rectum. *See* page 273.)

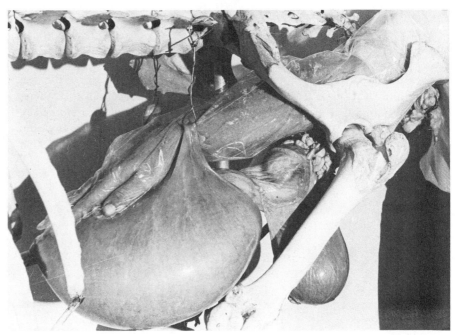

Figure 6-12   Simulated palpation of the uterus. *(Illustration by Tom Stallman)*

DETERMINING PREGNANCY

To determine if a cow is pregnant, the cattle producer inserts his or her arm into the rectum of the cow and feels the reproductive tract for evidence of pregnancy. This process is called palpation. Little equipment is needed for palpation. The person doing the palpating should wear a protective covering on the arm and hand—a rubber or plastic sleeve that covers the arm to the shoulder. The sleeve protects both the cow and the palpator from infection and disease and eliminates irritation of the arm. A lubricant such as liquid soap should be used.

With one hand grasp the cow's tail and use it as a handle. The other hand should be wearing the protective sleeve and will be used in palpation. Shape the hand into a wedge by bringing the fingers closely together. Push the hand through the anus into the rectum with a swift thrust. Fold the fingers into a modified fist as the hand enters the rectum, thus straightening out the rectum and pushing feces aside. Figure 6-12 shows the correct method of palpating to determine pregnancy. An experienced palpator can determine pregnancy as early as 30 days after breeding. At this point the uterus is filled with a small amount of fluid and will feel slightly thinner than in a nonpregnant animal. One horn is enlarged more than the other. The embryo is about a half inch long. The uterus is in the same position as before pregnancy.

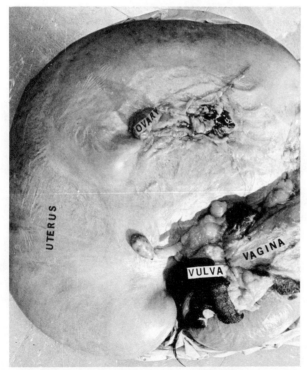

Figure 6-13   Detached placenta illustrating cotyledons. Note fetus floating in amniotic fluid.

At 45 days, the uterine horn is somewhat enlarged, thinner walled, and prominent. The fetus has grown to an inch in length. The outer membrane, containing considerable fluid, can be felt through the uterine wall.

At 60 days the uterus has enlarged until one horn is about the size of a banana. The fetus has grown to about 2½ inches in length. At this time the best way to feel the fetus is to bobble it by gently tapping the uterus, causing the fetus to swing and hit against the wall of the uterus and vesicle.

At 90 days the uterus will have enlarged a great deal and the fetus reached a size of about 6½ inches. Displacement of the uterus, enlargement of the uterine artery, and its characteristic "whirring" pulsation are indications of pregnancy at this time. The uterine artery is located in the broad ligament and can be moved 4 to 6 inches. It should not be confused with the femoral artery, which may not be moved.

At 120 days the fetus has enlarged to 10 to 12 inches long. The head is about the size of a lemon. The pulsating uterine artery may be palpated, as well as the corpus luteum and the displacement of the entire reproductive tract.

At 5 months and over the main changes will be based on enlargement of the size of the fetus.

STUDY QUESTIONS

1. A way to cause cows to come into heat when the producer wants them to is called _____. (heat synchronization)
2. A hormone that prevents heat and ovulation is _____. (progesterone)
3. A cow with a swollen, reddish, moist vulva with a clear mucous discharge is showing signs of _____. (heat)
4. The most reliable sign of heat in the cow is _____. (standing to be mounted)
5. Semen produced in this country is shipped and stored in _____. (liquid nitrogen refrigerators)
6. Cattle producers can determine whether a cow is pregnant by a process known as _____. (palpation)

7

Ova Transplant—The Prolific Cow

The transplanting of a fertilized egg from a superior female, sired by a superior male, into the uterus of a less valuable female is known as ova transplant. Basically ova transplant was developed to gain better use of top-quality cows than ever had been possible before. Through artificial insemination top bulls have been able to make tremendous contributions to their breeds. Until the development of the ova transplant technique, even the best cows of each breed were limited to production of one calf each year. Ova transplant enables quality cows to make much more extensive contributions to their breeds than ever before. Naturally, even ova transplants do not allow cows to contribute the same huge numbers as bulls do through artificial insemination, but the improved opportunities for use of a top-quality cow are tremendous.

Figure 7-1 These five calves began their existence inside the body of this cow, where ova were fertilized by sperm from a top bull. The fertilized ova then were transferred to less valuable recipient cows for pregnancy and delivery. *(Courtesy of CBR Ova Transplants)*

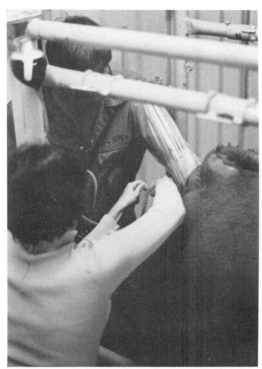

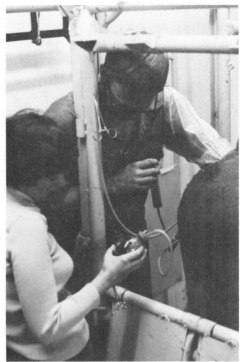

Figure 7-2 Donor cows are given a local anesthetic while ova are removed non-surgically. *(Courtesy of CBR Ova Transplants)*

Figure 7-3 A Foley catheter is passed through the cervix into the horn of the uterus. *(Courtesy of CBR Ova Transplants)*

NO LONGER USED ONLY FOR RESEARCH

Until about 1971 the embryo transplant technique primarily was used for research on reproductive functions and problems, fertility studies, infections, and the normal reproductive mechanism. The technique allowed the researcher to remove the embryo from the environment of the mother and to study the effects of temperature, nutrition, and all kinds of environmental and genetic factors.

More recently, however, with the development of nonsurgical ova transplant techniques, cattle producers have developed increased interest in the technique.

EXPENSIVE TECHNIQUE

Compared to conventional breeding, ova transplant is an expensive technique. But with higher cattle prices the use of ova transplants is a viable tool to develop valuable foundation stock to be used for semen production.

Figure 7-4 The catheter is connected to a collection device consisting of a reservoir for the culture media, a 60cc syringe for agitating the media, and a collection bulb for collecting the media after it has been flushed through the uterus. *(Courtesy of CBR Ova Transplants)*

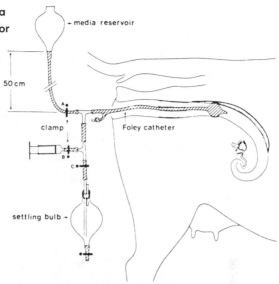

Today producers can use ova transplants to hurdle the long years normally needed to develop the volume of dams with desirable traits for a foundation herd. Ova transplants speed up the breeding process dramatically. If the same efforts were attempted in a regular natural breeding system, getting the desired results would take a human lifetime. Additionally, once the desired genetic mix is achieved, it is possible to make nearly identical copies and to do that rapidly.

Unfortunately, not all cows respond to the necessary superovulation techniques required to produce quantities of embryos for transplant. Cattle producers becoming involved in ova transplant programs should not place all their confidence or money in one donor cow.

GREATER APPLICATION NECESSARY

New techniques, reduced costs, and on-site transfers will allow greater application of the embryo transplant program in the future. One technique employed by some producers to select top-quality animals for breeding is called a *two-phase technique*. Since there are vast differences even in full brothers and sisters that normally take months and years to evaluate, embryo transplant has been of tremendous help in this phase of selection. The embryo transplant program allows the producer to speed up the evaluation of a cow's normal lifetime of production.

After a litter of calves has been performance tested and a bull calf selected for the AI program, the producer moves to phase two of the program and selects a female to be used in an embryo transplant program. Program results indicate that it takes about a year of a donor cow's life to produce six embryos that eventually result in live calves.

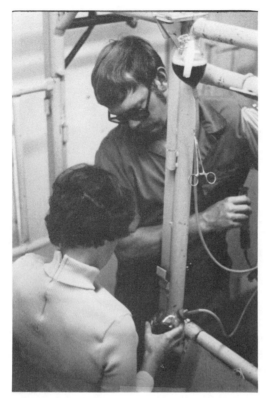

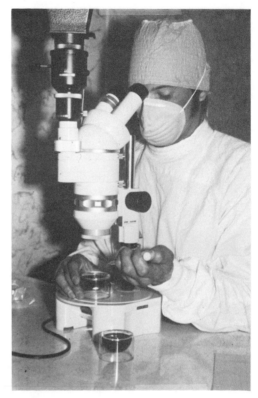

Figure 7-5 The collected ova are flushed out with the media. *(Courtesy of CBR Ova Transplants)*

Figure 7-6 An embryologist draws the media into ova cups, then puts the cups under a low-powered microscope to search for the ova. *(Courtesy of CBR Ova Transplants)*

HEAT SYNCHRONIZATION NECESSARY

A basic requirement for ova transplants is the necessity for both the donor and the recipient cow to be at the same stage of the estrus cycle when the transplant is made. To accomplish this, research continues with heat synchronizing compounds throughout the country. Prostaglandin has been approved for use by the Food and Drug Administration for this purpose.

Hormones are used to superovulate the donor cow, that is, to cause her to produce more than one egg. If the hormones work and the cow produces multiple eggs, all eggs can be removed and transplanted to recipient cows, freeing the donor to continue to be used only as a donor, or allowing the donor cow to carry a calf at the same time that recipient cows are carrying her other offspring.

DISLODGING THE EGG

To conduct an ova transplant, the cow is superovulated and fertilized by artificial insemination. Between 6 to 9 days after the sperm activates growth in the egg, the eggs are removed and transplanted to recipient cows. A few years ago the only method of removing the eggs was by surgery. With non-surgical ova transplant, however, the method of removing the 10 to 15 eggs is by flooding the uterus with a liquid media, then massaging the uterus to dislodge the eggs from the uterine lumen to flow with a solution. The solution containing the ova is then withdrawn through a tube to a syringe. The syringe is then taken to a temporary laboratory set up in a barn or elsewhere, where a technician selects the fertilized ova under a microscope in a light-tight room. A bisecting microscope is necessary because the eggs are only at the 8- to 16-cell stage of division.

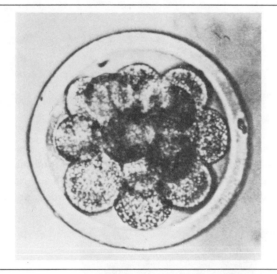

Figure 7-7   The ova, like this 16-cell egg, are removed from the ova cups with a special pipette and placed in fresh culture media to await transplant into recipient cows. *(Courtesy of CBR Ova Transplants)*

Recipient cows are brought to a holding cage, anesthetized, shaved, and an incision is made—usually in the left flank—to allow the horn of the uterus to be pulled to the surface. The fertilized ovum then is transferred to the new uterus by a small syringe inserted through a tiny hole in the uterine wall. Once the transfer is complete, the incision is sutured, the cow released, and normal pregnancy develops. (*See* Figure 7-8 overleaf.)

If, for instance, 10 embryos are found in a single fertilized donor cow, current research indicates that a success rate of four to six pregnant recipient cows can be expected.

Ova transplant does not lend itself to get-rich-quick schemes, but represents an excellent management tool when accompanied by proper planning.

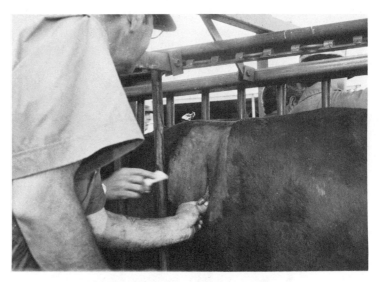

Figure 7-8 Recipient cows are given a local anesthetic. The surgeon makes a small incision in the flank area, exteriorizes the uterus, and inserts the ovum into the uterus with a pipette. The ovum is transferred to the recipient cow and the pipette is checked under the microscope to be sure the transplant is complete.

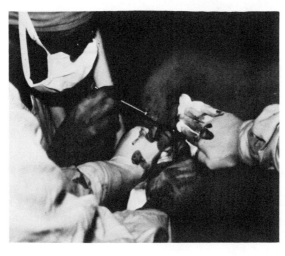

Figure 7-9 This detail shows how the ovum is transferred during flank surgery. (*Courtesy Carnation/Genetics*)

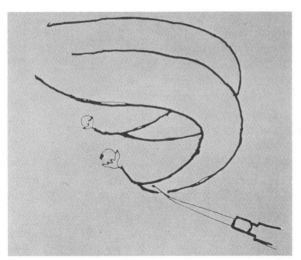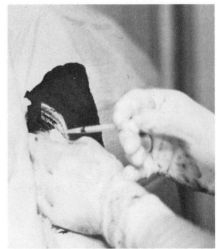

Figure 7-10 *(above left)*   The sketch shows exactly where the fertilized ovum is placed in the horn of the cow's uterus. **Figure 7-11** *(above right)* illustrates the actual procedure as the veterinary surgeon transfers the ovum from the pipette to the uterus. *(Drawing courtesy of Carnation/Genetics; photograph courtesy of CBR Ova Transplants.)*

Figure 7-12 *(below left)* Detail shows the surgical technique now usually replaced by the liquid media flushing method illustrated earlier.

Figure 7-13 *(right)* also shows how ova collection had to be done before the nonsurgical technique was developed. *(Photographs courtesy of CBR Ova Transplants.)*

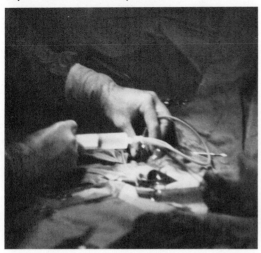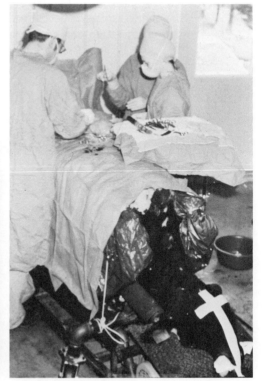

FROZEN EMBRYOS FOR THE FUTURE

Ova transplant promises to become an even more effective management tool when higher pregnancy rates are achieved. Many transplant centers are working on freezing embryos and expect to offer frozen embryos for sale in the near future. Researchers believe that frozen embryos will have a much better pregnancy rate than currently is being achieved with embryo transfers.

Actual costs of ova transplants vary depending upon who does the transfers, whether they are done on the farm or at a transplant center, and depending upon who supplies the recipient cows. Naturally, the donor's owner supplies the semen. Ova transplant centers are listed in Appendix C. Each can supply the reader with additional information on actual costs.

STUDY QUESTIONS

1. For ova transplant to be successful, the donor cow must be able to respond to drugs causing her to _____. (produce several eggs)
2. A _____ microscope is used to view the eggs that are at the 8- to 16-cell stage of division. (bisecting)
3. The recipient cow receives the fertilized egg in her _____. (uterus)
4. For ova transplant to be successful, the _____ and the _____ must be at the same stage of the estrus cycle when the transplant is made. (donor, recipient)

8

Facilities for the Farm and Ranch

Ideally, equipment used in beef and dairy operations should be sturdy, safe for both workers and animals, and relatively inexpensive. Cattle raising has changed drastically from the days when herds of Texas Longhorns were driven from Texas to markets in Kansas. In the 1800's, little equipment was utilized to make the job easier. "Old-timers" would be amazed at the variety and effectiveness of the "new fangled" equipment that modern producers have at their disposal to make life easier for them and to make their cattle more productive.

Figure 8-1 Remington illustrated a "modern" cattle corral in 1888.
(Courtesy of The Kansas State Historical Society, Topeka)

For example, cattle exposed to extremes of heat and cold do not produce as well as those protected from extreme elements. Where weather is relatively mild all year, shelters may not be mandatory. In harsher climates, like those of Minnesota, the Dakotas, and other northern states cattle need protection from the weather. Cold stress takes its toll on production, so it makes sense to lessen the effects of wind and cold through use of sheds, shelters, and windbreaks. At the opposite extreme, where weather reaches 80° to 85° F, cattle need shade in order to maintain normal growth and production.

SHEDS

Mature beef animals require about 40 square feet of shelter space per animal. Calves and yearlings need 20 to 30 square feet per animal. Open sheds located in a well-drained area with a southern exposure are helpful to beef animals in northern and midwestern sections of the U.S. Sheds for winter protection are generally not needed by cattlemen in southern and southwestern areas of the country.

Shelter sheds often serve as shade areas during the summer so it is important to design portions of the closed sides so that they can be opened easily in mild weather to take advantage of air flow.

In hot weather shade shelters are needed in pastures lacking shade trees. If a pasture lacks trees, some artificial form of shade shelter should be constructed. Placed on an elevated area of ground, a shelter can take advantage of normal wind movements. Roof materials range from straw and hay to sheet metal.

Figure 8-2 In warm climates, cattle may not need shelters. *(Courtesy of the American Hereford Association)*

WINDBREAKS

In some areas, natural windbreaks such as timber and earth embankments exist and there is no need to construct an artificial windbreak. When a windbreak is absent, it may be helpful to construct one by building an eight foot high wall from either wood or metal materials. The windbreak can be either solid or semi-solid. In either case, however, the supports holding the windbreak wall must be sturdy since the windbreak must withstand both animal crowding and wind stress. Six-inch pressure-treated wood posts or three or four inch pipe, eight feet long, can be used to support a windbreak. Wood posts should be set 3 feet in the ground, 6 to 8 feet apart. Pipe posts have greater stability if set in concrete. Bags of instant mix concrete are very convenient for this purpose.

FEEDING EQUIPMENT

Self-feeders are designed to provide a continuous supply of high-quality nutrients to cattle at all times. Most commonly, self-feeders are used as calf "creep feeders" and sometimes are used in fattening operations.

Automated feeding equipment saves time and effort while making the farm operation more efficient. The University of Illinois developed an automatic group feeding system on its dairy farm that has the capacity to mix programmed rations of forage and concentrate and to deliver them to five feedlots, accommodating a total of 127 cows.

In this system, automatic subsystems proportion forage and concentrate, resupply concentrate bins through a pneumatic conveying system, control forage flow of top type silo unloaders, and feed several groups of cows in automatic sequence.

Figure 8-3 These feeders allow cattle to approach from either side. *(Courtesy of U.S. Department of Agriculture)*

The cost of an automatic system must be measured carefully against its advantages, the length of time the farm or ranch is intended to operate, and age and physical abilities of the rancher. For some, automated feeding is wonderful: it shortens the time required for feeding large groups of animals. For others, the costs do not justify the investment. Their operations are too small to benefit from such a major cost item.

FEEDING HAY

Some cattle producers use combination feed bunk-hay racks to good advantage. Hay racks placed inside shelters should be located so they can be filled from the hay storage area or from equipment used to haul forage.

Chopping, baling, and stacking are the three basic ways hay can be handled on the farm. Chopped hay can be handled wet (haylage) or dry by using the typical silage blowers or flighted elevators, or both. Baled hay compresses hay into a dense package to reduce space requirements for storage. Stacking can be done by hand or by machine and can even be left in the field for the animals to eat directly from the stack.

WATER TANKS

Cattle must have an adequate supply of water available at all times. Water tanks should be placed where they are readily available to animals of all ages. Water tanks can be constructed of galvanized metal or poured con-

Figure 8-4 Water must be available to cattle at all times. *(Courtesy of U.S. Department of Agriculture)*

crete. Metal tanks usually can be moved from one location to another. Naturally concrete tanks are more permanent, and more durable. Pouring a 6- to 8-foot wide concrete slab around the tank prevents erosion of the soil around it. To keep water from freezing in the winter, many farmers use a heating device available from local farm supply dealers. Water tanks located in the common corner or fence of two or more lots or pastures can serve several groups of cattle.

CORRALS

The producer who puts extra thought into the design of corrals will be rewarded with a more efficient corral system later on. The design of the corral depends on the kind and number of cattle to be handled, the type of farm or ranch, and the location.

Ideally, corrals facilitate the efficient movement of large numbers of cattle in a short time. Locate the corrals where they can process many cattle into the holding area or crowding area that leads to a working chute in a short time.

Extra effort should be made to be certain that the gates are sturdy and well built.

Figure 8-5 In its heyday in the 1920's, the Kansas City, Missouri, stockyards were an excellent example of an efficient operation—holding up to 70,000 cattle at one time. *(Courtesy of The Kansas State Historical Society, Topeka)*

Figure 8-6   Chutes make it easier to work on cattle. *(Courtesy of USDA)*

CHUTES

Chutes can make a cattle producer's job easier and safer. To be really effective, a chute should be long enough to hold five or six mature animals. A curved chute encourages cattle movement more than a straight chute. Also, constructing the chute with sloping sides wider at the top and narrower at the bottom allows both large and small animals to be handled in the same chute. Without the sloping sides, smaller animals would be able to turn around inside the chute, blocking the traffic flow through the chute.

Strength of the chute is another important factor. The chute must be strong enough to hold the most active animal in the herd. A top or high sides prevent cattle from climbing out.

A loading chute is helpful for use on the ranch too. Usually these are constructed of wood. The ideal chute allows lots of room for truck approach. The ramp should have two layers of dimension lumber with cleats placed 6 to 8 inches apart to prevent animals from slipping or falling. Portable loading chutes are available, but are not quite as functional as a permanent facility.

Figure 8-7 Waste handling presents a problem even for small farm feedlots. *(Courtesy of U.S. Department of Agriculture)*

WASTE HANDLING

A major problem for feedlots and large dairy operations is the dilemma of disposing of the animal waste products. The U.S. Environmental Protection Agency and state pollution control agencies may require permits for disposal of animal wastes. Runoff control regulations have been implemented throughout the United States to prevent pollution of lakes, rivers, and ground water supplies. Since waste management and pollution control practices are carefully controlled by federal, state, and local regulations, it is important to check with the state pollution control agency before constructing a waste-handling system.

There are two types of waste-handling systems, solid and liquid. The solid systems include a tractor and mounted scoop and blade, a manure spreader, and a concrete manure pad for spreading. With this method the manure is spread on crop land for use as fertilizer. Unfortunately, odors persist for 2 or 3 days following spreading, depending on the weather. Odors can be reduced by mixing the manure with the soil. Discing and plowing under aid in reduction of odors.

Liquid waste-handling systems require a storage location, agitation and removal with liquid manure tankwagon, and safety precautions to keep people and animals out of the storage tank. The liquid system often requires a large initial investment and requires good management. Odor may be increased or decreased compared with solid systems, depending on total system design and management.

LIGHTING

Proper use of both natural and artificial lights makes a cattle operation safer for both people and animals. Also, a California study found that feedlot cattle ate more feed and gained faster when the feedlot was lighted at night. The research study found that cattle ate from lighted bunks after dark and spent more time eating. Additional advantages to use of lighting in feedlots were the elimination of "spooking" and stampeding with less tendency to crowd in bunches when cattle can see other cattle or people; cattle can be "worked" at night during hot weather; bird roosting over bunks is reduced; and the lighting tends to deter predators and vandals.

MILKING EQUIPMENT

Keeping all equipment clean is important in any cattle operation, but the necessity is emphasized with dairy cattle. For instance, the vacuum pumps used in a pipeline milking system need to have their supply lines cleaned at least every 60 days. Unstable vacuum can result when the supply line is not large enough to move vacuum from the vacuum pump to the milk line. Vacuum supply lines cleaned less frequently than every 60 days will most likely have decreased vacuum capacity due to accumulations of foreign material on the inside of the lines.

Dust from the air in combination with moisture and milk vapors make deposits that gradually decrease the capacity of vacuum supply lines. To clean these lines, flush with a hot 1 percent lye or nonfoaming detergent solution. Attach a rubber vacuum hose to the stall cock nearest the vacuum pump and draw 2 to 4 quarts of the solution through this stall cock. Repeat at the next stall cock and continue working away from the vacuum pump. Drain the sanitary trap before it overflows to avoid drawing the cleaning solution into the vacuum pump. After flushing the vacuum supply line with the cleaning solution, rinse with hot water using the same procedure. Dry the line by pulling air through the stall cock at the end of the line with the vacuum pump.

Whatever brand of milking equipment is selected, it is imperative to maintain the equipment in good, clean condition at all times. Too often, dairy farmers forget that it is necessary to perform routine maintenance chores on their equipment. When this happens, simple neglect can cause problems in the dairy herd.

For example, teat cup inflations on milking machines are supposed to massage teat-ends and interrupt continual vacuum on the teat-end. To do its job correctly, the teat cup inflation must be of the characteristic size, shape, and elasticity intended by the manufacturer of the specific milking machine. Most inflations have a useful life of about 1,500 cow milkings. Since it is easy to neglect changing these inflations as often as needed, a cow may suffer teat-end irritation due to a worn-out inflation. An inflation that has milked 1,500 cows will appear to work perfectly, but will have stretched to about ⅜-inch longer than a new one. By the time an inflation looks worn out, it has been ineffective for a long time.

To protect cows from irritation it is best to calculate the number of days a set of inflations will last, based on 1,500 cow milkings, record the information on a calendar, and change inflations accordingly. The teat cup inflation is the only part of the milking machine that works on living tissue so it should be maintained in good condition.

CALF BARNS

Care of calves is vital to the dairy farmer. Death losses mean loss of income as well as loss of potentially good replacement heifers and high-producing cows. The need for better calf care facilities is prevalent among many producers who had to build other facilities first in order to meet sanitation and health codes.

For producers with large herds and 25 to 30 or more calves each year, an enclosed environmentally controlled calf barn can prove economical and durable. Concrete block construction will provide durability and washdown properties required for such buildings. Additional insulation will be needed in midwestern and northern states, but the concrete blocks themselves would be adequate in southern and southwestern areas. A concrete floor provides for easy cleaning by simply hosing down. Many dairy farmers use individual calf crates or calf huts for raising calves.

STUDY QUESTIONS

1. The effects of wind and cold can be lessened through use of _____. (windbreaks, sheds, and shelters)
2. Cattle suffer from excess heat and need _____ in order to maintain normal growth and productivity. (shade)
3. Mature beef animals require about _____ of shelter space per animal. (40 square feet)
4. _____ provide a continuous supply of feed available to cattle at all times. (Self-feeders)
5. Waste handling systems can be of two types: _____ and _____. (solid, liquid)
6. Milking equipment must be kept _____ at all times. (clean)

9

Handling Livestock Safely

When thinking of life on the farm, romanticists who conjure up visions of lovely rolling hills and pastoral beauty generally add a picture of the farmer as an easy-going rube who putters around the ranch, encountering few if any hazards in day-to-day life.

What's wrong with the picture? Virtually everything, actually. Agriculture is big business. Like other big industries, agriculture has its share of accidents—more than its share as a matter of fact. It is unfortunate that agriculture is not as safe as a romantic dreamer might make it. In reality, agriculture is the third most dangerous industry in the United States. Only mining and construction work are more hazardous in terms of deaths of workers. And even though mining and construction workers are more likely than an agriculture worker to die as a result of an on-the-job accident, a rancher or farmer faces a greater risk of suffering a disabling injury than do workers in any other field.

Because agriculture is so hazardous, safety and accident prevention should be an important consideration for every rancher. The government agrees with this theory. If farmers employ even one worker outside their immediate families, they are subject to fines if they fail to comply with provisions of the Occupational Safety and Health Act as it applies to agriculture.

OSHA AND THE FARMER

The William-Steiger Occupational Safety and Health Act was passed in 1970 with the goal of making sure all workers have a safe and healthy place to work. The law applies to every employer engaged in a business affecting commerce. The law applies to nearly all farmers, since so many farm products are involved either directly, or indirectly, in interstate or foreign commerce.

TABLE 9-A.   REQUIRED RECORDKEEPING FOR OSHA

OSHA NO. 100

LOG OF OCCUPATIONAL INJURIES AND ILLNESSES

CASE OR FILE NUMBER	DATE OF INJURY OR ONSET OF ILLNESS	EMPLOYEE'S NAME (First name or initial, middle initial, last name)	OCCUPATION (Enter regular job title, not activity employee was performing when injured or at onset of illness.)	DEPARTMENT (Enter department in which the employee is regularly employed.)	DESCRIPTION OF INJURY OR ILLN [Nature of Injury or Illness and Part(s) of Body Affected (Typical entries for this column might be: Amputation of 1st joint right forefinger Strain of lower back Contact dermatitis on both hands Electrocution—body)]
(1)	Mo./day/yr. (2)	(3)	(4)	(5)	(6)

Company Name_____

Establishment Name_____

Establishment Address_____

NOTE This is NOT a report form. Keep it in the establishment for 5 years.

Basically, the employer has six general responsibilities to fulfill under the law, observe federal agricultural safety standards, supply every employee a safe and healthful place to work, keep records on occupational injuries and illness as required, provide safety information to employees, train employees, and cooperate with U.S. Department of Labor inspectors.

RECORDABLE CASES: You are required to record information about: every occupational <u>death</u>; every nonfatal occupational <u>illness</u>; and those nonfatal occupational <u>injuries</u> which involve one or more of the following: loss of consciousness, restriction of work or motion, transfer to another job, or medical treatment (other than first aid).
More complete definitions appear on the other side of this form.

Form Approved
OMB No. 44R 1453

		EXTENT OF AND OUTCOME OF CASES				
		LOST WORKDAY CASES			NONFATAL CASES WITHOUT LOST WORKDAYS	TERMINATIONS OR PERMANENT TRANSFER
			LOST WORKDAYS			
Injury or Illness Code See codes at bottom of page.	DEATHS (Enter date of death.)	Enter a check if case involved lost workdays.	Enter number of days AWAY FROM WORK due to injury or illness.	Enter number of days of RESTRICTED WORK ACTIVITY due to injury or illness.	(Enter a check if no entry was made in columns 8 or 9 but the case is recordable, as defined above.)	(Enter a check if the entry in columns 9 or 10 represented a termination or permanent transfer.)
(7)	Mo./day/yr. (8)	(9)	(9A)	(9B)	(10)	(11)

Injury Code
10 All occupational injuries
Illness Codes

21 Occupational skin diseases or disorders
22 Dust diseases of the lungs (pneumoconioses)
23 Respiratory conditions due to toxic agents
24 Poisoning (systemic effects of toxic materials)

25 Disorders due to physical agents (other than toxic materials)
26 Disorders associated with repeated trauma
29 All other occupational illnesses

If a rancher employs one or more people outside his or her family, then OSHA regulations must be observed. Also, his or her farm is subject to inspection by a Department of Labor Compliance officer. If the inspector finds a safety violation a citation may be issued. Citations are *serious* where there is a high probability of an accident resulting in death or serious injury, *nonserious* where injury potential exists but the injury would not result in death or total disability, and *De minimis,* that is, a minor violation that does not have direct or immediate relationship to safety or health.

In cases where the compliance officer issues a citation following the farm inspection, the citation will be accompanied by a letter explaining the specified time allowed for correction of the violation and a discussion of the rights of the employer in the matter. At this time, mention of any applicable fines would be made. The farmer has the right to appeal any citations, but if the appeal fails, must correct the violation or be subject to an additional penalty. Under the law, employers bear the brunt of responsibility for any violations. Even though an employee may be the person committing the safety violation, it is the employer who must pay the fines, if any are applicable.

If a rancher employs 11 or more employees, a log of occupational injuries and illnesses must be kept. These records should be filled out according to Department of Labor regulations and must be kept for 5 years after the year to which they relate.

Some questions arise as to who might be classified as an employee. Any member of the farm family is exempt from OSHA provisions unless paid a salary by an employer. The family includes brothers, uncles, nephews, wives, and others. If two families exchange labor, this would include payment in kind and would not be payment of a salary. The provisions of OSHA do not apply since there is no employee-employer relationship.

If however, a rancher "loans" a paid employee to a neighbor, he or she still must maintain the required records as long as the worker is employed. If the rancher turns over control of the employee to the neighbor, the neighbor must maintain the required records.

With even one employee, the rancher must post the OSHA "Safety and Health Protection on the Job" poster. If the farmer had 11 or more employees in the prior year, or if selected to participate in the annual OSHA survey, he or she must maintain three types of records: a log of occupational injuries and illnesses, a supplementary record of occupational injuries and annual illnesses, and a summary. The poster and forms are available from local OSHA offices throughout the United States.

WHY AGRICULTURE IS DANGEROUS

Fear of fines should not be the primary motivation for safety on the farm or ranch. Because the death rate for agriculture is 3.66 times higher than for the average of all industries, workers need to be aware of the particular hazards facing them each day. Without an awareness of the dangers involved in agriculture, cattle producers risk becoming a part of national accident statistics.

Figure 9-1 Dairy cattle may kick, butt, or trample handlers if they let up their guard. *(Courtesy of CBR Ova Transplants)*

One of the major difficulties in instructing agricultural workers in safety habits is the extremely diversified nature of the job. Whereas in other industries, each laborer would have a specific job, in agriculture each laborer usually has every job. Farmers must be jacks-of-all trades. The same person who handles cattle also must handle chemicals, vaccines, pesticides, must operate and repair machinery, and do the complex bookkeeping required of today's cattle producer.

Working with cattle can be a particularly hazardous task. Since the dairy farmer must work closely with cattle on a daily basis, opportunities for injury are frequent. Dairy cows may kick, butt, trample, or crush a handler if the farmer lets his or her guard down. And dairy bulls are even more dangerous. Because of their unpredictable temperaments, dairy bulls should never be trusted. Most dairy bull owners learn to handle them only in properly constructed pens with proper equipment. A dairy bull has such great size and strength that if he turns unexpectedly from docile to angry, he could seriously injure or even kill someone. Almost one-third of the accidents on dairy farms occur while the worker is performing routine chores. A momentary lapse in basic safety practices can result in a severe injury. For this reason, cattle producers must constantly be aware of the prudent method of doing chores.

The beef producer faces the same hazards as a dairy farmer, with the additional dangers of rope burns and falls from horses while working cattle. Chasing a steer, for example, is exciting; from a safety aspect, the excitement is less than desirable, because the horse and the steer become excited also. The chances of the horse falling are increased with the excitement. Because of this, any animal to be roped should be cut from the herd before roping, the horse should be reined to the point where the rider is in control, and

Figure 9-2 Working cattle on horseback is exciting but dangerous. *(Courtesy of American Murray Grey Association)*

roping should be done on level ground, if possible. Leather gloves will reduce the rider's chances for sustaining rope burns, too.

WATCHING FOR DANGER SIGNS

Observation of an animal before working with it may prevent accidents, also. However, often an animal will not show signs of aggression until approached. Cattle that are not accustomed to seeing a human or a horse are wilder in temperament than cattle that have become used to people. Newly purchased cattle should be watched even more closely than those that have been on the ranch. A newcomer might charge a worker in the lot or pasture. Some cattle producers believe that there are regional differences in cattle temperament that affect their reactions to specific situations.

Working with cattle in a confined area presents additional hazards. The cattle producer risks being squeezed between the animal and a solid structure, or being kicked or stepped on by the animal. For this reason it is important to let an animal know where the person is at all times. Usually it is helpful to speak calmly to an animal before touching it also to reduce nervousness in the animal.

Figure 9-3 Working with this dairy bull for semen collection can be hazardous if the collector is not careful.

LIVESTOCK FACILITIES

Poor maintenance of livestock facilities can lead to serious accidents. Something as simple as splinters from deteriorating fencing can cause painful and infectious injuries. Protruding pieces of lumber, nails, or bolts can cause uncomfortable bruises. Hazards such as these can be reduced by removal or by padding. Old automobile and bicycle tires and foam rubber can be used as protective padding. Not only humans, but cattle also, will have fewer chances for injury when a few commonsense safety precautions are taken.

MANAGEMENT PRACTICES

The tools used for various management practices around the ranch are safe when used properly. When mishandled, chances for accidents increase during branding, tattooing, trimming feet, and dehorning. To enhance the safety of any operation, it is a must to use restraints on the animal when needed.

The dangers involved in branding seem obvious, but one must keep in mind the hazardous nature of the task in order to be properly safety-conscious. Hot irons can burn human flesh, fires can rage out of control. There is danger for the animal, too. If the branding iron is too hot the animal's hair will catch fire, damaging the hide as well as endangering the rancher. If using an electric branding iron, it is important to be sure that any extension cords are the proper size to handle their load, and that the iron is properly grounded. A producer might get an electric shock if the unit is not grounded.

Freeze branding is not without hazards either. Dry ice and the refrigerant solution used for bringing the branding iron to the desired temperature are dangerous chemicals and should be handled with care.

Tattooing presents dangers for the animals involved only if proper sanitation standards are not maintained. Dirty tattoo equipment can transmit wart viruses and other diseases from animal to animal.

CHUTES AND ALLEYWAYS

Accidents are likely to happen in chutes and alleyways if a rancher allows safety consciousness to lapse. Chutes should be designed to reduce shadows and excitement. Livestock will move more readily through a chute if they can see light ahead. Head gates and squeeze chutes, if used at all, should be designed to handle livestock with the least amount of excitement to the cattle and the least exposure to the rancher when moving levers, gates, springs, and latches.

Cattle squeeze chutes are involved with one of every five accidents on the farm with people or cattle since squeeze chutes can injure the cattle as well as the ranch hands. A poorly designed squeeze chute can expose workers to a lot of excessive pushing and lifting of animals. Too much pushing and lifting of 500-pound or larger animals can cause hernias, pulled muscles, injured backs, and in some workers, even possible heart attacks.

To keep workers out of the chute area, some farmers build catwalks along the chutes and alleyways. These allow supervision of the cattle without exposing the workers to the hazards of being in the chute with the animals. However, if a catwalk is more than 18 inches above the ground it should have a guard rail to prevent falls. In designing a walkway, the builder should allow sufficient space for a person to carry equipment, and, if necessary, provide room to treat the livestock.

Figure 9-4   Cattle producers should keep out of chutes for safety's sake.

Additionally, chutes, corrals, and pen fencing should provide an escape route to prevent worker entrapment. A bull could crush a worker up against a chute that does not allow the person to escape. Because of this danger, provisions should be made for emergencies, and the corrals, chutes, and fences well maintained to prevent a needless catastrophe. In some operations, going over or under a fence would be an adequate escape route. In other cases, however, an upright opening large enough for a person to slip through but too small for a bull may be needed.

ON-THE-FARM HAZARDS

On many farms, old equipment and machinery are stored on a back pasture, out of sight. If cattle are allowed to roam or rest in the same area with the equipment, they could injure themselves. Additionally, if ranch personnel have to go into the area to work the cattle out of the pasture, the people might have accidents also. It is best to keep cattle out of these areas entirely.

If electric fences are used on the farm, especially the high-voltage units, the rancher risks a severe shock if he or she walks into the fence inadvertently. The danger is compounded on wet ground where grounding of the current is assisted by moisture.

Lagoons and manure pits present drowning hazards on the farm. They should be fenced. If practical, manure pits should be covered since noxious gases from manure pits pose a genuine hazard to both animals and humans if the victim falls in.

ACCIDENT PREVENTION

There are some steps ranchers can take to protect themselves, their families, and their employees from hazards on the farm. A hard hat is not just an item for construction workers, it can help prevent bumps on the head suffered by farm workers also. A good pair of leather gloves will protect the hands from splinters, rope burns, and other potential injuries. Steel insoled shoes reduce the possibility of a punctured foot from stepping on a nail or other sharp object. Leaving loose clothing at home can prevent accidents too. Loose clothing can get caught in any working equipment and draw the person into the machinery. Also the animal can get a horn or a hoof caught in the worker's clothes and cause injury to both. Being knowledgeable about the types of accidents that can happen often helps the livestock producers avoid them.

For this reason, proper training of employees is helpful. Anyone working with livestock needs to be instructed in the safest methods of handling the animals. Workers need to know how to stay in control of the animal at all times. Frequently a rancher will attempt a project that he or she cannot handle alone. It may be more bother to get a helper, but doing so reduces the chances of accidents and pays off in the long run by avoiding expensive hospital bills and lost time on the job. Examples of such tasks are artificial insemination, hoof trimming, and tattooing. Each of these tasks might be done by one person, but each is far better done by two people. There are others, of course. Tasks should be analyzed for possible dangers before they are begun.

Other training should include learning the danger signals exhibited by livestock. Watching for signs of aggressiveness, fear, or excitement will alert the cattle producer to be especially careful when approaching the animal involved. Even if an animal does not appear excited upon observation, it may become excited when a person approaches. For this reason, it is a good idea to never walk too closely to the animals, thus averting injury from a kick or a squeeze.

LIGHTING

Using natural and artificial lighting in good combination to keep work areas well lighted ranks as an excellent accident prevention method. Additionally, weatherproof lights, shielded from physical damage, should be installed in livestock work areas for maximum safety.

BENEFITS OF SAFETY

Due to the independent nature of the rancher in American business, agriculture is much more sensitive to the loss of an individual worker than any other high-risk industry. For example, if a miner or construction worker suffers a work-related injury, that person can be replaced by another worker and the work can continue uninterrupted. However, if a cattle producer sustains an injury, there is rarely anyone immediately available to replace him or her. Frequently the work must go undone until he or she recovers sufficiently to get back to work. For those managing small farms, the results can be economically devastating. Therefore, avoiding accidents has, as one benefit, the very real advantage of keeping a vital and necessary worker on the job.

Another benefit of a safe working operation is avoiding the unpleasant inconvenience of going to the hospital. Few of us enjoy going to the doctor or into the hospital and a continuing attitude of "safety first" can prevent expensive and time-consuming rehabilitation.

For farmers who employ workers to help them on their ranches or farms, accident prevention may also prevent legal entanglements. An injured worker might have grounds for a law suit if an accident was caused by negligence on the part of the employer. Keeping a cattle operation free of hazards avoids these possible legal problems.

An additional point sometimes overlooked, is that by preventing accidents to themselves and their employees, producers may be preventing accidents to their livestock as well. Any safety improvements made to protect workers are bound to have a side benefit of protecting cattle as well.

Cattle producers can cut the costs of making their operations safe by creative thinking—improvising with excess or inexpensive materials to correct safety hazards. Most cattle producers agree, however, that, weighed against the high cost of hospitalization, their inability to hire adequate temporary help to replace an injured worker, and the very real possibility of lawsuits or fines for an unsafe workplace, the cost of making a ranch safe is comparatively low.

STUDY QUESTIONS

1. If a rancher employs one or more people outside his or her family he or she must comply with _____ regulations. (OSHA)
2. Bulls have _____ temperaments. (unpredictable)
3. Animals should be observed carefully for signs of _____. (aggression)
4. Livestock facilities should be checked regularly for signs of _____. (deterioration)
5. Cattle squeeze chutes are involved with one of every five accidents on the farm because they can injure both _____. (cattle and workers)
6. Signs of aggressiveness, fear, or excitement in cattle should alert cattle producers to be _____ when approaching the animal. (careful)

Glossary

Aberdeen-Angus Refers to origin of Angus breed, the shires of Aberdeen and Angus.

Abomasum The true stomach of cattle, where most digestion is completed.

Africander A Zebu-type breed of humped cattle from South Africa.

Artificial insemination The process of impregnating a female by use of stored semen.

Bos indicus Species of humped cattle, for example, the Brahman.

Bos taurus Cattle without humps, for example, British breeds.

Bred Applies to the pregnant female safe in calf, or pregnant; also refers to mating process.

Breed A group of animals with similar external characteristics developed over generations, which will breed true in subsequent generations.

British breeds Those native to the British Isles such as Hereford, Angus, and Shorthorn.

Bulldog A genetically imperfect calf. The condition is lethal. *See* Dexter.

Calves Young cattle of either sex less than a year of age.

Carcass Data Service U.S. Department of Agriculture service that provides important performance information to feeders and cattle producers.

Castrate To remove the testes of male cattle.

Cervix Composed of strong, constrictor muscles, the cervix in the cow separates the uterine cavity from the vaginal cavity, protecting the uterus from bacteria and foreign matter.

Colostrum Produced by the cow during the first three days after calving, colostrum contains valuable nutrients and built-in protections for the calf against disease and infection.

Cows Female cattle that have borne one or more offspring.

Crossbred An animal that is any combination of two or more breeds.

Cryptorchid Male cattle with one or both testes undescended.

Cull To eliminate an animal of low quality, or with a specific problem, from the herd.

Dehorning Removing horns from horned cattle.

Double muscling An undesirable but very distinctive genetic trait in cattle. Symptoms include thick tongue, inability to nurse, and general dullness. Increases calving difficulties.

Dual-purpose cattle Those bred for more than one specific purpose, such as meat and milk.

Ectomorphic Long-bodied and long-muscled, refers to shape of cattle.

Electroejaculation One method to collect semen from bulls for artificial insemination.

Embryo transplant The transfer of a fertilized embryo from one cow to another.

Estrogen A hormone that brings about the physical symptoms of estrus.

Estrus Recurrent period of sexual excitement in mature cows when cows will accept the bull; heat.

307

European cattle breeds Cattle native to continental Europe such as Charolais, Simmental, and Limousin.

Exotic cattle breeds Refers to any of the new breeds such as Maine-Anjou, Gelbvieh, and Salers.

F-1 cattle The first generation cross of two genetically unlike parents.

FSH The follicle-stimulating hormone, important in ovulation.

Freemartin The female member of unlike twins in cattle, showing many male characteristics and incapable of reproduction.

Gene One of the biologic units of heredity contained in the chromosome, each of which controls the inheritance of one or more characteristics.

Genetic association The result of genes favorable for the expression of one trait tending to be either favorable or unfavorable for the expression of another.

Genetic interval The average age of all parents when their progeny are born.

Get Calves sired by the same bull.

Grade Carcasses are assigned a grade based on their quality.

Grade cattle Beef cattle that are not registered with any purebred association.

Grulla The sandhill color of Texas Longhorn cattle.

Heat Estrus.

Heifers Female cattle that have not had a calf.

Heritability The proportion of the differences between animals that are transmitted to the offspring.

Heterosis The increased growth or production that an F-1 animal exhibits over the average of its two parent breeds.

Hybrid vigor Heterosis.

Independent culling level A system of selection.

Inbreeding Breeding between a sire and dam that are closely related.

LH Luteinizing hormone, essential to ovulation.

Lactation Milk production following calving.

Linebreeding Selective breeding with a sire and dam with a similar heredity, but not as close as in inbreeding.

Longevity Refers to how long-lived cattle may be.

Manyplies The omasum, a large absorptive area in the digestive system of cattle.

Marbling The distribution of fat throughout the meat.

Mothering ability Generally refers to nursing ability and milk production adequate to raise a healthy calf.

Nutrients Elements essential to the well being of an animal.

Omasum The manyplies, an absorptive area in the digestive system.

Open A nonpregnant female.

Ova Egg produced by the cow.

Ova transplant The transfer of a fertilized egg from the womb of one cow to the womb of another.

Ovaries Primary organs of reproduction of the female.

Ovulation Production of egg.

Palpation Technique used to determine proper location of pipette for artificial insemination, or for determining pregnancy in cattle.

Parturition Birth.

Pedigree A line of ancestry.

Performance test Measure of individual performance.

Polled Cattle born without horns.

Pregnancy rate Percent of the herd that becomes pregnant.

Prepotent Above average in ability to transmit desirable traits of the individual to the animal's offspring.

Progesterone A hormone that prevents heat and ovulation.

Prostaglandin Compound used for heat synchronization in female cattle.

Purebred Cattle whose parents are of the same breed.

Registered An animal whose name and the names and numbers of its sire and dam have been recorded with the appropriate breed association.

Reticulum The honeycomb of the digestive system.

Rotational cross Systematic rotation of heifer replacements from one breeding unit to a succeeding unit for two or more rotations, and utilization of purebred bulls of a different breed in each unit.

Rumen A part of the digestive system of cattle.

Rumination Cattle chewing a cud.

Sebum secretion Yellow secretion on the neck of Brahman cattle that repels insects.

Second cross Second generation cross of two or more breeds.

Seed stock Foundation animals for establishing a herd.

Selection Choosing animals for specific traits.

Selection differential Difference between the selected individuals and the average of all animals from which they were selected.

Semen Seminal fluid that contains the sperm capable of fertilizing an egg.

Sperm That portion of the semen capable of fertilization.

Steers Male cattle castrated at early age before sexual development.

Superovulation Production of more than one egg per heat cycle.

Tandem selection Selection for one trait at a time.

Termination cross A systematic cross with a planned ending.

Testosterone The male sexual hormone.

True stomach Refers to the abomasum, where most digestion is completed.

Ultrasonics Complex measuring device to evaluate meat and fat content of a live animal.

Uterus Portion of the female reproductive tract that serves as a path for sperm at time of breeding.

Vagina The copulatory organ of the female, and passageway from the vulva to the uterus.

Vulva Rear-most and external part of the reproductive passageway of female genitalia.

Weaning Cattle generally are weaned or switched from mother's milk to solid feed, at about 205 days, more or less.

Zebu Humped cattle of India.

Cattle Breed Associations

For more information on any of the breeds listed in this book, contact the appropriate breed association. These groups not only register animals, they also promote their breed. They are eager to assist new breeders.

DAIRY CATTLE BREED ASSOCIATIONS

Ayrshire Breeders' Association
Brandon, Vermont   05733   (802) 247-5774
> *Special programs: Approved sire and dam programs; Herd book;*
> *Selective registry program; Youth programs.*

Brown Swiss Cattle Breeders' Association of America, Inc.
Box 1038, Beloit, Wisconsin   53511   (608) 365-4474
> *Special programs: Production and type performance registry;*
> *Herd book; Sire development program; Sire recognition program;*
> *Cow recognition program; Junior programs.*

American Dexter Cattle Association
P.O. Box 56
Decorah, Iowa   52101   (319) 736-5772
> *Special program: Herd book*

Dutch Belted Cattle Association of America, Inc.
P.O. Box 358
Venus, Florida   33960
> *Special program: Herd book*

The American Guernsey Cattle Club

70 Main Street

Peterborough, New Hampshire   03458   (603) 924-3344

> *Special programs: Sire evaluation recognition; Performance register;
> Gold star awards; Herd book; Youth programs, scholarships;
> Guernsey queen contest.*

Holstein-Friesian Association of America

Box 808

Brattleboro, Vermont   05301   (802) 254-4551

> *Special programs: Sire development service; International marketing
> service; Herd book; Performance pedigrees; Sire summaries;
> Production testing; Junior membership.*

The American Jersey Cattle Club

2105-J South Hamilton Road, P.O. Box 27310

Columbus, Ohio   43227   (614) 861-3636

> *Special programs: Youth scholarships; Herd book; Genetic recovery
> program; Production testing.*

American Milking Shorthorn Society

1722 JJ S. Glenstone

Springfield, Missouri   65804   (417) 887-6525

> *Special programs: Youth programs, awards; Queen contest; Herd book;
> Gain registry program; Feedlot recognition program.*

American Normande Association

P.O. Box 350

Kearney, Missouri   64060   (816) 676-3575

> *Special Programs: Herd book; Youth programs.*

BEEF CATTLE BREED ASSOCIATIONS

Abondance / Hy-Cross Beef Breeders Ltd.

Box 199, Stittsville

Ontario, Canada   KOA 3GO   (613) 836-2858

> *Special program: Promotion*

American Angus Association

3201 Frederick Blvd.

St. Joseph, Missouri   64501   (816) 233-3101

> *Special programs: Angus herd improvement records; Production
> measure; National sire evaluation; Ladies junior associations;
> Sire summary / cow summary.*

Barzona Breeders Association of America
P.O. Box 1421
Carefree, Arizona   85331   (602) 488-9274
   *Special programs: "Breed up to Barzona" program; Production and
   performance records.*

Beefmaster Breeders Universal
GPM Tower South, Suite 350, 800 N.W. Loop 410
San Antonio, Texas   78216   (512) 341-1277
   *Special programs: Issues certificates of breeding; Name franchise
   contract; Voluntary classification and approved sales programs.*

American Blonde d'Aquitaine Association
c/o Grand View Farms
Grand View, Idaho   83624   (208) 834-2320
   Special programs: Promotion; Registration

International Braford Association
P.O. Box 1030
Fort Pierce, Florida   33450   (305) 461-6321
   *Special programs: Uniform selection program; Record pedigrees,
   production data.*

American Brahman Breeders Association
1313 La Concha Lane
Houston, Texas   77054   (713) 795-4444
   Special program: Junior associations

International Brangus Breeders Association
9500 Tioga Drive
San Antonio, Texas   78230   (512) 696-8231
   *Special programs: Enroll purebred Angus & Brahman; Certify
   intermediate crosses; Register Brangus*

Charbray (Charolais)
American / International Charolais Association
1610 Old Spanish Trail
Houston, Texas   77054   (713) 797-9211
   Special programs: Registration of Charolais and Charbray; Promotion

American Chianina Association
Box 11537
Kansas City, Missouri   64138   (816) 229-1944
   *Special programs: Open AI program; Multiple sire program;
   "Chi" program*

Devon Cattle Association, Inc.
P.O. Drawer 628
Uvalde, Texas   78801   (512) 278-2201
   Special programs: Qualified registry; Growth index records

American Galloway Breeders Association
302 Livestock Exchange Building
Denver, Colorado   80216   (303) 534-0858
   Special programs: Registration; Galloway performance international

American Gelbvieh Association
311 Livestock Exchange Building
Denver, Colorado   80216   (303) 623-4461
   Special programs: Performance data; Registration

Hays Converter / American Breeders Service
DeForest, Wisconsin   53532   (608) 846-3721
   Special program: Promotion

American Hereford Association
715 Hereford Drive
Kansas City, Missouri   64105   (816) 842-3757
   *Special programs: Sponsors educational programs; Performance and
   production records; Total performance records; Junior department /
   junior association; Promotion.*

Kobe Beef Producers, Inc.
Route 1, Box 292, 1538 Lillian Avenue
Jourdanton, Texas   78026   (512) 769-3504
   Special program: Promotion

North American Limousin Foundation
100 Livestock Exchange Building
Denver, Colorado   80216   (303) 623-6544
   Special programs: Goldmaker / silvermaker program; Registration.

Lincoln Red/Shaver Beef Breeding Farms
Box 817, Galt-Cambridge
Ontario Canada   N1R   5W6   (519) 621-7720
   Special program: Promotion

American Maine-Anjou Association
564 Livestock Exchange Building
Kansas City, Missouri   64102   (816) 474-9555
   *Special programs: Multiple sire program; Appendix heifer program;
   Junior associations; National sire summary*

American International Marchigiana Society
P.O. Box 342
Atlanta, Texas   75551   (214) 796-4882
   Special programs: Performance data; Registration; Promotion.

American Murray Grey Association
P.O. Box 30085
Billings, Montana   59107   (406) 248-1266
   Special programs: Performance data; Registration; Promotion.

Norwegian Red / NORED Corporation
Route 2
Adair, Iowa   50002   (515) 742-5564
>   *Special programs: Promotion in conjunction with North American*
>   *Norwegian Red Association.*

Parthenaise / Shaver Beef Breeding Farms
Box 817, Galt-Cambridge
Ontario, Canada   N1R   5W6   (519) 621-7720
>   *Special program: Promotion*

American Pinzgauer Association
P.O. Box 1003
Norman, Oklahoma   73070   (405) 364-0730
>   *Special programs: Performance data; Registration; Promotion.*

American Polled Hereford Association
4700 East 63rd Street
Kansas City, Missouri   64130   (816) 333-7731
>   *Special programs: Junior association; Superior sire program; Guidelines*
>   *performance records program.*

Ranger Cattle Company
P.O. Box 21300, North Pecos Station
Denver, Colorado   80221   (303) 469-0071
>   *Special program: Promotion*

Red Angus Association of America
Box 776
Denton, Texas   76201   (817) 387-3502
>   *Special programs: Breeding herd inventory; Performance records*
>   *program; Junior association*

American Red Brangus Association
Box 1326
Austin, Texas   78767   (512) 288-2840
>   *Special programs: Promotion; Registration*

Red Poll Beef Breeders International
c/o Schuler Carroll
Ross, Ohio   45061   (513) 738-1691
>   *Special programs: Breeder information; Promotion*

American Romagnola Association
P.O. Box 13548
Houston, Texas   77019   (713) 522-5141
>   *Special programs: Registration; Promotion.*

American Salers Association
P.O. Box 30
Weiser, Idaho   83672   (208) 549-0142
>   *Special programs: Registration; Promotion.*

Santa Gertrudis Breeders International
P.O. Box 1257
Kingsville, Texas   78363   (512) 592-9357
   Special programs: Grading up program; Promotion; Registration;
   Classification program.

American Scotch-Highland Breeders Association
P.O. Box 249
Walsenburg, Colorado   81089   (303) 738-3110
   Special programs: Registration; Promotion.

American Shorthorn Association
8288 Hascall Street
Omaha, Nebraska   68124   (402) 393-7200
   Special programs: Sire evaluation program; Records of performance
   program; Appendix registry program; Builders of the breed awards.

American Simmental Association
1 Simmental Way
Bozeman, Montana   59715   (406) 587-4531
   Special programs: Registers Simmental and Brahmental; Mandatory
   within-herd performance testing; National sire summary / cow
   summary.

North American South Devon Association
P.O. Box 68
Lynnville, Iowa   50153   (515) 527-2437
   Special programs: Promotion; Registration

Sussex Cattle Association of America
Refugio, Texas   78377
   Special program: Promotion

American Tarentaise Association
Box 1844
Fort Collins, Colorado   80522   (303) 493-6622
   Special programs: National sire summary; Promotion; Registration.

Texas Longhorn Breeders Association of America
P.O. Box 659
San Antonio, Texas   78293   (512) 225-3444
   Special programs: Registration; Promotion; Preservation of the breed.

United States Welsh Black Cattle Association
Rt. 1
Wahkon, Minnesota   56386
   Special programs: Registration; Promotion.

APPENDIX B

Artificial Insemination Services

DIRECTORY OF U.S. SEMEN SUPPLIERS

American Breeders Service
DeForest, Wisconsin 53532 (608) 846-3721
  President, Manager: Dr. Robert E. Walton

Artificial Insemination Program of Puerto Rico
P.O. Box 726
Dorado, Puerto Rico 00646 (809) 765-2905 & 796-1134
  Chief: Anastacio A. Romero

Atlantic Breeders Cooperative
1575 Apollo Drive
Lancaster, Pennsylvania 17601 (717) 569-0413
  Manager: David J. Yoder

BOV Imports—International Beef Breeders
P.O. Box 29009
Denver, Colorado 80229 (303) 825-1038 & 452-8151
  General Manager: Bud Prosser

The Bull Bank, Inc.
18907 E. Lone Tree Road
Escalon, California 95320 (209) 838-7891 & 982-1071
  President, Manager: Frank Faria, Jr.

Carnation Company, Genetics Division
P.O. Box 938
Hughson, California 95326 (209) 883-4001
  Division Manager: Ron Eustice

Colorado State Animal Reproduction Laboratory
Colorado State University
Fort Collins, Colorado   80521   (303)   482-3011
>   *Director: Dr. B.W. Pickett*

Curtiss Breeding Service
Cary, Illinois   60013   (312)   639-2141
>   *President: Glenn Pirrong*

Eastern Artificial Insemination Cooperative, Inc.
P.O. Box 518, Judd Falls Road
Ithaca, New York   14850   (607)   272-2011
>   *Manager: Charles J. Krumm*

Excelsior Farms, Excelsior Genetics
Route 1, Box 128
Corona, California   91720   (714)   737-2343
>   *Manager: Robert W. Sherwood*

General Genetics
P.O. Box 23
Jenison, Michigan   49428   (616)   457-0310
>   *Owner: Jacob Van Hoven*

Hawkeye Breeders Service
4535 N.W. First Street
Des Moines, Iowa   50313   (515)   244-3209
>   *President: Lloyd M. Jungmann*

Illinois Breeding Cooperative
Route 1
Hampshire, Illinois   60140   (312)   464-5281
>   *Manager: Jesse C. Barnes*

Illini Sire Service
201 Park Street, P.O. Box 187
Cornell, Illinois   61319   (815)   358-2897
>   *Owner / Manager: Dennis Fulkerson*

Kansas Artificial Breeding Service Unit
1401 College Avenue, Kansas State University
Manhattan, Kansas   66502   (913)   539-3554
>   *Manager: Charles L. Michaels*

Louisiana Animal Breeders Cooperative, Inc.
Box BD, Louisiana State University
Baton Rouge, Louisiana   70803   (504)   344-2324 & 388-3292
>   *Manager: Dr. Arnold Baham*

Midwest Breeders Cooperative
Box 469
Shawano, Wisconsin   54166   (715) 526-2141
    General Manager: Thomas L. Lyon

Minnesota Valley Breeders Association
New Prague, Minnesota   56071   (612) 758-4443
    Manager: Sterling Gillingham

New Breeds Industries, Inc.
P.O. Box 959, Route 5
Manhattan, Kansas   66502   (913) 537-2540 & 537-2914
    President and General Manager: C. Ancel Armstrong

NOBA, Inc.
P.O. Box 607
Tiffin, Ohio   44883   (419) 447-6262
    Manager: Bryce Weiker

North American Breeders, Inc.
Route 1
Berryville, Virginia   22611   (703) 955-3647 & (301) 622-0579
    President: Charles A. Anderson

Pan American Breeders, Inc.
Box 818
Terrell, Texas   75160   (214) 563-2490

Select Sires, Inc.
11740 U.S. 42
Plain City, Ohio   43064   (614) 873-4683
    President: Jack Dendel

REGIONAL MEMBERS OF SELECT SIRES

All West Breeders
P.O. Box 507, Burlington, Washington   98233   (206) 757-1885
    Manager: Archie Nelson

Central Ohio Breeding Association
1224 Alton-Darby Road, Columbus, Ohio   43228   (614) 878-5333
    Manager: Dr. Wallace Erickson

East Central Breeders Association Coop.
P.O. Box 191, Waupun, Wisconsin   53963   (414) 324-3505

East Tennessee Artificial Breeders Association
Route 10, Tipton Station Road
Knoxville, Tennessee   37920   (615) 577-4892
    Manager: Don Ardrey

REGIONAL MEMBERS OF SELECT SIRES (continued)

Kentucky Artificial Breeders Association
1930 Herr Lane, P.O. Box 22146
Louisville, Kentucky   40222   (502) 425-1868
   Manager: Marshall C. Carpenter

Michigan Animal Breeders Cooperative, Inc.
Box 511, 3655 Forest Road, East Lansing, Michigan   48823   (517) 351-3180
   Manager: Kenneth B. Baushke

Tennessee Artificial Breeding Association
Box 67, Brentwood, Tennessee   37027   (615) 832-3881
   Manager: Fred Cowart

Virginia / North Carolina Select Sires, Inc.
P.O. Box 370, Rocky Mount, Virginia   24151   (703) 483-5124
   Manager: Emory Brubaker

Sire Power, Inc.
Operational Unit, Route 2
Tunkhannock, Pennsylvania   18657   (717) 836-3168
   AND
P.O. Box 555
Frederick, Maryland   21701   (301) 898-9101
   Manager: W. Lewis Campbell

REGIONAL MEMBERS OF SIRE POWER

Maryland Artificial Breeding Cooperative
P.O. Box 555, Frederick, Maryland.   21701   (301) 898-9101

Northeastern Breeders Association
Rt. 2, Tunkhannock, Pennsylvania 18657   (717) 836-3127

Soligenics Frozen Semen Service
484 Thompsonville Road, Suffield, Connecticut   06078   (203) 668-2602
   Owner: Roger Ives

Southwest A.I. Custom Freezing Center
Route 1, Box 50 A
Ponder, Texas   76259   (817) 627-2763
   Manager: Jerry Savage

Sun Up Farms
Smithville, Missouri   64089   (816) 873-2546
   Owner: David R. Miller

Topline A.I. Service, Inc.
Route 10, Galyon Lane
Knoxville, Tennessee   37920   (615) 577-7337
   Manager: Leland Stanfill

REGIONAL MEMBERS OF SIRE POWER (continued)

Tri-State Breeders Cooperative
ADMINISTRATIVE OFFICES:
Route 3, Box 50
Baraboo, Wisconsin 53913 (608) 356-8357
PRODUCTION HEADQUARTERS:
Westby, Wisconsin 54667 (608) 634-3111
Manager: Gerald Larson

Universal Semen Service Ltd.
1114-1/2 Central Avenue
Great Falls, Montana 59401 (406) 453-0374

Upjohn Company (Tuco Products Co. Div.)
Animal Research and Development, Ag. Div.
Kalamazoo, Michigan 49001 (616) 382-4000
Manager: Marlin Kleckner, DVM

Woods, John DVM
1915 N. Williams Street
Mesa, Arizona 85201 (602) 696-1379

World Wide Sires, Inc.
15840 10th Avenue, P.O. Box 1346
Hanford, California 93230 (209) 584-3341
President: Willard G. Clark

Wye Plantation
Queenstown, Maryland 21658 (301) 827-7166
Manager: John R. Whaley, III

DIRECTORY OF CANADIAN SEMEN SUPPLIERS

British Columbia Artificial Insemination Centre
Box 40
Milner, British Columbia (604) 534-2121
Manager: Gordon Souter

Chilliwack Artificial Insemination Centre
10119 Kent Road
Chilliwack, British Columbia (604) 795-5735
Manager: John A. Peter

New Brunswick Central AI Cooperative, Ltd.
P.O. Box 1567
Fredericton, New Brunswick (506) 454-3327
Manager: Dr. D. G. Moore

DIRECTORY OF CANADIAN SEMEN SUPPLIERS *(continued)*

Nova Scotia Animal Breeders Cooperative, Ltd.
Route 1
Truro, Nova Scotia   (902) 895-1510
Manager: Don Cameron

Ontario Association of Animal Breeders
Route 5
Guelph, Ontario   (519) 821-5060
Manager: Roy G. Snyder

REGIONAL MEMBERS

Eastern Breeders, Inc.
Kemptville, Ontario   (613) 258-3471
Manager: Dr. R. G. Smiley

United Breeders, Inc.
Route 5, Guelph, Ontario   (519) 821-2150
Manager: Dr. C. R. Reeds

Western Ontario Breeders, Inc.
P.O. Box 457, Woodstock, Ontario   (519) 539-9831

Quebec Artificial Breeding Centre
3450 Sicotte Quest Street, C.P. 518
Hyancinthe, Quebec   (514) 774-6426
Manager: Claude Hayes

Simmental Breeders Cardston, Ltd.
Box 537
Cardston, Alberta   (403) 653-4421
Manager: R. B. (Ron) Gibson

Universal Semen Service Ltd.
Box 910
Cardston, Alberta   (403) 653-4437
General Manager: M. R. Gebauer

Western Breeders, Ltd.
Balzac, Alberta   (403) 274-1555
General Manager: Douglas G. Blair

DIRECTORY OF U.S. SEMEN SUPPLIERS BY STATES

[Complete addresses are listed in the previous section of this Appendix.]

Arizona
John Woods, DVM (Mesa)

California
The Bull Bank, Inc. (Escalon)
Carnation Company (Hughson)
Excelsior Farms (Corona)
World Wide Sires, Inc. (Hanford)

Colorado
BOV Imports-International Beef
Breeders (Denver)
Colorado State Animal Reproduction
Laboratory (Fort Collins)

Connecticut
Soligenics Frozen Semen Service
(Suffield)

Illinois
Curtiss Breeding Service (Cary)
Illini Sire Service (Cornell)
Illinois Breeding Cooperative
(Hampshire)

Iowa
Hawkeye Breeders Service
(Des Moines)

Kansas
Kansas Artificial Breeding Service
Unit (Manhattan)
New Breeds Industries (Manhattan)

Kentucky
Select Sires / Kentucky Artificial
Breeders Association (Louisville)

Louisiana
Louisiana Animal Breeders
Cooperative, Inc. (Baton Rouge)

Maryland
Sire Power, Inc. / Maryland Artificial
Breeding Cooperative (Frederick)
Wye Plantation (Queenstown)

Michigan
General Genetics (Jenison)
Select Sires / Michigan Animal
Breeders Cooperative (East Lansing)
Upjohn Co., Tuco Products Co.
Division (Kalamazoo)

Minnesota
Minnesota Valley Breeders
Association (New Prague)

Missouri
Sun Up Farms (Smithville)

Montana
Universal Semen Service Ltd.
(Great Falls)

New York
Eastern Artificial Insemination
Cooperative Inc. (Ithaca)

North Carolina
Select Sires / Virginia-North Carolina
Select Sires, Inc. (Rocky Mount)

Ohio
NOBA, Inc. (Tiffin)
Select Sires, Inc. (Plain City)
Select Sires / Central Ohio Breeding
Association (Columbus)

Pennsylvania
Atlantic Breeders Cooperative
(Lancaster)
Sire Power, Inc. / Northeastern
Breeders Association
(Tunkhannock)

DIRECTORY OF U.S. SEMEN SUPPLIERS BY STATES (continued)

Tennessee

Select Sires / East Tennessee
  Artificial Breeders Association
  (Knoxville)
Select Sires / Tennessee Artificial
  Breeding Association (Brentwood)
Topline A.I. Service, Inc. (Knoxville)

Texas

Pan American Breeders, Inc. (Terrell)
Southwest A.I. Custom Freezing
  Center (Ponder)

Virginia

North American Breeders, Inc.
  (Berryville)
Select Sires / Virginia-North Carolina
  Select Sires, Inc. (Rocky Mount)

Washington

Select Sires / All West Breeders
  (Burlington)

Wisconsin

American Breeders Service
  (De Forest)
Midwest Breeders Cooperative
  (Shawano)
Select Sires / East Central Breeders
  Association Cooperative
  (Waupun)
Tri-State Breeders Cooperative
  (Baraboo)
Tri-State Breeders Cooperative
  (Westby)

*   *   *

Puerto Rico

Artificial Insemination Program of
  Puerto Rico (Dorado)

DIRECTORY OF OTHER SEMEN SUPPLIERS

Australian Association of Artificial Breeders
Artificial Breeding Board
P.O. Box 128
Harvey 6220, Australia
> *Manager:* W. A. *"Bill" Hambley*

Dalfarm A.B. Services
38 Bridge Street
Sydney, 2001, Australia
> *Manager: Storm Jackoin*

King Ranch (Australia) Pty., Ltd.
Milton Park
Bowral, N.S.W., 2576, Australia
> *General Manager: P. L. Baillieu*

Mudgee Artificial Breeding Center
Mudgee, N.S.W., 2850, Australia
> *Owner / Manager: A. E. Loneragan*

Northwest Stock Services
P.O. Box 249, N.S.W., 2343, Australia
> *Laboratory Veterinarian: Dr. Ian Knight*

Union Nationale des Cooperatives D'Insemination Artificielle
147–149 Rue de Bercy F⁵, Paris 12ème, France

Arbeitsgemeinschaft der Besamungsstationen in Bayern
Haydnstrasse II D-8000, Munchen 2, West Germany
> *President: Prof. Dipl. Ing., Eberhard Thyssen*

Israel Cattle Breeders Association Ltd.
25 Arlozorov Street, Tel Aviv, Israel
> *President: S. Doti*

Hokkaido Artificial Insemination Technician Association
C/o Hokuren Building, Kita 4, Nishi 1 (060) Sapporo, Japan
> *General Manager: Dr. Michiro Wakabayashi*

Insemina Co-Operative Ltd.
Private Bag #5, Irene, Transvaal, Republic of South Africa
> *Manager / Director: Dr. A. B. P. LaGrange*

Natal Animal Breeding & Milk Recording Co., Ltd.
Box 19, Thornville Junction, Natal, Republic of South Africa
> *General Manager: Dr. C. T. McDonald*

APPENDIX C

Ova Transplant Centers

DIRECTORY OF U.S. AND OTHER SUPPLIERS

American Embryo
2220 Patterson, Middleville, Michigan   49333   (616) 795-3347

Carnation / Genetics
P.O. Box 938, Hughson, California   95326   (209) 883-4001

CBR Ova Transplants, Inc.
Route 1, Box 176, Fennimore, Wisconsin   53809   (608) 822-6770

Elliott Embryological Labs
Route 2, Box 29, Mitchell, Nebraska   69357   (308) 623-1622

Maplehurst Ova Transplants
Route 1, Keota, Iowa 52248   (515) 636-3811

Marlana-Sean Transplants
Route 3, Box 52, Gentry, Arkansas   72734   (501) 736-2000

Northwest Veterinary Clinic of Stanwood, Transplant Division
8500 Cedarhome Drive, Stanwood, Washington   98292   (206) 629-2242

Pan American Breeders, Inc.
Route 2, Box 453-A, Terrell, Texas   75160   (214) 563-2490

Portable Embryonics, Inc.
P.O. Box 511, Zachary, Louisiana   70791   (504) 654-4150

Rio Vista Farms (Genetics)
R.R. 9, Box 242, San Antonio, Texas   78227   (512) 677-8014

Scientific Transplants, Inc. (STI)
R.R. 2, Box 195 E, Las Animas, Colorado   81054   (303) 456-0612

VIA PAX Inc.
R.D. #1, Box 657, Elizabethtown, Pennsylvania   17022   (717) 653-8124

*   *   *

Alberta Livestock Transplants
Site 12, Box 22, RR 4, Calgary, Alberta, Canada   (403) 288-4444

Bedirian Embryo Transfers Limited
R.R. 2, Norval, Ontario, Canada   (416) 846-4130

VIA PAX Corporation Ltd.
7531 Pine Valley Drive, Woodbridge, Ontario, Canada   (416) 851-2288

*   *   *

Centro de Transplantes de Embriones
Avenida Hincapie 5–71, Zona 13
Guatemala, Guatemala   Phone: 316377

Index